THE **COMPLETE IDIOT'S GUIDE** TO

Seed Saving and Starting

by Sheri Ann Richerson

ALPHA

A member of Penguin Group (USA) Inc.

I dedicate this book to seed savers everywhere; my children, Sarah, Anna, David, Josh, and Trisha; my grandchildren, Trinity, Alexis, and Noah; and my husband, Jerry Stanley.

ALPHA BOOKS

Published by the Penguin Group

Penguin Group (USA) Inc., 375 Hudson Street, New York, New York 10014, USA • Penguin Group (Canada), 90 Eglinton Avenue East, Suite 700, Toronto, Ontario M4P 2Y3, Canada (a division of Pearson Penguin Canada Inc.) • Penguin Books Ltd., 80 Strand, London WC2R 0RL, England • Penguin Ireland, 25 St. Stephen's Green, Dublin 2, Ireland (a division of Penguin Books Ltd.) • Penguin Group (Australia), 250 Camberwell Road, Camberwell, Victoria 3124, Australia (a division of Pearson Australia Group Pty. Ltd.) • Penguin Books India Pvt. Ltd., 11 Community Centre, Panchsheel Park, New Delhi— 110 017, India • Penguin Group (NZ), 67 Apollo Drive, Rosedale, North Shore, Auckland 1311, New Zealand (a division of Pearson New Zealand Ltd.) • Penguin Books (South Africa) (Pty.) Ltd., 24 Sturdee Avenue, Rosebank, Johannesburg 2196, South Africa • Penguin Books Ltd., Registered Offices: 80 Strand, London WC2R 0RL, England

Copyright © 2012 by Sheri Ann Richerson

International Standard Book Number: 978-1-61564-137-6
Library of Congress Catalog Card Number: 2011936777

14   13   12   8   7   6   5   4   3   2

Interpretation of the printing code: The rightmost number of the first series of numbers is the year of the book's printing; the rightmost number of the second series of numbers is the number of the book's printing. For example, a printing code of 12-1 shows that the first printing occurred in 2012.

Printed in the United States of America

Note: This publication contains the opinions and ideas of its author. It is intended to provide helpful and informative material on the subject matter covered. It is sold with the understanding that the author and publisher are not engaged in rendering professional services in the book. If the reader requires personal assistance or advice, a competent professional should be consulted.

The author and publisher specifically disclaim any responsibility for any liability, loss, or risk, personal or otherwise, which is incurred as a consequence, directly or indirectly, of the use and application of any of the contents of this book.

Most Alpha books are available at special quantity discounts for bulk purchases for sales promotions, premiums, fund-raising, or educational use. Special books, or book excerpts, can also be created to fit specific needs.

For details, write: Special Markets, Alpha Books, 375 Hudson Street, New York, NY 10014.

Publisher: *Marie Butler-Knight*
Associate Publisher: *Mike Sanders*
Executive Managing Editor: *Billy Fields*
Acquisitions Editor: *Brook Farling*
Development Editor: *Jennifer Moore*
Senior Production Editor: *Janette Lynn*

Copy Editor: *Krista Hansing Editorial Services, Inc.*
Cover Designer: *Kurt Owens*
Book Designers: *William Thomas, Rebecca Batchelor*
Indexer: *Julie Bess*
Layout: *Ayanna Lacey*
Proofreader: *John Etchison*

Contents

Appendixes

Introduction

Savvy gardeners have long known that starting seeds is the best way to save money and grow the most unusual or the newest plants on the market. Seed catalogs are full of enticing choices: colorful flowers, flavorful herbs, delightful heirlooms, and, of course, the newest hybrid vegetables. Many of these plants simply aren't available at local nurseries or big-box stores. If you want to grow them, you must start from seed.

And because plants evolve and adapt as they grow, the seeds produced in your own garden are better suited to growing there than anything you can buy. The seed they produce contains the DNA changes that took place in the plant while it was growing before it set seed. When this seed is replanted in your garden, it adapts as it germinates and grows. Each generation of new plants continues this process.

That is at the heart of why many gardeners prefer to save their own seed from year to year. They know the seed. They know it has adapted to local environmental conditions. They know that disease or pests are less likely to destroy crops from their saved seeds than if they use new seeds every year.

An additional plus is that plants grown from seeds you save are optimized for your garden, meaning that they may produce earlier than plants grown from seeds you buy. This is a real advantage for gardeners in cold climates. Sometimes your seed-grown plants will even tolerate colder temperatures than purchased transplants.

But what it really all comes down to is the pleasure of working with seeds—harvesting them, storing them, sowing them, and nurturing the tiny seedlings that grow from them. Whether those young plants go on to produce taste-bud popping vegetables and fruits or fragrant, colorful flowers, you'll take the satisfaction in knowing that you had a hand in every step of the process.

How This Book Is Organized

Part 1, Getting Started with Seeds, offers an overview of the historical importance of seeds and how open-pollinated seeds help promote plant diversity. This section covers all types of pollination and shows how you can create superior varieties specifically suited to growing in your garden. You find out how to maintain seed purity using various natural methods and learn why encouraging natural pollinators to stay in your garden is important.

Part 2, Harvesting and Storing Seeds, covers seed identification and harvesting methods. You find out why it's necessary to clean the seeds you collect. Finally, you learn how to correctly dry and store seeds so all your hard work is not lost to mold or rot.

Part 3, Germinating and Sowing Seeds, covers scarification and stratification techniques, how to raise garden plants from seed, indoors under lights, outdoors in the spring, or even in special protective containers during the winter.

Part 4, When Seeds Become Plants, gives you the information you need to nurture your tiny sprouts into strong, healthy plants. You find out the best techniques for transplanting the plants you grow from seed and protecting those plants from harsh conditions and critters.

Part 5, Building Your Seed Future, covers a wide range of topics, including cross-breeding plants to create new hybrids and labeling and identifying plants and seeds. You learn how to create a gardening journal and why it's so important for you to share your seed-saving and sowing knowledge with other people. This part also covers the pros and cons of sharing or selling your excess seeds.

Part 6, Seed Directories, is a thorough guide to botanical names, seed-harvesting tips, germination tips, and sowing information for hundreds of plants. It covers a wide variety of vegetables and flowers as well as the more common fruits and grains.

Extras

Peppered throughout the chapters, you'll find sidebars filled with cool, pertinent facts relating to seed saving. Here's what you get:

DEFINITION

These sidebars define gardening and seed-saving terms you might not be familiar with.

KNOW THY SEED

Here you'll find tips for simplifying the process of collecting and saving seeds and other gardening ideas.

THE BAD SEED

Learn from my mistakes, and avoid the common pitfalls described in these sidebars.

SPROUTING WISDOM

Turn to these sidebars for garden lore and interesting facts about saving and starting seeds.

Acknowledgments

I would like to thank a number of people who helped make this book possible: All the wonderful people at Alpha Books and Penguin Group (USA); my agents, Janet Rosen and Sheree Bykofsky, who are the wind beneath my wings; Elaine Partnow, without whom this book would not have been possible; my husband, Jerry Stanley, who holds down the fort while I sit in front of a computer and write; and Katey Boller for help and encouragement.

I would also like to thank all of my Facebook, LinkedIn, Myspace, and Twitter peeps, as well as the wonderful people at Wilks PR who have encouraged me when things seemed bleak and helped me reach the status of best-selling author.

Finally, I would like to thank my high school journalism teacher, Mrs. Marilyn Kissane, for her constant encouragement, as well as Mrs. Karen Owens, the previous editor of the *Twin City Journal Reporter*. If it weren't for these women, I would not have attempted to write my first book, let alone my twenty-eighth.

Trademarks

All terms mentioned in this book that are known to be or are suspected of being trademarks or service marks have been appropriately capitalized. Alpha Books and Penguin Group (USA) Inc. cannot attest to the accuracy of this information. Use of a term in this book should not be regarded as affecting the validity of any trademark or service mark.

Getting Started with Seeds

Seed saving is a fascinating process in which you can harness plants' amazing power to reproduce themselves. Saving seeds is relatively easy, but it does involve a number of steps—including pollinating, harvesting, drying, and storing—as well as a keen eye and a fair bit of patience.

This part provides an overview of seed saving, introduces you to basic plant biology involved in plant reproduction, and gives you the lowdown on basic seed-saving terminology.

You'll also learn how seeds are formed and the role humans play in the process of seed diversity. Learning to save seeds is an exciting journey that enables you to grow plants in your garden that are specifically adapted to local growing conditions.

Why Save Seeds?

In This Chapter

- Getting acquainted with seed saving
- Distinguishing between heirloom and hybrid seeds
- Avoiding genetically modified seeds
- Understanding seed nomenclature
- Properly identifying plants

When you harvest seeds from plants, dry them, store them, and sow them the next growing season, you're harnessing nature's power. Whether you plan to grow a vegetable garden, start an orchard, plant a few trees in your yard, or nurture a bed of cutting flowers, you're embarking on a tradition that goes back tens of thousands of years.

The rich genetic diversity in gardens today is the result of people saving and sharing seeds from plants grown by gardeners who came before them.

What Is a Seed?

A seed is a living organism that's capable of absorbing oxygen and giving off carbon dioxide, a process known as *respiration*. (Ironically, once the seed starts growing, it does the opposite: in the presence of sunlight, it absorbs carbon dioxide and gives off oxygen.) The undeveloped plant, called the *embryo*, is inside the seed. The embryo is protected by the seed coat—the part of the seed you can see—until the seed absorbs enough moisture to start the *germination*, or sprouting, process.

A *metabolic process* causes the seed to begin to sprout. This process turns the carbohydrates inside the seed into soluble food that the plant absorbs. The plant uses this food during the beginning stages of growth.

DEFINITION

An **embryo** is the living part of the seed that contains the undeveloped plant.

Germination is the process that occurs at the exact moment when a seed begins to sprout, or grow, into a plant.

Metabolic process is the complex of physical and chemical processes occurring within a living cell or organism that are necessary to sustain life. Some substances are broken down to yield energy for vital processes; other substances are synthesized.

Setting seed is a normal process for most plants; it simply means that the plant is going about its business of having progeny by blossoming and, in so doing, creating seeds.

KNOW THY SEED

Seeds are nature's way of trying to keep things in balance and preventing plants from becoming extinct. When a plant becomes stressed or sick, one of the last things it tries to do to ensure its survival is flower and set seed.

As long as a plant is able to produce seeds, it continues to spread and survive. The creation of new plants—especially native plants—through the formation of seed is essential to local ecosystems.

Seeds range in size from dustlike *spores* that are barely visible to the naked eye, to bowling-ball-size coconuts. What's more, seeds come in many shapes, including the round seeds of peas, oval seeds of pumpkins and watermelons, curved seeds of snap beans and limas, pitted seeds of peaches, and feathered seeds of dandelions.

SPROUTING WISDOM

The coconut is actually a large seed. You can grow your own coconut palm tree by germinating the coconuts you buy at the store. Even if you live in a cold climate, these make lovely houseplants.

Seed color varies greatly as well, in shades of brown, black, tan, cream, and white. Some seeds are even red or multicolored.

A sampling of seeds of various shapes and sizes.

Looking Back at the Origins of Seed Saving

The earliest recorded knowledge we have of seed saving dates to the Stone Age. Drawings on cave walls showed that our early ancestors collected seeds of wild plants and domesticated them. Through this process, people were able to hand-select the best wild plant varieties to grow in their ancient gardens.

Over the millennia, our ancestors learned to select and save seeds from the best-performing plants in their garden. Instead of planting all that seed, they saved some as a backup in case a crop failed.

Having a surplus of seed also gave people the option of sharing or trading seeds with others, further ensuring that preferred seeds could be located and replanted in the event of a failed crop. This custom made it possible to prevent years of work from being lost if something happened to a family's personal seed supply.

But saving seeds made sense for many reasons beyond having backup seeds in case of crop failure. People also used—and continue to use—seeds for a wide variety of purposes, including the following:

- As a source of food for fresh eating, cooking, and preserving
- As medicine, dyes, or cosmetics

- To sell or barter
- To grow crops not commercially available
- To save money
- To be self-reliant
- To experiment with crossing specific plants

SPROUTING WISDOM

People used to carry seeds with them from place to place by sewing them into their clothing or into the lining of their trunks or baggage. This kept the seeds safe from marauders and allowed the travelers to take a piece of their homeland with them. It was often the only way for them to enjoy the fruits, flowers, or vegetables to which they were accustomed.

It didn't take long for folks to figure out that seeds saved from their own gardens had numerous advantages—advantages that still hold true today. The end results are plants that are better suited to coping with any number of environmental factors, including the following:

- Local weather conditions, including cold snaps, hot spells, and droughts
- Local pests or disease problems
- The native soil of the region

KNOW THY SEED

Pests and diseases can wipe out an entire crop. One of history's most famous crop disasters is the 1845 Irish potato famine. However, any plants that survive such an invasion likely carry a gene that makes them resistant to the problem. When those surviving plants set seed, they pass on this resistant gene to future generations.

Making Sense of Various Types of Seeds

As you peruse seed catalogs and seed racks at your local gardening center, you realize you have a lot of choices when it comes to the kind of seeds you can plant. The following sections help you make sense of the types of seeds available so that you can make the best choice for your needs.

Open-Pollinated Seeds

Open-pollinated seed is the offspring of two plants of the same variety crossed naturally without the interference of man. They are pollinated by bees, butterflies, hummingbirds, and the like (for details on pollination, see Chapter 2).

Seed saving is an important means of preventing open-pollinated seeds from becoming completely extinct. In addition to using them yourself and sharing with others, you can donate some of the seeds you save to organizations and seed banks devoted to preserving heirloom seeds; those organizations, in turn, pass the seeds on to gardeners who are interested in preserving such plants (see Appendix B for some sources).

Heirloom Seeds

Heirloom seeds are open-pollinated seeds that are more than 50 years old. Over the years, gardeners have saved seeds from only the best-performing plants in their gardens, resulting in fruits, flowers, or vegetables that normally outperform store-bought varieties. Having ready access to your favorite heirloom plants is as easy as growing them in your own backyard.

SPROUTING WISDOM

Heirloom seeds are part of the public domain, so no one owns them. You're free to save seeds from these plants, to sell them, or to share them without the fear of legal retaliation.

Many gardeners prefer to grow heirlooms for any or all of the following reasons:

- The fruits or vegetables taste better.
- The fruits or vegetables have a better texture.
- The flowers have a stronger scent.
- The fruits, flowers, and vegetables look more appealing.
- The fruits or vegetables come in a wide variety of unusual colors.

You may find it difficult to locate heirloom fruits and vegetables to purchase; you can't usually find them in supermarkets, but you might find them at local farmers' markets. When you do find them, they're usually more expensive than mass-produced plants because they weren't bred to survive shipping. Instead, they were bred to go from the garden to the table, or to be preserved for winter use by freezing, canning, or dehydrating.

Some heirloom seeds are hard to find because they have been passed down from one family member to the next for generations. These varieties are known as *family heirlooms* and often aren't available commercially. When you buy an heirloom fruit or vegetable, you can save its seeds and plant them yourself.

Hybrid Seeds

Hybrid seeds come from plants that humans intentionally crossbreed. They are most often produced commercially for the purpose of creating a new plant with specific characteristics, such as hardiness, cold or pest resistance, or lack of seeds (seedless watermelon, for example). Plants that are used for crossbreeding usually consist of two genetically different varieties of the same type of plant, but sometimes two different plant species that are compatible with one another are crossbred to create a brand-new plant.

Here are some examples of crossbred species:

- **Triticale:** a cross between wheat and rye
- **Grapple:** a cross between grapes and apples
- **Tangelo:** a cross between tangerines and grapefruits.

Newer "designer" fruits are crossbreeds as well. These designer breeds include the aprium, a hybrid of apricot and plum; the nectaplum, a mix of nectarine and plum; and the pluot, a blend of plum and apricot.

Although hybrid seeds seem like a fun way to introduce variety into your garden, they have a dark side: the increasing use of hybrid seeds (in place of heirloom and open-pollinated seeds) may ultimately destroy garden seed diversity. And diversity is what makes it possible to have some seeds and plants that are immune to diseases such as late blight that can wipe out an entire crop.

Furthermore, if you save and plant hybrid seed, the resulting plant won't resemble the hybrid plant that produced the seed the previous season. In fact, the seed may be sterile and not grow at all, or it may revert to one of the parent plants from which the hybrid was created. Because the genes that make up the plant come from two totally separate plants, they can cross in any number of ways.

In the 1860s, people like Charles Darwin and Gregor Mendel influenced the world of crossbreeding to create a hybrid species. Mendel discovered he could cross breed different strains of pea plants and predict the traits of the offspring. He proposed that there was a genetic basis for inherited traits and demonstrated that he could control them.

As an example, shortly after the turn of the century, scientists realized they could plant two pure or "inbred" varieties of corn in a field, alternating rows. Then they could remove or cover the tassels of one variety so that the only pollen released into the field would come from the second variety. The ears harvested from the first variety would have the hybrid seeds. Hybrid plants, it was discovered, were usually more vigorous than their parents. The simple act of crossing different strains resulted in higher yields and stronger plants. *Hybrid vigor* had great appeal to seed companies, which began producing more and more varieties. Today, somewhere around 99 percent of U.S. corn is grown from hybrid seed. The same is true for wheat, soybeans, grain sorghum, cotton, peanuts, and many other crops.

DEFINITION

F1 hybrid seeds are the first generation made by crossing two different parent varieties, the offspring of which produce a new, uniform seed variety with specific characteristics from both parents.

Hybrid vigor is increased vigor or other superior qualities that arise from cross-breeding genetically different plants or animals; it is also called *heterosis*.

Hybrid seeds cost seed companies more to produce than heirloom varieties. But when gardeners buy hybrid seeds, the seed companies know that customers must buy more seeds in subsequent years if they hope to continue growing the same plants.

No law requires seed companies to disclose which two parent plants were crossed to make the new hybrid. This prevents other seed companies from stealing their successful varieties and selling them as their own. If another company wants to sell that particular seed in their catalog or store, they must buy the stock from the company that created it.

The ornamental cabbages in this photo were grown from hybrid seeds. Notice how closely they resemble one another.

Farmers and home gardeners choose hybrids over heirlooms largely because hybrid plants offer any or all of the following advantages:

- Hybrids produce fruits, flowers, or vegetables that have uniform results, which is especially important for commercial growers.

- Hybrid plants tend to have more vigor.

- The fruits, flowers, or vegetables typically have a longer shelf life than heirlooms.

- The fruits and vegetables of hybrid plants endure better than heirloom varieties during shipping.

- Hybrids can be bred to produce earlier in the season.

All these qualities have been bred into the plants to make them superior to heirlooms in some way. However, when a plant is bred to gain a specific quality, it may lose another—such as smell or taste. A good example of this is old-fashioned roses. Heirloom roses have a wonderful scent, but are known for being droopy, blooming just once a year, and quickly dropping their petals. Hybrid roses such as hybrid tea roses were developed that bloom all season long, have long stems, and the flowers hold their shape, making them ideal for bouquets. The downside of the hybrid roses? They don't smell nearly as good as their open-pollinated counterparts.

The best way to decide whether to grow plants from hybrid or open-pollinated plant seeds is to grow several varieties of each; compare their taste, growth habit, or fragrance; and make a decision based on your personal preferences.

GMOs

Genetically modified organisms (GMOs) are seeds—either heirloom or hybrid—that have been altered by man in a laboratory using specialized equipment. Many people consider GMO seeds to be superior to both heirloom and hybrid varieties because they contain many desirable traits.

To obtain these traits, technicians insert herbicides or other nonplant matter, such as animal or bacterial genes, into the DNA of the seed. When the cells of the foreign DNA merge with the seed cells, it creates a hardy seed that's able to withstand conditions—such as drought or extreme cold temperatures—that heirloom or hybrid seeds wouldn't be capable of surviving.

For example, GMO seeds that are herbicide resistant enable large-scale farmers to spray herbicides on their fields to kill weeds without harming their crops. Similarly, home gardeners growing GMO crops that are "Round-Up Ready" can spray commercial weed killers on their fruits, vegetables, and flowers without killing the plants.

Although this all sounds positive, there's another side to GMOs that isn't so rosy.

For one thing, it's not always clear that the nonplant matter that's injected into the seed is safe for human ingestion. For example, a gene found in flounder fish makes it impossible to freeze flounder. Inserting that same gene into a plant makes it more resistant to cold temperatures, to e. coli, and to a natural pesticide known as *Bacillus thuringiensis* (B.t.). (B.t. is a naturally occurring bacterium that produces crystal proteins that kill insect larvae when they try to eat crops that contain this gene.) Many people are concerned about the safety of ingesting food grown from GMO seeds.

Additionally, GMO seeds are patented. That means that it's illegal to save seeds from GMO crops from year to year due to licensing restrictions. Corporate agricultural companies have been known to sue people for saving GMO seeds!

THE BAD SEED

Large agribusinesses are primarily responsible for creating GMO seeds. They inject seeds with their technology and then patent them. As a result, the corporations not only own the seeds they created *but all offspring of those seeds.* Because the seeds are patented, it is illegal to save GMO seeds without first getting permission from the patent holder. This makes saving seed tricky.

If you intend to save seeds, it is essential to know exactly what you're growing in your garden and where it originated. You also need to know what your immediate neighbors are growing. GMO seeds will cross with open-pollinated varieties, so it can be difficult to know whether your seeds have been contaminated until it's too late. You can take steps, such as bagging the plants from which you save seeds or hand-pollinating them, to ensure that the seed you save has not crossed with a GMO variety.

Many types of crops, such as corn, are wind pollinated. GMO pollen, like any other pollen, can travel for miles. To avoid cross-pollinating with GMO plants, be aware of the proximity of the nearest GMO crops to your garden. Also pay close attention to what is growing in nearby ditches and in your yard. Take the time to destroy any plants that aren't killed by weed killers, even if this means digging them out by hand and burning them. If you prefer not to use chemical weed killers, try vinegar—it does the job well and is completely nontoxic.

As more people choose to grow GMO varieties, and with their ability to cross-pollinate with other types of plants, we could be looking at the end of the road for seed savers everywhere. Imagine the loss of thousands of varieties of heirloom seeds that people have been saving for countless generations. Once these seeds are extinct, there's no way to get them back.

Before you choose to grow GMO crops, do your research. Know the good points and the bad points, and take the time to make an informed decision.

Spores

Not all plants produce seeds. Some produce *spores.* Spores are a single-cell reproductive body capable of growing into a new organism.

Spores are tiny, almost powderlike substances. They grow in a spore case, known as sporangia, which are then enclosed in a sorus (or, if there are more than one, a sori). These are often located on the underside of the plants' leaves or fronds.

DEFINITION

A **spore** is a small, usually single-celled reproductive body that is highly resistant to desiccation (being dried out) and heat, and is capable of growing into a new organism. Plants produced by spores include certain bacteria, fungi, algae, and other nonflowering plants.

Orchids, ferns, fungi, mosses, and lichens are among the many plants that produce spores instead of seeds. If you intend to collect spores, timing is essential. Once mature, the plants wait for a dry day and then release hundreds of microscopic spores into the air, where they may travel for miles before landing. For details on saving and starting spores, see Appendix C.

Learning the Lingo: Botanical Names vs. Common Names

If you've ever wondered why some gardeners and gardening books insist on using seed *nomenclature*, the reason is simple: using common names can introduce confusion because they're often regionally based. This is especially true for flowers and herbs (the common name of most fruits and vegetables remains the same regardless of where you live as long as people speak English). For example, a plant known as Blazing Star in one part of the country is known as Button Snakeroot or Gayfeather elsewhere—and it gets even more confusing when you factor in language differences around the world. By referring to the plant by its correct botanical name—*Liatris*—you can rest assured that anyone who comes into contact with your seeds, whether by sharing, purchasing, or donating, will know exactly what they are.

DEFINITION

Nomenclature is the use of Latin names in botany for labeling plants. Nomenclature is a system used in many arts and sciences.

Botanical names for flowers and herbs are the same throughout the world, unlike common names, which change according to where you are, who you're talking to, and what language is being spoken. The usefulness of botanical names becomes abundantly clear when you consider, for example, the pansy: the pansy is a member of the *Violaceae* family, which includes approximately 500 known species. So which pansy are you talking about? Or to which of the approximately 500 species of *Primulaceae*, which includes the primrose, are you referring?

Always list the correct botanical name for flowers and herbs on your seed envelopes when you package them. If you intend to ship seeds, you may be required to list the botanical name on the content form that attaches to the outside of the box or envelope. If you don't include this information, your shipment may be denied, especially if you're shipping the seeds out of the country.

Don't be intimidated by botanical names—they aren't as difficult as they seem. Often a plant's common name, or some part of it, is derived from the botanical name. A good example of this is impatiens. The common name is exactly the same as the botanical name.

Knowing the botanical name also helps you cross-reference plants easily when someone uses the common name. If you have any doubt about what plant you're talking about, show him or her a photo of the plant. Then you'll know you're both talking about the same plant.

Distinguishing Between Genus and Species

The plant kingdom is sectioned into divisions, classes, orders, families, genera or genus, and then species; there's even a further classification of varieties under species. For practical purposes, the two classifications to concern yourself with are the genus and the species.

A Quick Nomenclature Lesson

Plant Classification	Example	Definition
Genus	*Salvia*	A group of closely related plant species.
Species	*Salvia coccinea*	A group of plants in the same genus with common characteristics that set them apart from other members of the genus.
Form or variety	*Fragaria vesca* var. *vesca*	A naturally occurring variation of the straight species. For example, the flower color may be different, but the rest of the plant is the same.

Plant Classification	Example	Definition
Cultivar	*Fragaria vesca* "Alpine Yellow"	The result when a human intentionally breeds to get a distinct variation with a desirable characteristic.
Hybrid	*Dicentra* x *spectabilis* *Viola* x *cornuta*	A named variety created by crossing two plants in the same genus or two plants in two totally different genera. The "x" denotes the fact that the plant is a hybrid.

Finding the Botanical Names of Your Plants

Learning botanical nomenclature takes time and patience. But doing so makes sharing your knowledge as well as your plants or seeds with other gardeners much more rewarding. The international plant names index (www.ipni.org) is a great resource for looking up and learning botanical names.

The botanical name does more than aid in accurate plant identification. It facilitates your ability to look up growing preferences, pest and disease problems, data on how to propagate the plant, and more.

KNOW THY SEED

Many botanical names are the same as the common names or are similar to words you already know, which makes learning the Latin names easier than you might think.

Start small. Don't overwhelm yourself. Pick one or two plants and learn their botanical names. Keep a good reference book with you when you're in the garden so you can look up plants you're unfamiliar with. Repetition is the key to learning; eventually, you'll find yourself able to identify your garden's plants by their botanical names.

The Least You Need to Know

- Seeds saved from the best plants in your garden are superior to anything you can buy.
- Saving and sharing seeds preserves an important part of our history.
- GMO plants can cross-pollinate with non-GMO plants, creating seed that is illegal to save.
- Try to identify plants by their correct botanical name to avoid potential confusion based on regional differences in common names.

A Seed Is Born

In This Chapter

- Identifying plant reproductive anatomy
- Understanding the importance of natural pollinators
- Creating the right habitat for natural pollinators
- Embracing beneficial insects in the garden

Seeds play an important role in the circle of life. All living organisms depend on the continued production of seed for their survival. And for plants to produce seed, they must be pollinated. Natural pollination occurs through insects, animals, wind, or water, although some plants are capable of pollinating themselves. Plants require certain habitats to pollinate successfully. Additionally, some insects play a particularly beneficial role when it comes to successfully pollinating plants and protecting seeds.

Plant Anatomy 101

Flowers have a purpose, and it's not to decorate our gardens or our tables—even though that's what we love about them. The sole purpose of the flower is to attract pollinators, become pollinated, and produce seed. Pollination is the transfer of pollen—minute, usually yellow, grains—from the tips of the *stamen*, which is the male reproductive part of the plant, to the *pistil*, which is the female reproductive organ.

Flowers that contain both the male and female reproductive organs are considered complete or perfect. Plants that contain flowers of just one sex are said to be incomplete or imperfect.

DEFINITION

The **stamen** is the male reproductive part of the plant. It's made up of filaments, which are long stalks, and anthers, which are the swollen tips at the end of the filaments where the pollen grain is formed. The **pistil** is the female part of the plant.

The stamen is comprised of modified leaves that form inside the flower and grow into a long stalk called the *filament.*

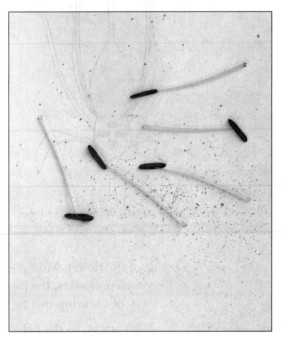

Here you can see the stamen, filament, and grains of pollen.

The swollen tips that sit on top of the filament are known as *anthers.* The anthers are pollen sacs where individual pollen grains form and develop. When the pollen is mature, the sacs burst open.

KNOW THY SEED

Some plants, such as hollies, require that you have both a male and a female plant for pollination to occur. The flowers these plants produce are known as "imperfect" because they are either male or female.

The pollen must touch the pistil at just the right stage of the flower's development for successful pollination to occur, much like the delicate timing of sperm and egg merging in humans. The pollen must also come from the right flower. Just as it's unlikely that breeding a feline and a canine will produce any progeny, pollination typically doesn't occur in unrelated species.

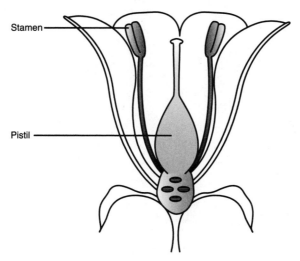

A flower showing both the stamen, the male organ that bears the pollen, and the pistil, or female organ.

The pistil typically forms in the center of the flower. Most plants have numerous carpels, which make up the pistil. In complete flowers, the pistils and the stamen grow close together, which is nature's way of ensuring that pollination takes place.

The stigma is the top part of the pistil. It's sticky, so the pollen attaches easily. The plant's pistils are connected to ovaries by a long tube known as a *style*. Once pollen touches the stigma, the plant forms a pollen tube.

The pollen tube carries the pollen down to the ovary, which contains the eggs. Once the eggs inside the ovary are fertilized, the ovary begins to swell and form a fruitlike structure, which is the developing seedpod.

The ovary encloses and protects the developing seeds until they reach the right size. At that point, the ovary stops growing. When the green seedpods begin to turn brown, the seeds inside the ovary are starting to mature.

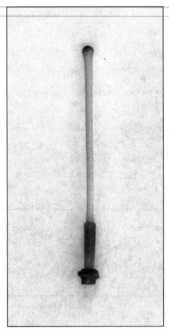

Here's where the pistil attached to the ovary.

The Birds and the Bees: Plant Sex

Often pollination occurs when an insect or other pollinator moves around inside a flower in an attempt to reach the nectar. The pollen rubs off on the insect's body when it bumps against the flower's stamen. As the insect burrows deeper into the plant, its body rubs against the stigma, effectively transferring the pollen.

Flowers have adapted over time to use specific methods to attract pollinators:

- Specific colors
- Different wavelengths of light
- Movement
- Smell

As insects fly around looking for nectar, they may notice an ultraviolet stripe inside a flower that's invisible to the unaided human eye. If the color appeals to the bugs, they land on the flower's petals and follow the ultraviolet guide down to the source of nectar.

Different flower features attract different types of pollinators. For instance, butterflies and birds are attracted to red and yellow flowers, moths and bats like white and other light colors, and bees prefer shades of blue and ultraviolet light.

> **SPROUTING WISDOM**
>
> Insects and animals aren't aware that their foraging activities pollinate plants—they simply want to sip the nectar that sustains them. The color, scent, and shape of the flower are what attract the insect to it. In return for their pollination efforts, the flower offers the insects nutrition in the form of wax, pollen, and nectar, some of which is narcotic and modifies the insect's behavior. Some flower nectars offer pheromones, which the insects use in any number of ways, from sexual attractants to defense mechanisms.

Color isn't the only way plants attract pollinators. Some flowers, such as *Amorphophallus*, a tropical member of the Arum family, and *Symplocarpus foetidus* (skunk cabbage) produce a foul-smelling odor that's unsettlingly similar to decaying flesh. This odor attracts the flies that pollinate them.

Cycas, a palmlike imperfect tropical plant, produces heat to activate a unique odor that attracts pollinators.

> **SPROUTING WISDOM**
>
> Flowers must bloom at the right time of day (or night) to attract the right pollinators. Some plants, such as the yucca, are pollinated only at night. To offer the pollinators easier access to them, yuccas turn their flowers toward the sky at night. When the sun comes up, the flowers turn back, facing the ground. Bats, moths, and other creatures of the night are attracted to the nectar or fragrance that night-blooming plants produce.

DIY Plants: Self-Pollinators

Some plants are self-pollinating. In these plants, the stigma grows so close to the anthers that the pollen naturally falls onto them, allowing fertilization to occur without any assistance from birds, insects, or other pollinators.

Self-pollinating plants normally have a stable gene pool, so they can inbreed for generations without any problems. Self-pollinating plants set seed readily and are some of the easiest plants to save seed from. The following list includes some self-pollinating edible plants:

Barley

Cowpeas

Endive

Escarole

Lettuce

Lima beans

Oats

Peas

Peppers

Snap beans

Soybeans

Strawberries

Tomatoes

Wheat

Some self-pollinators need a helping hand to get pollinated. You can help these flowers by gently shaking them as you walk past or work in your garden. This action encourages the remaining pollen to fall onto the surrounding flowers, hopefully fulfilling the job.

It Takes Two to Tango: Cross-Pollinators

Most plants reject pollen from their own flowers; such plants are called *cross-pollinators*. This characteristic of a plant rejecting its own pollen has evolved for the same reason we humans avoid inbreeding within our families: to prevent the prevalence of weak or diseased genes. Diversity has a better shot at giving healthy genes dominance. The flowers of plants also generally reject pollen from foreign species, just as humans don't reproduce with other species

Mother's Helpers: Natural Pollinators

A wide variety of insects and animals pollinate plants. For instance, people rarely think of bats as pollinators, but they are, and so are birds, beetles, lemurs, lizards, geckos, and skinks. Pollinators often have long tongues, grasping feet, or long tails that allow them to easily access the nectar and, in the process, pollinate the flower.

Some of our most important pollinators aren't even living creatures; wind and water also transfer pollen from plant to plant.

SPROUTING WISDOM

The world's largest pollinator, the black and white ruffled lemur, is responsible for pollinating the Traveler's Palm Tree *(Ravenala madagascariensis)*. The fruit of this tree is a major source of food in its country of origin, Madagascar.

In return for pollinating plants, living pollinators receive shelter, nest-building materials, and food—both in the form of natural sugar from the nectar and from insects that may be on the plant. Plus, flowers are an easy place to find a mate. Some pollinators dine on the pollen as well, which is full of protein, fat, vitamins, and minerals.

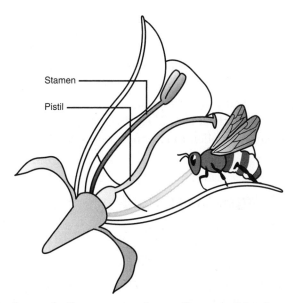

The design of a flower ensures that a pollinator will brush against the stigma and then move the pollen to the pistil in an attempt to get to the nectar at the bottom of the flower.

Birds, Bees, and Other Insects

Bees, butterflies, and moths are the largest group of pollinators. More than 2,000 species of birds around the world use the nectar the flowers produce or the insects that visit the flowers as their main food source. Hummingbirds, honeyeaters, honey-creepers, sunbirds, white-winged doves, and brush-tongued parrots are among the world's key pollinators.

KNOW THY SEED

A flower's shape and color attract the birds to it. Birds tend to navigate toward red, yellow, or orange tubular, funnel-shaped, or cup-shaped flowers with strong, recurved petals (petals that curve backward or downward). Such flowers are ideal for birds to land on.

The head and the back of the bird become covered with pollen as it seeks out the nectar, which is deep inside the flower. Just as with other pollinators, as the bird moves around inside the flower or from flower to flower, it transfers the pollen.

Wind and Water

Wind and water pollinate plants. In fact, wind pollinates around 12 percent of the world's flowering plants. Examples of wind-pollinated plants include corn, beets, Swiss chard, spinach, rye, grass, and many types of trees.

Wind is a very effective means of transporting pollen, as anyone knows who has walked out to their car only to find a yellow dustlike substance coating their windshield. Wind-pollinated plants produce an abundance of pollen that drifts on and on until it finds a suitable mate.

Plants that are wind pollinated don't produce nectar, fragrance, or vibrant-colored, showy flowers. In fact, the flowers on wind-pollinated plants are typically tiny. The stigmas are usually feathery or branched, with the anthers exposed, making it easy for the grains of pollen to attach to them.

Water pollination is a much more rare occurrence, but it does happen. Often plants that are pollinated by water are either male or female, so pollen from each is needed for pollination to occur. Most water-pollinated plants are pond, or aquatic, plants. Certain mosses and algae are the more commonly known types of water-pollinated plants.

Creating Healthy Habitats for Pollinators

Creating a habitat in your garden that encourages the bees, butterflies, birds, and other local pollinators to take up residence is an excellent way to ensure their survival. It also goes a long way toward guaranteeing that you'll have a bumper crop of plants from which to save seeds. While it may not be practical for every gardener to create a large habitat, or even one that welcomes larger animals, you can create a small habitat just about anywhere—even if it's just on a windowsill.

Bees constitute the largest group of insect pollinators, followed closely by butterflies.

Avian Sanctuaries

To create a bird-friendly habitat, follow any of these suggestions:

- Hang a hummingbird feeder and keep it filled with sugar or honey-sweetened water. Many people add red food dye, but that's bad for the birds. They do like red, though, so buy a red feeder and tie red ribbons to it. A great spot to hang a hummingbird house is under the eaves of your roof, it is somewhat protected from high winds and bad weather.

- Set up a birdbath—and be sure to keep fresh water in it and clean it out regularly.

- Plant small shrubs that birds can nest in.
- Plant colorful flowers in reds, purples, and yellows that attract birds: cone-flowers (*Echinacea*) and trumpet vine are two good choices.

Not all birds are pollinators. Only nectar-feeding birds will help grow your garden. Many such species exist in Asia and Africa, but fewer reside in North America. The most popular avian pollinators in the United States are hummingbirds. Honeycreepers, which belong to the tanager family, are found in some parts of the South but are prevalent mainly from Mexico to south Brazil and in Hawaii. The white-winged dove is a good pollinator, too; doves are ground feeders, so if there are white-winged doves in your area—which is mainly the southwestern United States and the Gulf states, be sure to sprinkle some sunflower seeds and thistle on the ground to attract them.

KNOW THY SEED

The plants most attractive to hummingbirds are red, yellow, or orange and have tubes, funnels, or cups with sturdy supports for perching. These plants are open during the day and produce lots of nectar.

Butterfly Gardens

To attract butterflies, grow plenty of flowers rich in nectar, which butterflies feed on. They like rotting fruit, too, so don't throw away those overripe bananas or peaches. Instead, put them outside, on a rock or a post near your garden. Whereas birds are attracted mainly by color, butterflies are attracted by scent, so grow strong-scented flowers and flowering bushes. Some good choices are butterfly bush (*Buddleia*), bee balm (*Monarda*), and sweet shrub (*Calycanthus*).

Bat-Friendly Habitats

Bats tend to get a bad rap, but these winged mammals do a lot to benefit humans. Fruit bats in warm climates pollinate one third of the world's fruit, and bats are the primary reforesters of rainforests around the world. Insect-eating bats on all continents (except the Antarctic) gobble up to 1,500 insects per bat in a single night! Without bats to patrol the everlasting invasions of bugs, humans would find summer evenings out too buggy, and forests would die out because bats eat insects that destroy forests.

You can encourage bats to spend time in your yard by providing a water source, like a small pool. You can also put up a bat house, but be sure to use the correct design for your area. Bird stores sell bat houses that are usually nothing but redesigned bird-houses that bats would never use.

SPROUTING WISDOM

For good information about bats and bat houses, check out the Bat Conservation International website at www.bci.com.

Befriending Other Beneficial Bugs

Beneficial insects do a lot more in the garden than just pollinate. They help rid the garden of the bad bugs that can destroy your fruits, flowers, or vegetables. The following table lists some common beneficial insects and the bad bugs on which they feast.

The Good Bugs and the Bad Bugs They Eat

Beneficial Insect	Predatory Bug
Green lacewings	Aphids, mealy bugs, immature scale insects, spider mites, whiteflies
Assassin bugs	Caterpillars, beetles
Ladybugs	Scale insects, aphids, mites, mealybugs, thrips
Praying mantis	Beetles, grasshoppers, roaches, leafhoppers, aphids, small flies, Japanese beetles
Minute pirate bugs	Mites, aphids, thrips
Ground beetles	Slugs, cutworms, root maggots, caterpillars, insect eggs
Predatory stink bugs	Grubs, sawfly larvae, caterpillars
Syrphid flies (hover flies)	Aphids, scale insects, thrips, soft-bodied insects, caterpillars
Damsel bugs	Leafhoppers, soft-bodied insects, Caterpillars, thrips
Big-eyed bugs	Insect eggs, mites, aphids
Parasitic wasps	Tomato hornworm, flies, aphids, beetles, sawflies, scale insects

Although beneficial insects aren't a cure-all, they are an organic, natural way to help prevent a total crop failure in case an excessive amount of bad bugs invade your garden.

KNOW THY SEED

Once you've made the decision to encourage natural pollinators and beneficial insects to take up residence in your garden, avoid all pesticides and herbicides. If necessary, remove by hand any pests that are causing a big problem.

To survive, beneficial insects require bad bugs to feast on, a natural source of nectar, a shallow source of water, plus a place to hide and lay their eggs. If one of these is lacking, there's a good chance the beneficial insects won't hang around long, especially after they've consumed the live insects. This means when the eggs laid by the bad bugs hatch, no one will be there to eat them.

Follow these guidelines to create an ideal habitat for beneficial insects:

- Set a shallow dish near your garden and keep it filled with fresh water. Place some rocks inside and outside the dish. Some bugs, like butterflies, can drown if the water source is too deep; the rocks give them a safe place to perch as they sun and bathe.

- Don't mulch every square inch of your garden. Soil contains minerals that bugs need to survive; your soil is more attractive to them if it's easier to get to.

- Make sure there are hiding places in the flowerbeds, around shrubs, or in an area of the yard where the grass is allowed to grow. These can be as simple as scattered rocks and stones or decorative items used in landscaping.

- Set aside a small section of your yard and plant a little garden for them. Good plants to grow for beneficial insects include aster (*Aster*), goldenrod (*Solidago*), mint (*Mentha*), dill (*Anethum*), bachelor's button (*Centaurea*), sweet alyssum (*Lobularia*), borage (*Borago*), cup plant (*Silphyum*), anise hyssop (*Agastache foeniculum*), golden marguerite (*Anthemis tinctoria*), and fennel (*Foeniculum vulgare*). Many of these plants thrive in poor soil and bloom on and off all summer if you keep the faded flowers cut off; they're very easy to care for.

- Allow dead plant material to stand over the winter. This provides beneficial insects a place to lay their eggs where they can hatch naturally come spring.

Beneficial insects are an important part of both plant diversity and a healthy garden, regardless of the size of the garden. Remember that nothing in nature happens overnight. Encouraging beneficial insects and pollinators to hang out in your garden could take several years. However, to speed the process along, you can purchase some of these critters, like ladybugs, whitefly parasites, green lacewings, trichogramma, fly parasites, predatory mites, and nematodes; see Appendix B for some sources.

> **SPROUTING WISDOM**
>
> You might even consider raising honeybees. It's an easy and inexpensive hobby, and the benefits to your garden are myriad—plus, you can reap the harvest of delicious honey for your kitchen. You can find numerous resources online to help you get started. Another good resource is *The Complete Idiot's Guide to Beekeeping* (Alpha Books, 2010).

Allowing your garden to be as natural as possible allows seeds to develop that are better able to cope with the natural world and not rely on chemicals to keep them free of pests and diseases. Learning to coexist with the beneficial insects and pollinators in your garden is a journey you will be glad you embarked on.

The Least You Need to Know

- Pollination must occur for seeds to form; however, not all plants are capable of setting viable seed.
- Potential pollinators are insects, wind, water, bats, birds, and other mammals.
- Create a pollinator-friendly landscape to encourage pollinators to remain in your yard.
- Beneficial insects pollinate and help keep the bad bugs out of the garden.

Harvesting and Storing Seeds

A lot more is involved in saving seeds than just going out and collecting whatever seeds you see in your garden. You need to get to know your plants intimately. What qualities make them special to you? Are they healthy specimens? Why do you want to save seeds from a particular plant? There's no point in saving seeds from diseased or pest-ridden plants, because those same weak characteristics will likely end up in the next generation of plants as well.

This part helps you select the appropriate plants for seed saving and provides a detailed explanation of how to harvest the seeds from a wide variety of plants. And after you've collected seeds, you find out how to process them, clean them, and store them until you're ready to sow them.

How to Save Seeds

In This Chapter

- Identifying mature seeds
- Knowing how to harvest seeds
- Collecting seeds
- Steering clear of wild seeds

Saving seeds from the plants that you grow in your garden, or collecting seeds from a friend's garden, is a very rewarding activity, but it also requires patience, commitment, and a sense of adventure. Usually you know what the parent plants are, but if hybridization has occurred, a shroud of mystery surrounds the resulting seed. Will the seedlings look just like the parent, or will they grow into brand-new plants? Sometimes seeds, such as peonies, can take several years to sprout and even longer before you see the true flowers. Other seeds, such as those collected from vegetable plants or annual flowers, grow, produce, and set seedpods during their first growing season.

Harvesting Seeds: An Overview

When you collect seeds, you should select them from healthy plants that have the qualities you desire, whether those qualities include a certain taste, a nice fragrance, or exceptional beauty.

Avoid collecting seeds from plants with odd shapes—unless, that is, you like odd shapes—and that have pest or disease problems. The parent plant's traits are in the genes of any seeds you collect. So if the seeds you save are from plants with undesirable traits, whether disease or pest magnets, there's a very good chance those traits will show up in the plants grown from those seeds.

As explained in Chapter 1, seeds either are enclosed in a seedpod that splits open when the seeds are ripe, or grow inside the fruit or vegetable. If the plant has been pollinated, it will more than likely set seed.

The technique you use for harvesting seeds depends on the type of plant you're working with. You use either of the following techniques:

- **Dry collecting:** Used for plants whose seeds grow outside the plant
- **Wet collecting:** Used for seeds that grow inside a fruit or vegetable

The following sections explain each of these techniques in detail.

Dry Collecting Seeds

Dry collecting is the easiest method to use to collect seeds. Nature has done most of the work for you. You simply allow the seeds to dry on the plant and then collect the seedpods before they break open. (Some plants, such as sunflowers, do not encase their seeds in a seedpod. Instead they protect them with hard shells. These seeds often develop in the center of the flower head.)

Plants that produce seeds on the outside of the plant (instead of inside a fruit or vegetable) typically grow a seedpod that holds the developing seeds. The seedpod swells and grows in size as the seeds develop. You can watch the process if you pay attention to a particular flower when it's in bloom. Look inside the flower and identify the ovary, which is located in the center of the plant. It should look like a swollen bump, usually in some shade of green. Some ovaries stand completely above the attachment of other floral parts (these are called *superior ovaries*); some are completely below the rest of the flower (these are called *inferior ovaries*), making them harder to see; and some are situated both above and below the attachment point.

After the flower is pollinated and the flower petals begin to drop, the ovary should continue to grow in size. When you see the ovary increasing in size, you can be confident that the flower has been pollinated and is forming seeds. The ovary turns into the seedpod as the seeds develop and mature.

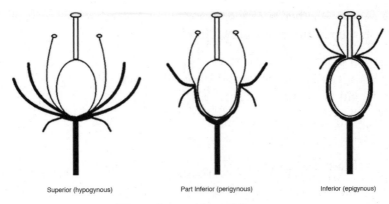

Superior (hypogynous)   Part Inferior (perigynous)   Inferior (epigynous)

The various positions of the ovary.

Although you may be tempted at this stage to harvest the seedpod, restrain yourself! If you harvest the seeds too early, they won't be mature enough to grow. Allow the seedpod to remain on the plant until the seedpod turns brown. The stem that holds the seedpod will also turn brown. When the seedpod and stem holding it turn brown, the seeds are mature and ready to harvest.

If the ovary or seedpod didn't grow and didn't split open when it dried, it's doubtful that any seeds inside are viable, even if they look like they are. Go ahead and break open one of the seedpods to see if there are mature seeds inside. You have to remove them from the seedpod anyway when you get ready to dry them (see Chapter 4).

THE BAD SEED

Green seedpods aren't ripe. You shouldn't remove seedpods from the plant until they turn brown. Seeds need to mature on the plant in order to be able to grow when they are planted again.

Trapping Seeds on the Plant: The Pantyhose Method

To ensure that you don't lose any seeds, you can add a homemade "net" to capture them. Simply cut the feet off a pair of pantyhose just above the ankle. Place the toe over the top of the seedpod, with the ankle dangling around the stem. Use twist ties, string, or a strip of the discarded part of the pantyhose to secure the bottom of the material to the plant stem; be careful not to tie it too tight, lest it damage the stem. You have created a little tent that will prevent the seeds from dropping to the ground—and stop birds from eating the seeds.

Using pantyhose to capture seeds.

Regularly check the twist tie or string that you secured the pantyhose with, because as the plant's stem dries, it may shrink. If the tie becomes loose enough, the seeds can slip through the bottom of the pantyhose.

You don't want the seedpod to be wet for long, or mold might form and ruin the seeds. If there's a heavy rain, remove the pantyhose and wring it out before you replace it—or, better yet, replace it with dry pantyhose. Even using the pantyhose method, it is important to keep an eye on the seedpod. As soon as you see it begin to split open, go ahead and harvest it—as long as it's dry (see the following section for details on harvesting seedpods).

This method works for almost any type of seed that you dry-harvest. The pantyhose method is especially helpful for plants, such as touch-me-nots, that have exploding seedpods.

Harvesting Your Seeds

Take with you into the garden a container of some type when you collect seeds so that you have something to put them into. Put just one type of seed/seedpod in each container and take the time to label the seeds as you collect them. Don't underestimate the importance of labeling your seeds: identifying them can be difficult because seeds can look very similar to one another—especially when they are out of the seedpod.

THE BAD SEED

If you allow seeds to remain on the plant during numerous rainy days, they may mold or begin to grow inside the seedpod. Once the seeds get moldy or begin to germinate, they are done for. Watch the weather to help determine the best time to collect mature seeds.

You can harvest the mature seedpod in any of the following ways:

- Cut the seedpod off the plant and turn it upside down. The pantyhose will catch any seeds that fall.

- Hang the plant upside down from its stem in a cool, dark, dry area and let the pod finish opening on its own; keep the pantyhose attached to catch the seeds.

- Gently crush the seedpod with your hands, releasing the seeds into the pantyhose.

Getting the Timing Right

There's no single best time to harvest seeds. Each plant is different, so you must abide by the plant's natural cycles and harvest the seeds only when the plant is ready. The seeds must reach maturity on the plant—or in the plant, as the case may be—for them to be viable. Most of the time, this means allowing them to form and dry on the plant.

The best way to know when to harvest seeds is to know the plant—know what the seedpod produces and what it looks like at maturity. If you have any doubts about whether seeds are mature enough to harvest, you can test the seeds to see if they're viable (see Chapter 6).

Seedpods vary greatly from plant to plant. Some plants, such as lotus and poppies, have seedpods with holes that allow water to penetrate; if the water remains in the pod for too long, the seeds can mold or rot and die. Other seedpods, such as those of the hibiscus and peony, remain tightly sealed during the seed-formation process and crack open only when the seeds are mature.

A variety of seedpods.

The ideal time of day to collect seeds is the early afternoon, well after the dew has evaporated. Wet, cool conditions lead to loss, so try to collect seed after three to four days of warm, dry weather. Of course, Mother Nature doesn't always cooperate, and sometimes seed has to be collected under less than ideal conditions; just do the best you can. Even if the seeds are wet, proper drying can save them as long as mold has not started to develop. If you must collect seeds that are wet, remove them from the seedpod immediately and lay them out on a seed-drying screen (see Chapter 4).

Wet Processing Seeds

Several types of seeds grow and mature inside plants with a fleshy pulp, such as passionfruit, tomato, balsam pear, and cucumber. You must use a technique known as wet processing to save the seeds from these types of plants.

You must allow the fruit to reach full maturity on the plant before you collect these types of seeds. That's the only way the seeds can mature and be viable. But you don't want to wait too long, because the seeds can begin to *germinate* inside the plant—and they will be lost to you.

DEFINITION

When a seed **germinates,** it begins to sprout, or grow, into a plant. **Germination** is the moment the seed goes from dormant to active.

When the fruit is ripe, cut it open and scoop out the seeds. Although some of the flesh will be too close to the seeds to remove at this time, try to remove as much as possible. Be very careful not to damage the seeds in the process of trying to remove the flesh; if it's too difficult to remove, leave it on the seeds.

As you remove the seeds from the fruit, place them in a clean, clear glass container. Some of these seeds, such as apple seeds, have a hard seed coat. Others, like tomato seeds, have a soft seed coat. Wet seeds vary just as greatly as those that are dry processed.

Some seeds that are wet processed, such as citrus or apple, simply need washed off to remove the sticky sugars that accumulate on the seeds. Other types of wet processed seeds, such as tomatoes or cucumbers, require fermentation to remove the gel-like coating that forms around the seeds. This coating will make it difficult, if not impossible, for the seeds to germinate. The easiest way to know if you need to ferment or not is to drop the seeds in a cup of warm water and look at them. The gel-like coating is easy to see within a couple of minutes of them being submerged. If the seed has the gel-like coating, you need to ferment them before drying them.

Fermenting

The purpose of *fermentation* is to remove the flesh from the seeds so they are clean. You can add water to speed the process along or allow natural, unaided fermentation to take place.

DEFINITION

Fermentation occurs naturally when mold, fungus, yeast, or other bacteria convert carbohydrates to alcohol or organic acid (carbon dioxide).

Fermenting with Water

If you choose to add water to the seeds and clinging pulp, use just enough room-temperature water to completely cover the plant material. Leave this same water in the glass with the seeds throughout the fermentation process. Allow the plant material to sit undisturbed in a dark place for three to five days. Scum will form on top of the water; this is a natural part of the fermentation process and is nothing to worry about.

After three to five days, scoop the scum off the top of the water along with any floating plant debris—including any seeds that are floating on top of the water. Pour the remaining water off through a fine sieve to catch the seeds at the bottom of the container.

Most seeds are heavier than water and fall to the bottom of the container. Typically, seeds that float are not viable. But there are exceptions to this rule. Papery *Amaryllis* seeds, for example, float and germinate on top of the water.

Fermenting Without Water

To ferment seeds without adding water, place the seeds into a jar, sprinkle them with salt (to get the plant material to release its natural juices), and let them sit, undisturbed, in a dark place for three to five days. After three to five days, scrape off the mold that forms, along with any plant material that has mold on it, and throw it away.

THE BAD SEED

Some seeds germinate during the fermentation process. Don't save these seeds. Instead, dispose of them along with the mold and scum.

Cleaning and Drying

Regardless of which method you used to ferment the seeds, the next step is to rinse them in room-temperature water, to eliminate any remaining mold or plant debris from the seed. When you're satisfied that the seeds are clean, give them one final rinse with hydrogen peroxide. You don't have to rinse the hydrogen peroxide off the seeds; it won't harm them. Simply strain it off and then proceed to dry them (see Chapter 4).

Collecting Seeds from the Wild

When people collect seed from wild, endangered plants, they further endanger the plants by taking away the plants' chance to propagate. Additionally, harvesting wild seeds is often illegal and could result in large fines or even a jail sentence. If you find a plant in the wild that you really want, first look at local nurseries and check online to see if you can find a source for that plant. If not, contact your local Department of Natural Resources office to see if you can get a permit to collect seeds from that plant.

THE BAD SEED

Many wildflowers are endangered. Don't collect seed from the wild without proper permission and permits. Keep a paper trail, especially if you collect seeds from endangered plants. It could save you a lot of legal trouble later.

If you get permission, collect only enough seeds to get a new one started in your garden. Removing all the seeds could result in a total loss of that plant in its native habitat. If that happens, the wild animals and insects that know where that plant is and rely on it for food or nectar will be forced to move on and look for a new source of food, if they can find one. Wild plants, even those growing on the side of the road, are an essential part of a healthy, thriving ecosystem.

Another problem with moving wild collected plants into a domesticated situation is that they may simply fail to thrive. Wild plants have adapted over time to grow where they are. Some don't like fertilization, even if it is nothing more than compost. Others, such as orchids, need certain elements in the soil, such as fungi, to thrive.

Certainly, some plants grown from wild seed will adapt to their new growing environment, but not always. Before you remove even one seed, research the wild plants you want to grow. The only exception to the rule is if that plant was going to be destroyed due to development; even then, do your research first. If that particular plant won't thrive in your garden, pass the seed on to a seed-saving organization or seed-saving bank where it can get into the hands of someone who can propagate it.

Vegetable Seed-Saving Tips

Saving vegetable seeds is a great way to save money on your grocery bill, especially if you preserve the food you grow. Saving your own vegetable seed also allows you to choose which varieties are better adapted to your garden and growing conditions. However, saving vegetable seeds takes some practice. Here are some tips and tricks to help you get off to a good start and ensure success from the beginning.

Most vegetable plants produce seedpods, so you should use the dry collection method to harvest their seeds. Once vegetable plants start producing seed, they stop producing food. For example, when bush beans mature past the picking stage, they begin to dry up and change into seeds. As the seedpods begin to dry, so does the plant. The bean pod splits open if it's left on the plant too long. To test whether it's time to pick a bean pod for seeds, put a little pressure on both sides of a pod at the split; if it begins to open, they're ready. The seeds inside will still need to dry a little longer before they are stored.

asparagus The seeds form inside the red berries produced on the female plant. When the top of the plant starts to bend, cut off the red berries. Soak the berries in water, removing the skin and pulp using the wet method. Air-dry the seeds for at least a week.

beans, lima and snap Leave the beans on the plant until the pod and plant begin to turn brown. Remove the pod and gently break it open to remove the seeds; then let them air-dry for two weeks.

broccoli Allow the bud clusters, which are the part of the plant you eat, to flower. When the pods are completely dry, pull up the plant by its roots, hang it upside down in a paper bag in a dry place for several weeks, and then remove the seeds by crushing the pods.

cantaloupe Spoon the seeds out of a ripe cantaloupe; process the seeds using the wet processing method described earlier in this chapter, and then let them air-dry for a week.

corn Don't pick the corn until a month after the time you would normally pick it to eat it. Peel back the husk and hang the ears in a dark, well-ventilated area until they're completely dry; you will know they're dry when you crush a corn seed and it turns into powder.

SPROUTING WISDOM

To ensure that the seeds you save reap the vegetables you want, choose open-pollinated heirloom varieties when selecting seeds. Hybrid seed doesn't come true; instead, it reverts back to one of the parent plants. Additionally, if you intend to save seed from more than one variety of a vegetable, be sure to use some sort of isolation method, such as those discussed in Chapter 13. This is especially important if you grow vegetables that cross-pollinate with one another, such as radishes and turnips.

cucumbers Allow the cucumbers to remain on the plant until they turn yellow. Pick them, scoop out the seeds, wet-process them, and then allow them to air-dry.

eggplant Allow the eggplant to remain on the plant until it is dull and somewhat wrinkled. Cut open the eggplant, scoop out the seeds, and process the seeds using the wet processing method. Allow the seeds to air-dry.

lettuce Allow the plant to bolt. (This happens naturally when summer arrives.) When it bolts, the lettuce plant sends up a flower stalk, which forms feathery seed heads. Remove the feathery seeds when they look similar to dandelions. Dry the seeds for an additional week after harvesting.

okra   Allow mature pods to dry on the plant. Collect the seedpods, remove the seeds, and dry them for an additional week.

parsnips   Mulch the plants well so they can survive in the garden over winter. The following spring, flower stalks will emerge. Cover the seed heads with pantyhose as soon as they begin to turn brown. The seed heads will shatter, so keep an eye on them and remove all mature seed immediately; finish drying indoors.

peas   Allow ripe pea pods to remain on the plant until both the plant and the pods begin to turn brown. Remove the seeds from the dry pods and continue to dry them indoors for two more weeks.

peppers   Cut open the pepper, scoop out the seeds, and dry them indoors for two weeks.

pumpkins   Cut open the pumpkin, scoop out the seeds, and use the wet processing method. Dry the seeds indoors for two weeks.

radish   Instead of picking the radish, allow it to send up a seed stalk. Small pods will form. When the pods turn yellow, pull up the plants and hang them to dry. When the pods are completely brown, break them open, remove the seeds, and let them dry an additional week.

spinach   Allow the plant to bolt (this will happen naturally in the summer). The seeds form on the long flower spikes. Allow the seeds to ripen and turn brown on the plant. Pick them and dry them for an additional week.

summer squash and zucchini   Allow the fruit to ripen on the vine and remain there for an additional eight weeks. Then cut the fruit off the vine, scoop out the seeds, and process using the wet processing method. Dry the seeds for two weeks.

tomato   Cut open a ripe or overripe tomato. Scoop out the seeds and use the wet processing method; then allow the seeds to dry for one week.

watermelon   Cut open a ripe or slightly overripe watermelon, scoop out the seeds, rinse them off, and dry them for one week.

winter squash   Cut open the fruit and scoop out the seed. Process the seed using the wet processing method. Dry the seed for two weeks.

SPROUTING WISDOM

Seed saved from your garden adapts to the specific growing conditions in your garden. That means the next generation tends to perform better and produce more than store-bought seeds.

Flower Seed-Saving Tips

Flower seeds are some of the easiest to collect. Most are collected and dried using the dry processing method. Flowers have a natural tendency to set seed after they bloom.

Some flowers continue to bloom while they're setting seed. Others stop blooming when seed begins to form.

KNOW THY SEED

Bulbs also form seed, and when they do, all the plant's energy goes into the seed, not the bulb. Thus, the blooms may not be as large or prolific the following year. That's why gardeners dig up some bulbs and replant them the next season. If you want to save seed from bulbs, it's best to allow only a handful to set seed. If you deadhead the faded flowers from all the others or dig up the bulbs, you get the best of both worlds.

Seed companies mass-produce numerous flowers through tissue culture. Many of these are sterile and won't set viable seed. The best flowers to save seed from are those that have been open pollinated. Many native plants—wildflowers and cottage garden types of plants, such as hollyhock (*Althea*), larkspur (*Consolida*), and Indian tobacco (*Nicotiana*)—are open pollinated. But just because you save seed from a pink hollyhock doesn't mean the resulting seedlings will have pink flowers, especially if you grow multiple colors of hollyhocks in your garden. This is all part of the fun of saving seeds; however, if you really want to precisely control the outcome, bagging the plant (see Chapter 13) is the way to go.

angel's trumpet (*Brugmansia* and *Datura*)   The seedpods of this plant are spiny and filled with hallucinogenic liquid, so always wear gloves when working with any part of this plant, including the seeds. Cover the seedpod with pantyhose while it is still green. Allow the seedpod to turn brown and split open before you cut it off the plant. Dry the seeds for two weeks indoors.

arum lily (*Zantedeschia*)   Remove the red berries from the plant and squish them so the seeds come out. Be sure to wear gloves, because these berries will irritate the skin. Process the seeds using the wet processing method to remove any remaining pulp, and then lay the seeds out to dry for two weeks. Arum seeds contain a germination inhibitor that you must wash away before the seeds germinate. Before planting the seeds, place the seeds in a sealed tea strainer and put it under running water.

bee balm (*Monarda*)   Cut the dried seed heads off the plant, place them in a paper bag, and allow them to dry for a week. Place the dried seed heads in a clear glass jar with a lid and shake the jar vigorously to release the wheat-colored seeds. Note that the seeds are difficult to separate from the chaff.

bells of Ireland (*Moluccella*)   Each *bract* forms two to four seeds. Allow the green bracts to turn light brown; as they do, you will be able to see the seeds forming inside. Keep an eye on the seeds, because you want to harvest them as soon as they turn brown, lest they fall to the ground. Wear gloves and be careful when collecting the seeds; you want to avoid touching the two sharp spines that develop directly below the bract. Let the gathered seeds dry for about a week.

> **DEFINITION**
>
> A **bract** is a modified leaf that resembles a flower petal. A good example is the red petals on a Poinsettia or the green petals on the bells of Ireland.

black-eyed Susan (*Rudbeckia*)   Once the flower petals drop, the seed head, which is the center of the flower, turns deep brown. The stem right below the seed head also dries up. Cut off the seed heads and let them dry for a week, then run your hands along the edges of the seed heads to release the small, splinterlike seeds. Allow them to dry for a week.

blanket flower (*Gaillardia*)   Allow the seed head to dry on the plant. Keep a close eye on the process, because once the seeds are dry enough, they begin to separate from the seed head. You can use the pantyhose method to prevent seed loss.

butterfly weed (*Asclepias*)   Long seedpods that are fat or thin, depending on the species, form. At first they are green, but as they mature, they turn gray-brown. Place pantyhose over them at this point, because they split open on their own when they reach maturity. Harvest the seeds, remove the fluff, and let them air-dry for a week.

castor bean (*Ricinus*)   Castor bean seedpods are prickly, so wear gloves when handling them. The seedpods turn brown as they mature. Remove the pod as soon as it turns brown, because it splits open on its own if left for too long. Lay the pods indoors on a screen-drying rack for several days until they open. Each pod has three chambers inside; each chamber is filled with seeds. Lay the seeds on a screen-drying rack and let them air-dry for three to four weeks.

cockscomb (*Celosia*)   Allow the flower to dry on the plant. Cover the flower head with pantyhose or a paper bag, and then cut off the stem. Cockscomb flowers contain numerous tiny black seeds that easily fall out of the flower when it's turned on its side and shaken. Dry the seeds for a week.

columbine (*Aquilegia*)   Tie pantyhose over the top of the seedpods. When the pods are brown and start to break open, cut them off, remove the seeds, and let them dry for a week.

coneflower (*Echinacea*)   Coneflower seed heads are very prickly, so wear gloves when handling them. To keep hungry birds at bay, cover the seed heads with pantyhose once the flower petals fall off. Cut off the seed heads after they are completely brown and then soak them in water for half an hour or so to soften the seeds. The seed bristles will be limp and the seed heads will easily break in half once they have absorbed enough water. The seeds will easily fall away from the seed head at this point. Spread the seeds out on a seed-drying screen, cover them with a second screen, and place the unit in the sun to encourage the seeds to dry quickly and prevent them from molding. As soon as the seeds are superficially dry, move them indoors and allow them to finish drying for two weeks.

daisy (*Leucanthemum*)   Allow the seed head to dry on the plant, then cut it off and dry it intact on a seed-drying screen for a week. The seed head is dry when the wheat-colored seeds easily fall out if you run your fingers across the seed head.

daylily (*Hemerocallis*)   Once the green pod begins to form where the flower was, cover it with pantyhose. Allow the pod to dry on the plant. When it reaches maturity, the end opens up. Remove the pod at this point, split it open, and gently remove the shiny, round, black seeds. Dry them for two weeks.

dolichos bean (*Lablab*)   Allow the pods to dry on the plant until they are brown and papery looking. They split open naturally, so use pantyhose to prevent seed loss. Remove the seeds from the pods and let them air-dry for three to four weeks.

foxglove (*Digitalis*)   Allow the seedpods to mature on the plant. When they start to split open, hold a paper plate under the seedpods and let the seeds fall out naturally. Never collect all the seeds—allow a few to drop onto the ground, to prevent loss of the plant. You can also cut off the entire seedpod if you prefer.

THE BAD SEED

Foxglove can affect your heart, so wear gloves when handling it. Many drugs used to treat the heart, including digitoxin and digoxin, are derived from this plant.

hellebore (*Helleborus*)   Seedpods form inside the flower. They split open and disburse the seed once they are mature. Place pantyhose over the seeds once the seedpods begin to form. You will know this is happening because the center of the flower forms a swollen, starlike shape. Once the seedpods break open, collect the round, black seeds and dry them for a week.

hollyhock (*Althea*)   A disk-shaped green pod forms where the flowers once were. This pod turns brown as it matures and, once it reaches maturity, splits open to reveal a ring of dark brown seeds. Cut the mature pod off the plant and allow it to dry for a week. Remove the seeds, lay them out in a single row, cover them with a screen, and place them in the sun for a couple hours to get rid of any weevils that may be in the seeds. Stir the seeds every hour and watch for signs of insects. When you stop seeing the weevils, leave the seeds for one more hour and then bring them indoors to dry for another week.

THE BAD SEED

Hollyhock can irritate some people's skin, so wear gloves and long sleeves when working with this plant. If your skin becomes irritated, stop immediately and wash your skin with warm, soapy water.

larkspur (*Consolida*)   Tubular pods form where the flowers once were. These pods turn brown and split open to reveal small black seeds. Use pantyhose to prevent the seed from falling on the ground when the pods split open. Dry the seeds for a week.

love-in-a-mist (*Nigella*)   Allow the seedpods to dry on the plant. The mature pods, which are a dull green with maroon stripes, are often used in floral arrangements. Inside the pods are small, dull black seeds. To harvest, cut the dry seedpods off the plants, pull the seedpods apart, and remove the seeds. Allow the seeds to dry for a week.

lupine (*Lupinus*)   The mature seedpods are a gray-black color and easily separate from the plant. Lay the entire seedpod on a seed-drying rack and leave it there for about a week. Break open the pod and remove the seeds. Each pod contains three to four round, dull brown seeds.

marigold (*Tagetes*)   Allow the seed heads to dry on the plant, cut them off, remove the flower seed husk, and spread the individual seeds out on a seed-drying rack to dry for a week.

moonflower (*Ipomoea*)   Cover the seedpods with pantyhose to prevent loss. Mature seedpods turn brown, dry up, and crack. When you shake the pods, you'll hear the seeds rattling around inside them.

morning glory (*Ipomoea*)   Morning glories produce their seedpods in clusters that turn brown and often split open when ripe. Collect the seed as soon as the seedpods turn brown. The seeds inside are brown or black and wedge shaped. Dry the seeds for two weeks.

nasturtium (*Tropaeolum*)   Allow the seedpods to remain on the plant until they turn brown. Then collect them and dry them for two weeks.

peony (*Paeonia*)   Allow the seedpod, which forms in the center of the flower, to mature on the plant. Pollinated seedpods swell; if they don't swell and aren't plump, they aren't pollinated. Cover the seedpods with pantyhose. Once the seedpods are mature, they split open to reveal shiny plump black seeds. Dry the seeds for a month.

pinks (*Dianthus*)   Allow the seedpods to dry on the plant. The top of the seedpod opens slightly when dry. Turn the seedpod upside down and let the small, black seeds fall out. Dry the seeds for a week.

poppies (*Papaver*)   Let the seedpod and the plant turn brown. Cut off the seedpod and turn it sideways. The seed will fall out of the small holes in the top of the seedpod. Gently crush the seedpod to remove even more seed.

rose (*Rosa*)   Rose seeds are formed inside the red rose hips. Harvest the hips after the first frost. Cut open the hips and remove the seeds. Use the wet processing method.

snapdragon (*Antirrhium*)   Allow the seedpod to mature on the plant. When the seeds are mature, the pod turns brown and begins to open at the top. Cut off the seedpod, turn it upside down, and let the small black seeds fall out.

sunflower (*Helianthus*)   Cover the sunflower head with pantyhose as soon as the seeds begin to form. Once the seeds are mature, cut off the sunflower head and hang it upside down from the stem in a cool, dark place for two weeks. Gently rub the seeds off the seed head and lay them on a drying rack to dry for two more weeks.

sweet pea (*Lathyrus*)   An elongated seedpod forms on both annual and perennial varieties of sweet peas. As the seedpod matures, it swells and changes color from green to brown. When brown, cut the pods off the plant and lay them on a seed-drying rack to finish drying. When they begin to split, open the seedpods and remove the tannish-gray seeds. Allow them to dry for two weeks.

winter aconite (*Eranthis*) Cover the green seedpods with pantyhose. When dry, the seedpods split open. Collect the seeds and dry them indoors for a week.

zinnia (*Zinnia*) Allow the flower heads to dry on the plants. Cut off the dried seed heads, break them apart, and lay them out on a seed-drying rack (see Chapter 4) for about a week to finish drying. This takes about a week.

> **SPROUTING WISDOM**
>
> If you see a flower in a public garden that you feel you can't live without, check to see if they have some for sale; they often do. Never remove seedpods from a public garden unless you have permission to do so. If you don't get permission, ask for the botanical name of the flower so you can look for it at your local nursery or online.

Grain Seed-Saving Tips

Growing grains in the home garden is fun and offers an alternative crop for gardeners looking for something unique. And growing grain need not be limited to your vegetable garden. Mix a few plants into your flowerbeds to create unique effects.

Most heirloom grains are wind pollinated. With the new GMO grains coming on the market, it is really important that you protect your grains in some way if you plan on saving seed. Many heirloom grains are being lost due to fewer people growing them in their home gardens. Many commercial operations no longer grow heirloom grains, and fewer people are growing them in their home gardens.

Grains add interest and sometimes color to the garden. Once the seed is harvested, you can work some of the remaining plant material into dried floral bouquets; if you have chickens, offer it to them.

> **SPROUTING WISDOM**
>
> The seed you save from grains is also the seed you eat. This makes it easy to save enough seed for human consumption and still have some left over to plant the following year.

amaranth Allow the ripe seed to fall out of the seed head. The ripe seed will germinate and self-seed in your garden, if allowed. Use the pantyhose method to collect seed from this plant. Tie the pantyhose on the flower heads once you are sure pollination has occurred. You will know this has happened by observing bees and other pollinators around the plant. When the seeds are dry, they will fall out of the plant. You can help this process occur by gently bending the flower head toward the ground. Dry the seeds for a week after collecting them.

KNOW THY SEED

Amaranth produces a nutty-tasting grain that's high in protein. The grain was a staple of the Aztecs. Today many gardeners grow it in their flowerbeds. The grain is easy to harvest, and you can use it in all sorts of homemade breads.

barley   To test for dryness, bite into a seed. When ready to harvest, the seed readily snaps and the inside of the seed appears chalky. If the seed seems doughy or too springy, it is not ready to be harvested.

oats   Allow the oat plants to dry up; then wait an additional week longer to harvest the oats. Lay the grains out to dry indoors for two weeks.

rye   Bite into the seed to see if it's doughy. If it is, the seed isn't dry. The seed heads easily strip off the plant when they are ready to be harvested. Remove the plant material from the seed by hand, and then lay the seeds out to dry for at least a week. Moisture in the air and in the seed can cause these seeds to take up to two weeks to fully dry.

wheat   Gently bend the dry stalks and shake the wheat head, which is where the seeds form. If at least 75 percent of the seeds fall out, the wheat is ready to harvest. When the wheat plants turn brown, cut the wheat to the ground and lay it on a tarp. Cover the wheat with the other half of the tarp and thrash the wheat with a plastic whiffle bat. This causes the seed heads to release the seed. Another option that works well when collecting small amounts of seed is to remove the seed heads by hand and then remove the chaff from around the seeds. Lay wheat seeds out to dry for a week or two.

Other grain plants that are easy to grow at home include rice, spelt, and flax.

KNOW THY SEED

Winter wheat, along with other winter cover crops, add nitrogen to your soil, improving its quality. Nitrogen-rich soil improves the performance of other crops. Winter cover crops help recycle soil nutrients and prevent water, wind, and soil erosion.

Herb Seed-Saving Tips

Herbs are some of the easiest plants to grow. They thrive in poor soil, don't require fertilization, and, once established, are drought tolerant. Most herbs produce flowers toward the end of summer. Bees, butterflies, hummingbirds, and beneficial insects swarm these flowers, so pollination typically isn't a problem.

Herb seeds are easy to collect once they are dry. They grow right where the flower was, at the top of the plant.

Some herbs, such as mints, won't come true from seed. For instance, if you save and plant a peppermint seed, a mint plant will grow from the seed, but it may not be a peppermint plant. It may be a lavender mint, a lemon bergamot mint, or a penny-royal, especially if you have more than one variety growing in your garden. The best way to ensure that you get the desired variety of mint is to grow plants from cuttings. Mint grows like crazy and can be invasive, so keep an eye on it and keep it cut back.

dill   Allow the seeds to dry on the seed head; then carefully cut off the seed head and place it in a paper bag. Gently rub the seeds off the seed heads and allow them to dry for two weeks.

fennel   Allow the seeds to dry on the seed head, and then carefully cut off the seed head and place it in a paper bag. Gently rub the seeds off the seed heads and allow them to dry for two weeks.

parsley   The seed heads form the year after planting. Allow them to dry on the plant; then carefully cut off the seed head and place it in a paper bag. Gently rub the seeds off the seed heads and allow them to dry for two weeks.

Always harvest as much of the herb as you want to use in your kitchen before you allow it to set seed. As with bulbs, once an herb sets seed, all the plant's energy goes into reproduction mode, so the flavor of the leaves declines. You can still use them in the kitchen, but they won't have the same intensity they had before they set seed.

Interplanting herbs with flowers, fruits, or vegetables increases the number of pollinators that visit those plants as well.

SPROUTING WISDOM

Growing and drying your own herbs is the best way to make sure they are fresh. Many herbs sold in stores are several years old and flavorless. Save the seed from your favorite herb plants to make sure you always have some to plant the following year.

Many herbs are available only as seeds. If you save your own, you won't have to spend hours rummaging through seed catalogues the next year to find your favorites. It's exciting to experiment with new varieties of herbs as well, so have fun cross-pollinating (making sure you keep good records). Many spices fall into the herb category, so try some of them as well. Exchange herb seeds with others to increase the diversity of the herbs you grow.

Fruit Seed-Saving Tips

Generally, you won't find fruit seeds growing in a seedpod. Most fruit seeds form inside the fruit itself. They come in all shapes and sizes: just look at some of the most common—apple, peach, lemon, kiwi, tomato, and watermelon seeds. Once the fruit is mature, you can cut it open to access the seeds.

> **KNOW THY SEED**
>
> When you grow a fruit from a seed, it may not taste anything like the parent plant. Fruiting plants usually require the presence of two different varieties of the same plant for cross-pollination to occur, although some new hybrids are self-pollinating.

Some seeds, such as apple or citrus, are easy to remove cleanly, without any of the pulp clinging to them. As you cut them away from the fruit, be careful not to nick or cut the seeds themselves: a damaged seed may not to grow. Clean seeds can simply be given a quick rinse under water or with hydrogen peroxide and then laid out to dry (see Chapter 4). Other fruit seeds, such as cucumbers or tomatoes, which have pulp clinging to them, are better processed using the wet processing method. Removing the pulp from the seeds gives you clean seeds, ready to dry.

apple   Cut open the apple and remove the seeds. Give them a quick rinse under water so they're not sticky. A small tea strainer works well for this. Lay the seeds out to dry for a week.

banana   Most commercial varieties of bananas are seedless, but homegrown, non-commercial varieties often do have seeds. Simply collect the seeds when you eat the banana. Wet-process them and then dry them for two weeks.

citrus   Cut open the fruit and remove the seeds. Place the seeds in a tea strainer to rinse them. Lay them out to dry for two weeks.

passionflower   Allow the fruit to fall off the vine on its own. Cut open the fruit and scoop out the seeds. Process using the wet processing method and dry for two weeks.

Some people like to start their fruit seeds indoors under grow lights; others prefer doing so outdoors in a raised bed. Either method is fine. Once the young plants are large enough to go into the garden, it's time to transplant. Fruit grown on its own rootstock is usually hardier than grafted fruit.

Try growing some new varieties of fruit from seed you've cross-pollinated. You may be surprised by what will grow and overwinter in your area. It is best to try just one plant at a time, so if it doesn't make it through the winter, you won't have wasted a lot of time and energy. Mulch young fruit plants the first winter or two in the ground.

SPROUTING WISDOM

Although you can dry the seeds of fruit, most are sown fresh, if they are sown at all. In fact, fruit is usually grafted.

The Least You Need to Know

- Always collect seeds from healthy plants with traits you like.
- Give seeds time to fully mature before you collect them.
- Different types of seeds require different processing methods.
- Leave seeds from wild plants alone unless you have the proper permits to collect them; even then, never remove all the seeds.

Preparing Your Seeds for Storage

In This Chapter

- Threshing and winnowing your seeds
- Keeping your seeds free of disease and pests
- Drying wet- and dry-processed seeds
- Making your own drying screen

When you open a commercial packet of seeds from a respected company, you find the seeds clean and dry, with no debris or moisture present to spoil them. You can achieve the same excellent results at home.

Properly cleaning and drying your seeds is an essential component of seed saving, even if you intend to merely store the seeds until the next gardening season. Best of all, you don't need any expensive equipment or paraphernalia to prepare your seeds for storage. All you need are some basic items, many of which you probably already have.

A Clean Seed Is a Happy Seed

When you collect seeds from the garden, no matter how careful you are, you also collect a certain amount of debris along with the seeds. This debris, known as *chaff*, includes small sections of stems, crushed pieces of seedpods, bits of leaves, and other natural plant material. It's vital to remove those troublemakers before drying and storing your seeds.

Seeds collected at home often contain small amounts of chaff, even after cleaning them.

Cleaning the seeds before you store them gives you a chance to remove any seeds that are starting to show signs of mold or have other noticeable problems, such as broken seed coats or holes.

Threshing

If you're collecting seeds from just a few seedpods, carefully apply just enough pressure with your fingertips to break open the husk and collect the seeds that haven't fallen out on their own.

If you've collected large amounts of seed that require the seedpods to be crushed, place the pods inside a paper or plastic bag and gently crush them with your hands or a rolling pin so that all the seeds are released from their husks. This process is known as *threshing.* Don't use a hammer or other heavy object; this will crush the seeds and destroy the embryo.

Winnowing

Seeds that are collected from seedpods contain chaff. The chaff is easy to remove using a technique known as *winnowing*. Winnowing is the process of using wind to remove the chaff. Most seeds are heavier than chaff, so typically the seeds will fall into a dish set underneath your hands while the chaff will blow away.

THE BAD SEED

Be aware that if you winnow your seeds near your garden, some of the seeds that blow away will end up in the garden and possibly grow.

You can winnow your seed using either of the following basic techniques:

- Take the dry seeds outdoors on a windy day (not too windy, though) and let them flow through your fingers, allowing the chaff to blow away and the seeds to fall into a container positioned under your hands.

- Sift the seeds through your fingers as the breeze from a fan blows the chaff away. Be sure to use a low fan setting—you don't want the seeds to blow away, too!

It's not unusual to lose some seeds using these methods. The best way to preserve as many seeds as possible is to winnow them as close as possible to your storage container. The farther from the container you are, the more likely the wind is to carry away the seeds, especially if they're tiny seeds like poppies.

Avoiding Threats to Seeds

When fall comes, it's time to put away your summer clothes. But you don't put them away dirty. You wash, dry, fold, and properly store them so they'll be ready for you to wear again when the weather warms back up. You might even add mothballs or cedar to protect them. You should take just as much care with your seeds when preparing to store them until the next growing season.

Seeds that are properly cleaned and dried have a longer shelf life than those that aren't correctly processed. While it's true that seed viability varies according to species, clean, dry seeds that are properly stored can last and remain viable for years. The following sections outline the many threats to stored seeds.

Moisture

Unless something such as moisture encourages seeds to grow, they remain in a dormant state during storage. Dirty or damp seeds are an open invitation to disaster: bacteria can invade, mold may form, and pests—in the form of insect eggs—can find their way into your seed storage area. These troublemakers destroy seeds. By properly cleaning and drying your seeds, you help prevent these spoilers from ruining your harvest.

THE BAD SEED

Seeds must be completely dry before you store them. If they contain any moisture when put away, they may begin to germinate or rot, rendering them unusable.

Mold

Mold is any of various fungi that can cause organic matter to disintegrate. Mold travels through the air as tiny spores; those spores like to make their home in wet areas where they breed. Some molds are beneficial, but many can be hazardous to human health, especially to people who suffer from allergies and asthma. Mold is never healthy for seeds. In fact, it's a major problem that can occur when seeds aren't properly cleaned and dried before they're stored. A single moldy seed can spoil an entire batch.

The nature of mold is to continually release new spores. These released spores turn into more mold, feeding on whatever organic material is available. This process continues until everything, including the inside of the jar, the lid, the seeds, the silica gel or rice packets (more on these later in the chapter), and the seed packages are infected with the mold.

Insects and Other Infestations

When cleaning your seeds, keep an eye out for signs of possible insect or critter damage. Insects or critters such as mice or birds sometimes chew or peck at the seeds while they're still on the plant, so while you clean your seeds, look carefully at each one to see if you can spot signs of small holes. A microscope or magnifying glass can help you see the tiny imperfections caused by insect damage.

Sometimes the seeds are still green when birds peck at them. Later insects may infest the seeds by laying their eggs inside the holes the birds made. This may not happen until after the seeds have dried on the plant (or in your storage container, if you have a bug problem). Seeds damaged by insects are no longer viable. However, that doesn't mean the insect eggs are dead. They could be dormant for a while and become active later. Be sure to remove and throw away any and all seeds that show signs of insect infestation or other potential problems.

THE BAD SEED

One bad seed can destroy every seed it comes into contact with. Be sure to weed out damaged, damp, or otherwise compromised seeds.

Carefully cleaning seeds and inspecting each individual seed for signs of potential damage is time consuming and takes a good deal of patience, but the end result is clean, dry seeds with a long shelf life. Believe me, it's worth it!

Pests

Another problem with germinating or rotting seeds is that they attract pests. Rodents, for example, have a keen sense of smell—and they love to eat seeds. Insects, too, are drawn by the odor. Once pests invade your seed storage space, it's hard to discourage them from coming back. By the time you discover the situation, they may already have destroyed numerous seeds.

Drying Dry-Processed Seeds

You don't have to wash dry-processed seeds (see Chapter 3 for details on dry-processing seeds). Just inspect them for signs of damage, remove as much of the chaff as possible (see the preceding section), and finish drying them for a few weeks to make sure they're completely dry before packaging and storing them.

Drying on Styrofoam Plates

If you don't have a seed-drying rack or screen (described later in this later) you can dry your seeds on Styrofoam plates. It's best not to use paper plates because the wet seeds tend to stick to the paper. Styrofoam plates are ideal for drying tiny seeds that will fall through drying screens or seeds that were dry processed. To avoid having the seeds stick to the drying surface, jiggle them around several times a day.

So that you always know what kind of seeds you're working with, be sure to label your drying seeds. Place a heavy object, such as a rock, paperweight, or coffee mug, in the center of your container to keep it from blowing away.

How Long Should They Dry?

The amount of time seeds take to dry varies by both the type of seed you're working with and the processing method you use. In general, however, you can expect the seeds to dry in 7 to 10 days, although some can take as long as two months. Refer to the guidelines for specific seeds that appear in Chapter 4.

Many variables influence how quickly seeds dry. Larger seeds take longer to dry than smaller seeds, and wet-processed seeds take longer to dry than dry-processed seeds. Additionally, if the humidity level in the room where you're drying the seeds is high, your seeds will take longer to dry. When the humidity is too high, there's also a good chance the seeds will mold instead of dry. Ideally, you should dry your seeds in a room with a low humidity level or run a dehumidifier in that room while the seeds are drying.

SPROUTING WISDOM

Here's a tip for determining whether your seeds are dry: take a good look at the seeds when you first lay them out to dry. If you can, take a picture so that later you can compare what the seeds originally looked like to what they look like as they dry. As they dry, the seeds will look and feel drier every day. Some seeds will shrink slightly as they dry, but the shrinkage often isn't significant enough to notice.

It's better to leave the seeds on the drying screens longer than necessary than to rush the process and end up storing seeds that are still too damp.

Turn the seeds once or twice a day throughout the entire drying process. As you turn the seeds, inspect the material the seeds are lying on. If the material seems damp, replace it with a clean, dry plate or towel.

Drying Wet-Processed Seeds

Wet-processed seeds (see Chapter 3 for details on this technique) like tomatoes and cucumbers naturally contain more moisture than those that are dry processed. Many beginning seed savers don't let their wet-processed seeds dry for long enough before storing them. The key to success is to keep an eye on the seeds to make sure they're properly drying and not molding. When you're finished with the wet processing steps outlined in Chapter 3, the seeds are ready to be dried.

Here's what to do:

1. Drain the excess water off the seeds and spread them out on a paper towel to help absorb some excess moisture. Pat the seeds with another clean paper towel, much as you might do when preparing greens for a salad.

2. Immediately move the seeds onto a seed-drying screen (see the following section). Make sure the seeds are in a single layer.

THE BAD SEED

Don't leave wet-processed seeds on any type of paper product because, as they dry, they'll stick to the paper. You might damage the seeds when you remove them from the paper.

The best way to encourage the seeds to dry faster is by making sure the room they're in has plenty of air circulation. Use a table fan or a ceiling fan on the lowest setting to blow across the top of the seeds. It's important, however, to keep the fan far enough away from the seeds that the air movement doesn't cause the seeds to scatter as they dry.

When your seeds are dry, you're ready to package them and store them (see Chapter 5).

Making Your Own Drying Screen

The simplest and least expensive way to make a seed-drying screen is to use an old window screen. Clean the screen thoroughly, place it on some wood blocks or bricks to allow air to flow underneath the seeds (at least 6 inches), put more blocks or bricks or anything heavy on top of the four corners, and—voilà!—you have a seed-drying screen.

The size of your drying screen depends on how many seeds you plan to dry. Most screens range in size from 1×1 feet to 2×2 feet.

If you happen to have a bread rack in your home, you can cover the shelves with screening (making sure to weight them down) and use that.

You can purchase screening material at any hardware store and make your own drying screen. Follow these steps:

1. Remove the backing, hanging wire, and picture from an old wood picture frame. Clean the frame thoroughly, using soap and water. Let the frame dry.

2. Stretch screening material across the frame from side to side and end to end so that it's taut. Using a staple gun, staple the screening material to the wood to hold it tightly in place.

Your new seed-drying screen is now ready for use!

Alternately, if you're handy with woodworking tools, you could build a wood frame in a square or rectangular shape and attach 6- to 12-inch legs to it. Add the screening in the same manner as described for the picture frame.

The benefit to building screens from scratch is that you can make them just the size you want for the space you've allocated for drying your seeds. Another benefit, if you build several, is that you can stack them.

If you stack your screens, be sure they are exactly the same size, for stability, and that the legs allow for a minimum of 6 inches in between screens; 12 inches is even better.

THE BAD SEED

Stacking screens increases the possibility of mold, since the airflow between the screens is reduced and more moisture is present. Dry your seeds in a single layer for one week before stacking them.

Be sure to clean seed-drying screens after each use. This prevents seeds from remaining on the screen, which could contaminate the next batch. You can take the screen outside to the compost pile or garden and give it a good shake, but if you do so, be aware that any seeds that remain on the screen may germinate. To avoid this, use a dry brush to remove any plant material that may have stuck to the screen in a spot—like a mud sink—where you don't have to be concerned with germination. Don't forget to give the sides and corners and the frame a good brushing as well. Small seeds can embed themselves in these areas.

When you've removed all remaining plant material from the screen, use a garden hose to spray it down. If you have an indoor hook-up, you can spray and wash the screen in hot, soapy water. But a good spraying is usually all that's required. To make sure you've removed all potential bacteria, give the screen a final rinse with hydrogen peroxide, and then allow it to dry naturally, if possible, in a warm, sunny spot. When the screen is dry, it's ready to use again.

A seed-drying screen doesn't have to be fancy; in fact, the screens are easy to make at home using materials you may already have on hand.

The Least You Need to Know

- Use winnowing techniques to separate the seeds from the chaff.
- Pests, moisture, and mold are all problems that can destroy your harvested seeds.
- Although the seeds you collect may look dry, you must dry them after you bring them indoors to make sure all the moisture that could ruin them has evaporated.
- Use a fan on a low setting to help seeds dry faster.
- Avoid using paper products to dry seeds that were wet processed. Clean and sterilize seed-drying screens immediately after you use them.

Storing Your Seeds

In This Chapter

- Keeping seeds viable
- Choosing proper storage containers
- Labeling seeds
- Freezing and refrigerating seeds

You can be as careful as you want while harvesting and drying your seeds (see Chapters 3 and 4, respectively), but if you don't store them properly, you risk damaging them. Proper seed storage is essential to your seeds' longevity.

The best place to store your seeds is in a cool, dry, dark place. It doesn't matter if you store them in a closet, basement, or refrigerator, as long as the seeds remain cool and dry. A little light—such as when the refrigerator light comes on when you open the door—won't hurt them; however, you should keep dry seeds away from direct sunlight, which might cause the seed coat to break down or condensation to build up inside the storage containers.

Most important is to make sure you store the right seeds in the right place so the embryo doesn't die during storage.

Keeping 'em Lively

The average life span of a seed that's been properly stored is five years, with the exception of herb seeds, which typically don't last longer than one year. Tomato seeds that are stored properly can germinate for up to 10 years, although the average viability is only 4 years.

The length of time seeds are viable isn't set in stone, so don't throw them away just because the ideal germination time is up. Check the viability of all stored seeds at least once a year using the paper towel germination testing method described in Chapter 6.

The following tables list the average viability for many common herb, vegetable, and flower seeds when stored properly.

KNOW THY SEED

If you suspect that a seed is going to be lost due to low viability, grow it out and save new seeds from that plant. Be sure to remove all the old seeds from the jar before you add new seeds to it, or simply start a new container with a new label and date.

Average Viability for Herb and Vegetable Seeds

Variety	Viability in Years
Asparagus	3–4
Basil	8–10
Beans	3–6
Beets	3–4
Broccoli	3–5
Brussels sprouts	4–5
Cabbage	4–5
Cantaloupe	6–10
Caraway	3–5
Carrots	3–5
Cauliflower	4–5
Celery	3–5
Collards	4–5
Corn	4–6
Cucumber	5–7
Cumin	3
Eggplant	3–5
Kale	4–10
Kohlrabi	4–5

Variety	Viability in Years
Lavender	5
Leeks	2–4
Lettuce	1–4
Lovage	3
Okra	1–2
Onions	1–4
Parsley	3–5
Parsnips	1–3
Peas	3–6
Peppers	2–5
Potato seed	5–7
Pumpkins	3–5
Radish	3–5
Rue	2
Spinach	3–4
Squash	3–5
Swiss chard	3–4
Thyme	2–7
Tomato	4–10+
Turnip	4–8
Watermelon	4–6
Woodruff	3
Wormwood	3–9

Average Viability for Flower Seeds

Variety	Viability in Years
Ageratum (*Ageratum*)	4
Agrostemma (*Agrostemma*)	4
Alyssum (*Lobularia*)	4
Arabis (*Arabis*)	2–3
Aster (*Aster*)	1–2

continues

Average Viability for Flower Seeds   (continued)

Variety	Viability in Years
Baby's breath (*Gypsophila*)	5
Bachelor's buttons (*Centaurea*)	5–10
Balloon flower (*Platycodon*)	3
Balloon vine (*Cardiospermum*)	3–4
Balsam apple (*Momordica*)	6
Blanket flower (*Gaillardia*)	3
Bleeding heart (*Dicentra*)	1–2
Bidens (*Bidens*)	2
Bush clover (*Lespedeza*)	20+
Bush violet (*Browallia*)	2–3
Butterfly flower (*Schizanthus*)	10+
Calendula (*Calendula*)	8–10
Campanula (*Campanula*)	4–10
Canna (*Canna*)	3
Candytuft (*Iberis*)	3
Cassia (*Cassia*)	158
Celosia (*Celosia*)	4
Chrysanthemum (*Chrysanthemum*)	1–10
Clarkia (*Clarkia*)	1
Clianthus (*Clianthus*)	1
Coleus (*Solenostemon*)	2
Columbine (*Aquilegia*)	2
Coreopsis (*Coreopsis*)	2
Cosmos (*Cosmos*)	3–4
Cyclamen (*Cyclamen*)	4–5
Dahlia (*Dahlia*)	3–6+
Daisy (*Leucanthemum*)	2
Datura (*Datura*)	3–4
Delphinium (*Delphinium*)	1
Dianthus (*Dianthus*)	4–5
English daisy (*Bellis*)	6–7
Evening stock (*Matthiola*)	7–10

Variety	Viability in Years
Fleece flower (*Persicaria*)	25
Foxglove (*Digitalis*)	2
Geranium (*Pelargonium*)	2
Gerbera daisy (*Gerbera*)	1
Geum (*Geum*)	2
Gilia (*Gilia*)	4–5
Gomphrena (*Gomphrena*)	2–3
Gourds (*Lagenaria*)	3–4
Hakea (*Hakea*)	5–10+
Heliotrope (*Heliotropium*)	50+
Heuchera (*Heuchera*)	3
Hibiscus (*Hibiscus*)	3–4
Hollyhock (*Althea*)	2–3
Hyacinth bean (*Lablab*)	4–10
Impatiens (*Impatiens*)	2
Johnny-jump-up (*Viola*)	1
Jupiter's beard (*Centranthus*)	4
Larkspur (*Consolida*)	1–2
Lily (*Lilium*)	2–5
Lobelia (*Lobelia*)	3–4
Lotus (*Nelumbo*)	150–1,000
Lupine (*Lupinus*)	2
Marigold (*Tagetes*)	2–3
Mignonette (*Reseda*)	4
Morning glory (*Ipomoea*)	3–50+
Moss rose (*Portulaca*)	3–45
Mouse ear (*Cerastium*)	4–7
Nasturtium (*Tropaeolum*)	7
Nicotiana (*Nicotiana*)	5–10
Nigella (*Nigella*)	1–2
Pansy (*Viola*)	2
Penstemon (*Penstemon*)	2
Petunia (*Petunia*)	2–3

continues

Average Viability for Flower Seeds   (continued)

Variety	Viability in Years
Phlox (*Phlox*)	1–2
Poppy (*Papaver*)	5
Primrose (*Primula*)	1–5
Salpiglossis (*Salpiglossis*)	5–7
Salvia (*Salvia*)	1
Scabious (*Scabiosa*)	3
Shooting stars (*Dodecatheon*)	6
Sneezeweed (*Achillea*)	3–4
Statice (*Limonium*)	3
Stock (*Matthiola*)	7–10
Sweet pea (*Lathyrus*)	3
Sweet William (*Dianthus*)	2
Thunbergia (*Thunbergia*)	1–2
Tithonia (*Tithonia*)	2
Torenia (*Torenia*)	1–2
Turmeric flower (*Curcuma*)	10
Verbena (*Verbena*)	1
Vinca (*Vinca*)	2
Wallflower (*Erysimum*)	3–5
Yarrow (*Achillea*)	4
Zinnia (*Zinnia*)	5–6

Putting Your Seeds in Proper Containers

No matter how dry seeds are, they all contain some essential internal moisture. You may not be able to detect it, but it's there—and you want it to stay there. Seeds that lose all their internal moisture and completely dry up are no longer viable. To retain that moisture, you need to store them properly.

Packaging Your Seeds

First, place the seeds in a small paper or plastic bag, pressing out as much excess air from the bags as possible. Be careful not to crush the seeds when doing so.

Labeling Your Seeds

You won't necessarily know what a seed is when you look at it, unless it has a label. Labels should include the botanical name and the date you collected the seed.

THE BAD SEED

Avoid using pencils, ink pens, or ink-jet printers to make labels. These can all smear or fade over time. Instead, use a botanical marker, which you can purchase at most nurseries or online; use it on all your seed and plant tags.

If the seed came from a plant that was hand pollinated, include the name of both parent plants. That label would look something like this: "Clivia X Hippeastrum" (of course, you would replace the words *Clivia* and *Hippeastrum* with whatever two plants you crossed). Adding additional information, such as common names and where you collected the seed, can also be useful. In fact, the more information you can add, the better. If you're storing seeds in individual containers, make a label for both the outside and the inside of the container, to prevent possible loss of data.

Another option is to label the jar, both inside and out, with a number; put that number on a clean page of a seed saver's diary (see Chapter 14); and write all the pertinent information about the seeds in that entry. You might add photos of the flowers, the seeds, the fruits, or whatever you want to make a complete record.

Small plastic bags, paper envelopes, and glass jars with lids are all excellent choices for storing seeds.

Containing Your Seeds

Place the individual packets inside a larger container. Consider any of the following types of containers:

- Mason jars

- Plastic shoeboxes or tubs with lids

- Drawers

Look for these characteristics in a storage container:

- Airtight.

- Easy to handle.

- The right size for the amount of seeds you want to store.

- Opaque or a dark color. This is optional, but darker colors help keep light away from seeds.

THE BAD SEED

Don't vacuum-pack your dried seeds. It prevents the natural process of cellular respiration from occurring. Cellular respiration is what cells do to break up sugars into a food that the cell can use as energy.

Adding Drying Agents

Because moisture can build up inside the larger storage containers, place about a tablespoon of rice or silica gel in each storage container (but separate from the individual packets). Don't let the seeds come in direct contact with the rice or silica because it could absorb the essential moisture within the seeds. You can simply add a tablespoon of the rice or silica gel to the bottom of the container or put the items in a fabric bag or paper envelope.

You can save the silica gel packets that come with many dry goods, or you can buy silica gel in large containers at craft or floral design stores.

It's a good idea to remove the small packets of desiccant every six months and replace them, even if they feel dry. When you open your containers to remove the seeds, check the desiccant packets to see if they are moist; if they are, remove and replace them.

KNOW THY SEED

Some seeds, such as corn and legumes, shouldn't be stored in glass. These seeds need to breathe to remain viable; storing them in a glass or plastic container can prevent this process from happening. Instead, you should store them in paper bags or envelopes in the refrigerator. If you have a sealed metal closet that you're using for seed storage—one that will keep mice at bay—you can put the paper bags in it instead of in the refrigerator.

Finding Storage Space

Finding the best seed storage location in your home may take a little trial and error. Whenever you choose a new location in which to save seeds, keep a close eye on it. If that location doesn't work, move the seeds to another. A brief exposure to less than ideal conditions won't kill the seeds, but long-term exposure to adverse conditions will affect their viability and possibly kill them.

When you start looking for a place to store seeds, think small. Closets are a good place, especially if they're in an extra room that doesn't get used a lot and receives minimal heat. Basements are okay as long as the humidity is low enough. Some people store their seed boxes under their beds, under a couch, or in a drawer. When you start thinking of all the places in your home where you can store a shoebox or two of seeds, you'll be amazed by how easy it is to find a suitable dry, dark, and cool place.

Don't store seeds in a garage, barn, or other outdoor building unless the building is temperature controlled and free of pests.

KNOW THY SEED

An excellent way to prevent possible pest infestation is to refrigerate or freeze your seeds for 24 hours before you move them to their long-term storage location. This kills any eggs that might have been laid on the seeds while they were still in the garden.

Maintaining Proper Temperature, Light, and Humidity

Keeping the seed storage containers cool and dry is of the utmost importance. The cooler the seeds, the longer they'll remain viable. If you store more than a year's supply of seeds at one time, storing seeds at the proper temperature is even more important.

The ideal storage temperature range is between 32°F and 41°F. Ideal humidity levels should be 50 percent or less.

Fluctuating temperatures decrease a seed's viability, and high humidity could lead to a buildup of moisture inside the storage containers, which could ruin the seeds. Direct sunlight can break down the seed coat, which is there to protect the embryo inside and prevent premature germination.

If you have a large seed-storage area, you might want to consider using a dehumidifier and a humidity meter. With these, you can know and control the amount of humidity in the room. The ideal combination of temperature and humidity should never add up to over 100 combined—and this is a rather high number. A temperature of 50°F or less and 50 percent humidity or less is ideal. Most humidity meters indicate low, normal, and high levels. You want the room in which your seeds are being stored to have a low humidity level.

Colder storage conditions are always the best bet for increasing seed viability. Storing seeds in an area that is a mere 10°F cooler than room temperature can double a seed's shelf life. Of course, you don't want the seeds to get too cold, because that could kill them. Some seeds, such as those from tropical plants, can't handle freezing temperatures but do fine if saved at a temperature around 40°F. Temperatures that are too warm break down a seed's coat, exposing the embryo to the elements before it's time to germinate.

Freezing

The freezer is a good place to keep dormant perennial seeds. (Remember that a perennial is a plant that comes back every year from its own root system.) Not all seeds should be frozen, though. Annual, vegetable, fruit, and tropical seeds may sustain damage and actually die if they're stored in the freezer, because the temperatures are too low. If you're in doubt about whether you can safely freeze a seed, it's best not to do it. Instead, store them in the refrigerator or a cool, dry, and dark area.

You can store the following seeds in the freezer:

Baptisia (*Baptisia*)

Bellflower (*Campanula*)

Bleeding heart (*Dicentra*)

Cardinal flower (*Lobelia*)

Clematis (*Clematis*)

Columbine (*Aquilegia*)

Coneflower (*Echinacea*)

Evening primrose (*Oenothera*)

Goldenrod (*Solidago*)

Goldenseal (*Hydrastis*)

Hollyhock (*Althea*)

Jack-in-the-pulpit (*Arisaema*)

Joe-pye weed (*Eupatorium*)

Lavender (*Lavendula*)

Liatris (*Liatris*)

Milkweed (*Asclepias*)

Penstemon (*Penstemon*)

Rose (*Rosa*)

Rudbeckia (*Rudbeckia*)

Soap plant (*Chlorogalum*)

Trillium (*Trillium*)

Viola (*Viola*)

Virginia bluebells (*Mertensia*)

Wild ginger (*Asarum*)

Witch hazel (*Hamamelis*)

The interesting thing about storing seeds in the freezer is that the freezing temperatures emulate nature and help modify the seed coat. The temperatures inside the freezer cause the seeds to prepare for germination. Once these seeds are removed and exposed to normal household temperatures, they germinate readily without requiring additional stratification (more on this in Chapter 7).

Seeds that are properly stored in the freezer tend to last longer than those stored under other conditions. This is because the cold temperatures place the seeds in a state of animated dormancy.

When preparing seeds to freeze, make sure they're stored in airtight, freezer-proof containers. You can put individual varieties of seed in small plastic or paper envelopes if you want, but seal them inside a larger plastic or glass container, not a plastic freezer bag.

Refrigerating

The refrigerator crisper drawer is an ideal place to store seeds. The temperature of the average refrigerator is just right for keeping seeds viable and extending their shelf life. This area is easy to access for most people, and you will never forget where your seeds are. Seeds stored in a refrigerator should be kept in an airtight container so they don't draw moisture. It's a good idea to check them from time to time to make sure no moisture is forming.

THE BAD SEED

Make sure the container you choose is waterproof in case of an accidental spill.

You can store all types of seeds in the refrigerator, including those from tropical plants, because refrigerators don't get cold enough to damage the embryo.

Moist Storage

Magnolia and various spring woodland plant seeds should be stored in damp paper towels in the refrigerator. Be sure to place the damp paper towels in a plastic bag to prevent them from drying out. Seeds stored in this manner should be kept separate from the dry seeds.

Seeds stored moist must be kept in an anaerobic environment to prevent germination. Keep the seeds in tightly sealed polyethylene bags or vacuum-seal them.

The following seeds benefit from moist storage:

Aspen (*Salicaceae*)

Clematis (*Clematis*)

Coltsfoot (*Tussilago*)

Corydalis (*Corydalis*)

Cottonwood (*Populus*)

Gentiana (*Gentiana*)

Iris (*Iris*)

Lily (*Lilium*)

Liverwort (*Hepatica*)

Trillium (*Trillium*)

White Rush Lily (*Hastingsia*)

Willow (*Salix*)

Winter aconite (*Eranthis*)

Troubleshooting

Be sure to check on the jars or other containers for signs of condensation. Even if they contain silica gel or rice packets and you are 100 percent sure the seeds were completely dry when you packaged them for storage, keep an eye on them.

Condensation can occur inside the storage container if the humidity level inside the room in which the seeds are stored is too high. Sometimes moisture also gets into the storage container because the lid doesn't have an airtight seal.

If you see condensation start to form inside the container, remove the seeds immediately and start the drying process all over again. It's better to spend the time required to adequately dry the seeds than to lose your entire stash.

The Least You Need to Know

- Properly storing seeds leads to greater viability.
- Always label seeds and store them in a cool, dry, dark place.
- Use storage container that are impervious to pests.
- Freezing and refrigerating seeds helps stratify them.

Germinating and Sowing Seeds

This part is all about sowing seeds, both indoors and outdoors. From choosing the right seed-sowing media to figuring out which containers are the best to use, you'll find all the details you need to get your seeds in the ground and sprouting. Additionally, you get the scoop on proper lighting, the right depth to sow seeds, temperature needs, and more.

This part also shows you how to prepare seeds to germinate using various stratification and scarification techniques, and tells you which seeds require which technique. You also get step-by-step instructions for testing seeds to make sure they are viable before investing a lot of time and energy into growing an entire crop.

Germinating and Testing Your Seeds

In This Chapter

- Testing seeds to see if they're viable
- Planning your germination schedule
- Creating the right conditions for germination
- Germinating specific varieties of vegetables, herbs, and flowers
- Giving your newly germinated seeds their first home

There's a lot more to germination than meets the eye. Sure, you can simply plant your seeds and hope they grow, but there are better ways to find out if the seeds you saved are good before you plant them. Best of all, testing seeds using the methods laid out in this chapter is quick and quite accurate, and requires nothing more than a few simple household supplies.

Some seeds germinate overnight, but others take several weeks, several months, or even several years. To get the best performance out of your seeds, you need to know the average germination time for your seeds and the conditions to which the seeds must be exposed for germination to occur. Some seeds germinate better at a certain temperature or require light or darkness to induce germination. Some seeds require that you move them from warm temperatures to cool temperatures and back again for germination to occur. The following pages give you all the information you need to get those little seeds sprouting.

Putting Your Seeds to the Test

Determining whether the seeds you save are viable is one more part of the seed-saving process. You should always test a few of your seeds before you store them and then again about six months before you intend to sow them. Testing seeds is a simple process. Before beginning, gather the following supplies:

- Roll of paper towels

- Plastic bag or container with a lid. Choose a container that's large enough to hold the seeds without crushing them.

- Water

- Five or six of the seeds you want to test

KNOW THY SEED

Before you plant any seeds, whether you saved them yourself or bought them from another source, you should test them. If the seeds sprout, you can plant them with confidence. If they don't sprout, they're no longer viable and you should dispose of them.

Here's what you do:

1. Fold the regular-size paper towel once, and then fold it again. The folded paper towel needs to fit easily inside the container you're using, so cut it down to size, if necessary.

2. Place the folded paper towel inside your container or plastic bag.

3. Dip one corner of the paper towel in hot water; alternatively, use an eyedropper to add one drop of water at a time to the top of the paper towel inside the plastic container. Allow the water to disperse throughout the paper towel. You want the paper towel to be barely damp, not dripping wet.

KNOW THY SEED

Some seeds, such as foxglove, need darkness to germinate well; if they germinate in the light, the results will be poor. Cover such seeds with vermiculite or a paper towel and then set them in an area where direct light can't reach them.

4. If the seeds you're germinating don't need darkness, just lay them on top of the paper towel. Put the paper towel on a petri dish or some other small container and make sure you put the lid on to keep the seeds from drying out. You can also put the towel in a plastic bag and seal it.

After the seeds germinate, a process that can take anywhere from overnight to several years depending on the type of seed, make note that the batch from which you've tested is viable and then transplant the seedlings. Sometimes in the case of small seeds, such as foxglove, you can transplant the entire batch on the paper towel, thus eliminating the risk of damaging them; you can thin them out later, when they've grown some.

The germination rates of older seeds naturally decline from year to year. Keeping track of the number of seeds that germinate compared to the ones that don't germinate gives you a good idea of whether you need to plant and grow these seeds again soon to restock your seed supply.

If the paper towel test proves you have a good germination rate, you can plant seeds per original instructions (such as 1 inch apart, 1 foot apart, and so on); if your germination rate is poor, you might want to plant two or three seeds in each hole.

Deciding When to Test

The standard time to perform a seed test is approximately six months before your intended sowing date. This timeline isn't set in stone, however, and as a hobby gardener, you don't need to adhere to this strict schedule. Instead, if you're concerned about the viability of your seeds, test them a few weeks before you plan to sow them.

SPROUTING WISDOM

Most commercial seed companies perform their seed testing in the fall, as you will see if you look at the back of the seed packet. They often stamp the package with the date the seed test took place and the seed germination rate. This is important information for the seed companies to document: if there's any problem with the seed they sell to their customers, the date stamp enables them to identify what seed lot the seeds came from and figure out why the problem occurred.

If the seed you sow for the test doesn't germinate, try to germinate it at least one more time before you throw out the seed.

It's also a good idea to test seed that has shown signs of problems in the past, such as pest or insect infestation or signs of high moisture.

Giving Your Seeds a Grade

After you've completed a germination test, the next step is to analyze the results. This is a simple process. You divide the number of seeds that actually germinated by the number of seeds you started with. The result is your germination percentage.

So if you started with 10 seeds, and 8 of those 10 seeds germinated during the test, you divide 8 by 10, which equals 80; your germination rate is 80 percent. That's pretty high. Now if only 5 seeds germinated, 5 divided by 10 is 50, for a 50 percent germination rate; if only 3 seeds germinated (3 divided by 10), you have a 30 percent germination rate. (A 30 percent germination rate is quite low, so you would want to sow those seeds as soon as possible, to get some productivity out of them.)

The germination percentage tells you more than just how many seeds are germinating. You can use the figure as a guide to determine how many seeds to sow. If your germination rate is less than 100 percent, you know you need to plant additional seeds to compensate for the failed seeds. For example, suppose you want 10 plants and you have an 80 percent germination rate. If you plant only 10 seeds, you're likely to get just 8 plants, so you have to compensate. If you plant 12 seeds, you're much more likely to end up with your desired 10 plants.

Planning Your Germinating and Smoking Schedule

You need to plan ahead a little in order to give the plants adequate time to germinate. Gardeners typically start seeds based on when they want them to fruit or flower. If you're using seeds from seed packets, the information is usually included on the back of the packet; however, with seeds you've saved yourself or that someone has given you it's a little trickier. The seed directories in the back of this book include germination times for a large variety of herbs, fruits, flowers, and vegetables, so that's a good place to start. As for maturity dates, a quick online search will give you that data. Gather that data, and then follow these steps:

1. Add the average germination time (in days) to the average time to harvest/maturation time (in days). This is your total growing time. For example, if you're planting a seed with an average germination time of 5 days and an average days to maturation of 62 days, your total growing time is 72 days.

2. Using a calendar, choose your desired date of harvest and count backwards the number of days in the total growing time. The date you end up on is the date on which you should start your seeds. If you want to harvest a crop by July 1 and the total growing time is 72 days, you need to start the seeds on April 21.

Most seeds germinate over a wide range of days: for example, basil could germinate in as little as 5 days or take as long as 42 days. If you want to plant your basil outdoors on May 15, you should start your basil indoors, under lights, 42 days before that date. This way, you can count on not only the seeds being germinated, but the plants being mature enough to transplant. Another option is to germinate one or two seeds in moist paper towels ahead of time (see Chapter 6) to find out exactly how many days that particular variety requires before germination occurs.

In the following tables, I list a variety of common flowers and give the recommended time to start them from seed in order for them to mature by their ideal bloom time.

Seeds to Start 10 to 12 Weeks Before the Last Frost

Alyssum (*Lobularia*)

Baby's breath (perennial) (*Gypsophila*)

Basket of gold (*Aurinia*)

Bee balm (*Monarda*)

Bells of Ireland (*Moluccella*)

Brugmansia (*Brugmansia*)

Butterfly flower (*Schizanthus*)

Campanula (*Campanula*)

Candylily (*Iberis*)

Catchfly (*Silene*)

Climbing snapdragon (*Asarina*)

Coleus (*Solenostemon*)

Coneflower (*Echinacea*)

Coreopsis (perennial) (*Coreopsis*)

Dahlia (*Dahlia*)

Datura (*Datura*)

Daylily (*Hemerocallis*)

continues

Seeds to Start 10 to 12 Weeks Before the Last Frost   (continued)

Delphinium (*Delphinium*)

Dianthus (*Dianthus*)

Dog fennel (*Anthemis*)

Draba (*Draba*)

English daisy (*Bellis*)

Evening primrose (*Oenothera*)

Flannel flower (*Actinotus*)

Fleabane (*Erigeron*)

Flowering maple (*Abutilon*)

Forget-me-not (*Myosotis*)

Foxglove (*Digitalis*)

Geranium (*Pelargonium*)

Gerbera daisy (*Gerbera*)

Geum (*Geum*)

Heliotrope (*Heliotropium*)

Hyssop (*Hyssopus*)

Impatiens (*Impatiens*)

Jacob's ladder (*Polemonium*)

Ladybells (*Adenophora*)

Leopard's bane (*Doronicum*)

Lion's tail (*Leonotis*)

Lisianthus (*Lisianthus*)

Livingstone daisy (*Dorotheanthus*)

Lobelia (perennial) (*Lobelia*)

Monkey flower (*Mimulus*)

Nemesia (*Nemesia*)

Penstemon (*Penstemon*)

Pentas (*Pentas*)

Petunia (*Petunia*)

Pocketbook flower (*Calceolaria*)

Polka-dot plant (*Hypoestes*)

Primrose (*Primula*)

Salpiglossis (*Salpiglossis*)

Scabious (*Scabiosa*)

Self-heal (*Prunella*)

Snapdragon (*Antirrhinum*)

Soapwort (perennial) (*Saponaria*)

Thrift (*Armeria*)

Verbena (*Verbena*)

Veronica (*Veronica*)

Yarrow (*Achillea*)

Seeds to Start 6 to 8 Weeks Before the Last Frost

African daisy (*Osteospermum*)

Agastache (*Agastache*)

Ageratum (*Ageratum*)

Amaranth (*Amaranthus*)

Angelica (*Angelica*)

Angelonia (*Angelonia*)

Aster (*Aster*)

Astilbe (*Astilbe*)

Baby's breath (annual) (*Gypsophila*)

Balloon flower (*Platycodon*)

Balloon vine (*Cardiospermum*)

Balsam pear (*Momordica*)

Basil (*Ocimum*)

Bidens (*Bidens*)

Bishop's weed (*Aegopodium*)

Blanket flower (*Gaillardia*)

Calendula (*Calendula*)

California tree poppy (*Romneya*)

Candytuft (*Iberis*)

Cassia (*Cassia*)

Catmint (*Nepeta*)

Celosia (*Celosia*)

continues

Seeds to Start 6 to 8 Weeks Before the Last Frost   (continued)

Chilean glory flower (*Eccremocarpus*)

China aster (*Callistephus*)

Cilantro (*Coriandrum*)

Cleome (*Cleome*)

Coreopsis (annual) (*Coreopsis*)

Corn cockle (*Agrostemma*)

Cosmos (*Cosmos*)

Cupid's dart (*Catananche*)

Diascia (*Diascia*)

Dill (*Anethum*)

Echium (*Echium*)

Fennel (*Foeniculum*)

Four o'clock (*Mirabilis*)

Gilia (*Gilia*)

Godetia (*Clarkia*)

Goldenrod (*Solidago*)

Gomphrena (*Gomphrena*)

Hollyhock (*Althea*)

Hops (*Humulus*)

Hosta (*Hosta*)

Hyacinth bean vine (*Lablab*)

Ice plant (*Delosperma*)

Inula (*Inula*)

Lantana (*Lantana*)

Larkspur (*Consolida*)

Lavender (*Lavendula*)

Liatris (*Liatris*)

Lobelia (annual) (*Lobelia*)

Love-in-a-mist (*Nigella*)

Lupine (*Lupinus*)

Marigold (*Tagetes*)

Mask flower (*Alonsoa*)

Mexican sunflower (*Tithonia*)

Mignonette (*Reseda*)

Moss rose (*Portulaca*)

Nicotiana (*Nicotiana*)

Phlox (annual) (*Phlox*)

Pigsqueak (*Bergenia*)

Poppy (*Papaver*)

Prairie coneflower (*Ratibida*)

Rock cress (*Arabis*)

Salvia (*Salvia*)

Sandwort (*Arenaria*)

Shoofly plant (*Nicandra*)

Soapwort (annual) (*Saponaria*)

Stock (*Matthiola*)

Strawflower (*Helichrysum*)

Swan river daisy (*Brachyscome*)

Sweet alyssum (*Lobularia*)

Sweet peas (flower) (*Lathyrus*)

Sweet William (*Dianthus*)

Tassel flower (*Emilia*)

Thunbergia (*Thunbergia*)

Thyme (*Thymus*)

Torenia (*Torenia*)

Tree mallow (*Lavatera*)

Tweedia (*Tweedia*)

Unicorn plant (*Proboscidea*)

Wallflower (*Erysimum*)

Zinnia (*Zinnia*)

Germinating Vegetables, Fruits, and Herbs

Every type of seed has specific germination requirements that vary considerably. Some seeds need cold temperatures to germinate; some need warm temperatures. Some seeds need an abundance of moisture; others don't. Some seeds need darkness; others need to be fully exposed to the light. Some seeds take a long time to germinate; others germinate overnight.

Using the wrong technique to germinate seeds not only gives you false test results, but it could kill the embryo inside the seed.

Most herb, fruit, and flower seeds readily germinate as long as the soil temperature and other conditions are right. Most vegetables prefer a soil temperature between 60°F and 85°F, frost-free conditions, and consistently moist soil. Some vegetables, such as lettuce, kale, and broccoli, are cool-season crops and prefer cooler soil temperatures to germinate; tomatoes, peppers, and eggplants, on the other hand, are warm-season crops and prefer soil temperatures over 60°F.

Keep in mind that germination temperatures refer to soil temperature, not air temperature. You can use a plain kitchen thermometer with a probe that reads between 0°F and 220°F to test the temperature of the soil. Leave the probe in the soil for approximately 5 minutes so that it takes a proper reading.

Although you don't want the soil to be soggy, some crops—such as beans, Brussels sprouts, cabbage, broccoli, cauliflower, carrots, corn, and cucumbers—germinate much faster if the soil is wet rather than just moist.

The following table lists the germination time for many common vegetable seeds.

Vegetable Germination Chart

Species	Germination Time	Difficulty
Beans	7–14 days	Easy
Beets	5–10 days	Easy
Broccoli	7–14 days	Easy
Brussels sprouts	7–14 days	Easy
Cabbage	7–14 days	Easy
Carrots	7–14 days	Easy
Cauliflower	7–14 days	Easy
Celery	18–24 days	Easy
Corn	7–14 days	Easy
Cucumber	7–21 days	Easy
Eggplant	10–21 days	Easy
Kohlrabi	7–10 days	Easy
Leeks	6–10 days	Easy
Lettuce	7–14 days	Easy
Muskmelon	7–10 days	Easy
Onions	7–14 days	Easy

Species	Germination Time	Difficulty
Peas	7–14 days	Easy
Peppers	7–90 days	Easy
Pumpkins	7–21 days	Easy
Radish	7–14 days	Easy
Spinach	7–14 days	Easy
Squash	7–21 days	Easy
Turnips	7–14 days	Easy
Watermelon	7–10 days	Easy

As noted in Chapter 3, fruit grown from seed usually doesn't resemble the parent plant; in fact, it may revert to a wild type of the fruit and not taste good at all. The exceptions are certain varieties of tropical fruits that are often propagated by seed; these include apricots, bananas, citrus, and passionfruit.

Many fruit seeds have a hard outer coat that needs some type of stratification and/ or scarification (nicking, soaking, or refrigerating them; more on this in Chapter 7). Passionfruit seeds (*Passiflora*), for example, sprout better if they are soaked overnight either in their own juice or in orange juice; the acid in the juice breaks down the seed coat, making it easier for the embryo to break through. Sometimes seed coats are so hard that the embryo dies before it can break through. This is why knowing a little bit about the types of seeds you are trying to germinate is so important.

If you want to try your hand at germinating fruit seeds, some are easier to start with than others and produce better results. Apricots, bananas, members of the citrus family, nectarines, passionfruit, and peaches are all good fruits to start with.

Fruit Seed Germination Chart

Species	Germination Time	Germination Notes
Apricots	4–6 weeks	Dry the pit for several days and then crack open the pit and harvest the almondlike seed. Store the seeds in the refrigerator for 2–3 months; then soak the seeds overnight. Place the seeds in moist potting soil and return to the refrigerator until the seeds sprout.

continues

Fruit Seed Germination Chart   (continued)

Species	Germination Time	Germination Notes
Banana	14–21 days	Soak seeds until they swell. Sow in a sterile potting medium. Keep warm and moist.
Citrus	14 days–6 months	Plant fresh seed (germination of dried seed is tricky because it must break dormancy).
Nectarines	1–3 months	Dry the pit for several days, and then crack open the pit and harvest the almondlike seed. Store the seeds in the refrigerator for 2–3 months; then soak the seeds overnight. Place the seeds in moist potting soil and return to the refrigerator until the seeds sprout.
Passionfruit	21 days–8 months	Soak passionfruit seeds overnight in either their own juice or an acidic juice such as orange juice to soften the seed coat.
Peaches	1–3 months	Dry the pit for several days and then crack open the pit and harvest the almondlike seed. Store the seeds in the refrigerator for 2–3 months, and then soak the seeds overnight. Place the seeds in moist potting soil and return to the refrigerator until the seeds sprout.

You can grow your own herbs from seed, but it's best to buy them. Herbs don't typically come true from seeds you save. You will get the same type of plant, but not necessarily the same variety. Some types of herbs, such as stevia and yerba, require warm soil to germinate. It's best to wait until summer to sow the seeds of these plants, unless you have a way of controlling soil temperature, such as a heat mat. Other herb seeds germinate without any problem if you direct-sow them. Examples of herb seeds that are easy to direct-sow and that readily germinate are dill and fennel. Other herbs, such as black cohosh and aconite, require consistent moisture and a cycle of warm temperatures, followed by cold temperatures, followed by another round of warm temperatures. Another group of herbs, which includes parsley, prefers to be planted in late summer or early fall when they may begin to grow, go dormant for the winter, then start growing again come spring.

Germinating Flowers

Flowers are the heart of the garden. They attract pollinators, add color, and create year-round interest. Many perennial flowers are easy to germinate using the winter sowing method described in Chapter 9. Even if you choose to use that method, knowing the light requirements of specific flower seeds will tell you whether to cover the seeds. Learning how to germinate flower seeds correctly the first time around will save you a lot of time and money. After all, saving money is why a lot of people choose to start flowers from seeds.

Unlike growing vegetables from seed, the timetable for germinating flowers can vary greatly. Patience is the key to success with flowers. Some flowers bloom from seed the first year; others don't bloom until the second year. Some flowers, such as roses and peonies, take six or seven years before they show their true blooms. Think of growing flowers from seed in a way similar to having a baby: you have no idea what that baby will look like or how much that baby's looks will change over the years. That is exactly the way it is when you start flowering plants from seed.

KNOW THY SEED

Always water seeds that are planted in containers or sowing trays from below.

The following list includes germination times for some of the more popular flowers.

Plant	Time to Germination
African blood lily (*Haemanthus*)	7–24 days
African blue lily (*Agapanthus*)	20–90 days
African daisy (*Osteospermum*)	7–35 days
Agastache (*Agastache*)	2–90 days
Ageratum (*Ageratum*)	5–14 days
Ajuga (*Ajuga*)	21–28 days
Albuca (*Albuca*)	7 days
Aloe (*Aloe*)	9 days
Alyssum (*Lobularia*)	5 days

continues

continued

Plant	Time to Germination
Amaranth (*Amaranthus*)	10–15 days
Amaryllis (*Amaryllis*)	9–120 days
Amole (*Chlorogalum*)	30–90 days
Anemone (*Anemone*)	15–180 days
Angelica (*Angelica*)	20–60 days
Angelonia (*Angelonia*)	10–14 days
Angel's fishing rod (*Dierama*)	18–180 days
Annato (*Bixa orellana*)	24 days
Antiganon (*Antiganon*)	6 days
Arisaema (*Arisaema*)	30–180 days
Aristolochia (*Aristolochia*)	4–90+ days
Arum (*Arum*)	30–180 days
Aster (*Aster*)	14–36 days
Astilbe (*Astilbe*)	25–60 days
Athyrium (*Athyrium*)	10–365 days
Aubrieta (*Aubrieta*)	14–21 days
Australian flame tree (*Brachychiton acerifolius*)	17 days
Baby's breath (*Gyposophila*)	10–20 days
Balloon flower (*Platycodon*)	15–30 days
Balloon vine (*Cardiospermum*)	21–30 days
Balsam pear (*Momordica*)	14–21 days
Banana (*Musa*)	7–2 years
Baptisia (*Baptisia*)	5–36 days
Basil (*Ocimum*)	5–42 days
Basket of gold (*Aurinia*)	5–14 days
Bauhinia (*Bauhinia*)	8 days
Bayberry (*Myrica*)	12 days
Bear's breeches (*Acanthus*)	21–25 days
Beaumontia (*Beaumontia*)	7 days
Bee balm (*Monarda*)	10–40 days
Begonia (*Begonia*)	15–60 days
Bells of Ireland (*Moluccella*)	8–35 days

Plant	Time to Germination
Bidens (*Bidens*)	5–21 days
Billardiera (*Billardiera*)	30–300 days
Bishop's weed (*Ammi*)	7–25 days
Blanket flower (*Gaillardia*)	7–20 days
Bleeding heart (*Dicentra*)	30–365 days
Blue star (*Amsonia*)	28–42 days
Bridal wreath (*Francoa*)	14–30 days
Browallia (*Browallia*)	13 days
Brugmansia (*Brugmansia*)	21–60 days
Brunfelsia (*Brunfelsia*)	19 days
Bugbane (*Cimicifuga*)	30–365 days
Bush violet (*Browallia*)	6–21 days
Butterfly flower (*Schizanthus*)	7–20 days
Caladium (*Caladium*)	30–90 days
Calamint (*Calamintha*)	7–28 days
Calendula (*Calendula*)	6–14 days
California poppy (*Eschscholzia*)	14–21 days
California tree poppy (*Romneya*)	30 days
Calla lily (*Zantedeschia*)	30–90 days
Camassia (*Camassia*)	30–180 days
Campanula (*Campanula*)	14–28 days
Candylily (*Pardancanda*)	15 days
Candytuft (*Iberis*)	10–60 days
Canna (*Canna*)	21–365 days
Caraway (*Carum*)	14 days
Cardiocrinum (*Cardiocrinum*)	90 days–2 years
Cassia (*Cassia*)	5–90 days
Catchfly (*Silene*)	5–20 days
Catmint (*Nepeta*)	7–21 days
Celosia (*Celosia*)	6–14 days
Centaurea (*Centaurea*)	7–30 days
Cestrum (*Cestrum*)	5 days
Chaparral lily (*Lilium*)	90–180 days

continues

continued

Plant	Time to Germination
Chilean bell flower (*Lapageria*)	30–90 days
Chilean glory vine (*Eccemocarpus*)	14–60 days
China aster (*Callistephus*)	6–14 days
Chocolate persimmon (*Diospyros digyna*)	35 days
Chocolate tree (*Theobroma*)	1–30 days
Chrysanthemum (*Chrysanthemum*)	10–28 days
Cilantro (*Coriandrum*)	10 days
Clematis (*Clematis*)	30–365 days
Cleome (*Cleome*)	10–14 days
Clianthus (*Clianthus*)	2 days
Climbing snapdragon (*Asarnia*)	9–21 days
Clivia (*Clivia*)	3+ days
Coleus (*Solenostemon*)	10–20 days
Columbine (*Aquilegia*)	30–90 days
Coneflower (*Echinacea*)	10–21 days
Coreopsis (*Coreopsis*)	5–25 days
Corn cockle (*Agrostemma*)	14–21 days
Cosmos (*Cosmos*)	3–10 days
Crambe (*Crambe*)	21–180 days
Crinum lily (*Crinum*)	7–21 days
Crocosmia (*Crocosmia*)	30–90 days
Crocus (*Crocus*)	30–180 days
Crossandra (*Crossandra*)	7–10 days
Cupid's dart (*Catananche*)	20–25 days
Cyclamen (*Cyclamen*)	21–380 days
Dahlia (*Dahlia*)	5–20 days
Daisy (*Leucanthemum*)	10–14 days
Dancing girl ginger (*Globba*)	21 days
Datura (*Datura*)	21–42 days
Daylily (*Hemerocallis*)	15–49 days
Delphinium (*Delphinium*)	7–28 days

Plant	Time to Germination
Desert candle (*Eremurus*)	30–365 days
Dianthus (*Dianthus*)	10–21 days
Dicentra (*Dicentra*)	122 days
Dill (*Anethum*)	21–25 days
Dioscorea (*Dioscorea*)	21–36 days
Dog fennel (*Anthemis*)	8–14 days
Dombeya (*Dombeya*)	6 days
Draba (*Draba*)	30–90 days
Dragon arum (*Dracunculus*)	30–180 days
Echium (*Echium*)	7–21 days
Edelweiss (*Leontopodium*)	10–42 days
Elephant ear tree (*Enterolobium cyclocarpum*)	5 days
English daisy (*Bellis*)	10–25 days
Epiphyllum (*Epiphyllum*)	7 days
Evening primrose (*Oenothera*)	5–30 days
Evening stock (*Matthiola*)	3–20 days
Fan flower (*Lobelia*)	21–60 days
Fennel (*Foeniculum*)	10–14 days
Firmiana (*Firmiana*)	15 days
Flannel flower (*Actinotus*)	7–42 days
Flax (*Linum*)	20–25 days
Flax lily (*Phormium*)	30–180 days
Fleabane (*Erigeron*)	15–50 days
Flowering maple (*Abutilon*)	20–90 days
Flowering onion (*Allium*)	14–365 days
Foamflower (*Tiarella*)	14–90 days
Forget-me-not (*Myosotis*)	8–30 days
Four o'clock (*Mirabilis*)	5–21 days
Foxglove (*Digitalis*)	5–21 days
Freesia (*Freesia*)	25–30 days
Fritillary (*Fritillaria*)	322 days–18 months
Fuchsia (*Fuchsia*)	21–120 days
Galtonia (*Galtonia*)	7 days

continues

continued

Plant	Time to Germination
Gardenia (*Gardenia*)	40 days
Gas plant (*Dictamnus*)	30–180
Gelasine (*Gelasine*)	25 days
Gentiana (*Gentiana*)	14–180 days
Geranium (*Pelargonium*)	3–90 days
Gerbera daisy (*Gerbera*)	15–30 days
Geum (*Geum*)	21–28 days
Gilia (*Gilia*)	17–21 days
Gladiolus (*Gladiolus*)	20–40 days
Globe thistle (*Echinops*)	15–60 days
Gloriosa lily (*Gloriosa*)	30–38 days
Goat's beard (*Aruncus*)	30–90 days
Godetia (*Clarkia*)	5–21 days
Goldenrod (*Solidago*)	14–42 days
Gomphrena (*Gomphrena*)	6–15 days
Grevillea (*Grevillea*)	38 days
Gum Arabic (*Acacia senegal*)	2–5 days
Hard fern (*Blechnum*)	10–365 days
Hedychium (*Hedychium*)	20 days
Helenium (*Helenium*)	7–10 days
Heliotrope (*Heliotropium*)	2–42 days
Hellebore (*Helleborus*)	30 days–18 months
Hollyhock (*Althea*)	10–14 days
Honesty (*Lunaria*)	10–14 days
Hops (*Humulus*)	25–30 days
Hosta (*Hosta*)	15–90 days
Hottentot bread (*Dioscorea elephantipes*)	12 days
Hound's tongue (*Cynoglossum*)	5–10 days
Hyacinth bean vine (*Lablab*)	3–30 days
Hyssop (*Hyssopus*)	14–42 days
Ice plant (*Delosperma*)	10–40 days
Impatiens (*Impatiens*)	7–30 days

Plant	Time to Germination
Inula (*Inula*)	14–42 days
Iris (*Iris*)	29 days–18 months
Jacob's ladder (*Polemonium*)	20–25 days
Johnny-jump-up (*Viola*)	14 days
Kaffir lily (*Schizosylis*)	7–30 days
Key lime (*Citrus aurantifolia*)	18 days
Lady's bedstraw (*Galium*)	14 days
Lady's mantle (*Alchemilla*)	21–30 days
Ladybells (*Adenophora*)	13–90 days
Lantana (*Lantana*)	30–90 days
Larkspur (*Consolida*)	14–21 days
Lavender (*Lavendula*)	4–90 days
Leopard's bane (*Doronicum*)	15–20 days
Liatris (*Liatris*)	20–25 days
Ligularia (*Ligularia*)	14–42 days
Lily (*Lilium*)	30 days–8 months
Lion's tail (*Leonotis*)	2–21 days
Lisianthus (*Lisianthus*)	10–21 days
Livingstone daisy (*Dorotheanthus*)	15–20 days
Lobelia (*Lobelia*)	15–21 days
Lotus (*Nelumbo*)	14–30 days
Love-in-a-mist (*Nigella*)	8–15 days
Luffa (*Luffa*)	8–28 days
Lungwort (*Pulmonaria*)	30–42 days
Lupine (*Lupinus*)	14–60 days
Marigold (*Tagetes*)	4–14 days
Masterwort (*Astrantia*)	30–180 days
Mayapple (*Podophyllum*)	30–180 days
Meadowsweet (*Filipendula*)	30–90 days
Meconopsis (*Meconopsis*)	21 days
Mesembryan (*Mesembryan*)	365+ days
Mexican red bird of paradise (*Caesalpinia*)	6 days
Mexican sunflower (*Tithonia*)	5–14 days

continues

continued

Plant	Time to Germination
Mignonette (*Reseda*)	5–21 days
Milkweed (*Asclepias*)	7–90 days
Milky Way tree (*Stemmadenia littoralis*)	18 days
Monkey flower (*Mimulus*)	7–21 days
Monkshood (*Aconitum*)	5–270 days
Morning glory (*Ipomoea*)	5–21 days
Moss rose (*Portulaca*)	7–21 days
Nasturtium (*Tropaeolum*)	7 days–2 years
Nemesia (*Nemesia*)	5–21 days
Nicotiana (*Nicotiana*)	10–20 days
Oxen red eye (*Mecuna*)	24 days
Orchid (*Bletilla*)	30–365 days
Oregano (*Origanum*)	10 days
Ornithogalum (*Ornithogalum*)	365+ days
Pansy (*Viola*)	10–50 days
Partridge pea (*Cassia*)	16 days
Papaya (*Carica*)	16 days
Paris (*Paris*)	365+ days
Parsley (*Petroselinum*)	21–42 days
Passionfruit (*Passiflora*)	4–365 days
Pearly everlasting (*Anaphalis*)	10–60 days
Pelargonium (*Pelargonium*)	3–21 days
Pennisetum (*Pennisetum*)	15–20 days
Penstemon (*Penstemon*)	9–36 days
Pentas (*Pentas*)	6–40 days
Peony (*Paeonia*)	30–365 days
Petunia (*Petunia*)	7–21 days
Phlox (*Phlox*)	10–50 days
Pigsqueak (*Bergenia*)	15–180 days
Pimpernel (*Anagallis*)	30–42 days
Pineapple lily (*Eucomis*)	20–25 days
Plumbago (*Ceratostigma*)	30–90 days

Plant	Time to Germination
Poached egg plant (*Limnanthes*)	14–21 days
Pocketbook flower (*Calceolaria*)	14–21 days
Polka-dot plant (*Hypoestes*)	7–21 days
Poppy (*Papaver*)	10–30 days
Prairie coneflower (*Ratibida*)	7–42 days
Primrose (*Primula*)	4–40 days
Peruvian lily (*Alstroemeria*)	15–365 days
Pitcher plant (*Sarracenia*)	30–90 days
Prickly poppy (*Argemone*)	14 days
Pussy toes (*Antennaria*)	30–60 days
Puya (*Puya*)	21 days
Rain lily (*Zephyanthes*)	120+ days
Red hot poker (*Kniphofia*)	10–30 days
Rhodochiton (*Rhodochiton*)	18 days
Rock cress (*Arabis*)	14–25 days
Rock jasmine (*Saxifraga*)	30–365 days
Rosemary (*Rosmarinus*)	1–21 days
Royal poinciana (*Delonix regina*)	30 days
Safflower (*Carthamus*)	10–24 days
Salpiglossis (*Salphiglossis*)	2–30 days
Salvia (*Salvia*)	4–21 days
Sandwort (*Areneria*)	8–30 days
Sea holly (*Eryngium*)	5–90 days
Sandersonia (*Sandersonia*)	30–90 days
Scabious (*Scabiosa*)	10–15 days
Sedge (*Carex*)	1–90+ days
Self-heal (*Prunella*)	30–60 days
Shoofly plant (*Nicandra*)	15–20 days
Shooting star (*Dodecatheon*)	90–365 days
Shrimp plant (*Justicia*)	5 days
Snapdragon (*Antirrhinum*)	10–21 days
Soapwort (*Saponaria*)	10–21 days
Spurge (*Euphorbia*)	10–28 days

continues

continued

Plant	Time to Germination
Star fruit (*Averrhoa carambola*)	18 days
Starflower (*Mentzelia*)	5–21 days
Star-of-Bethlehem (*Ornithogalum*)	30–180 days
Statice (*Limonium*)	10–20 days
Stock (*Matthiola*)	3–20 days
Strawflower (*Helichrysum*)	5–20 days
Sunflower (*Helianthus*)	10–14 days
Swan river daisy (*Brachyscome*)	10–21 days
Sweet pea (flower) (*Lathyrus*)	10–30 days
Sweet William (*Dianthus*)	10 days
Tacca (*Tacca*)	40 days
Tassel flower (*Emilia*)	8–15 days
Thift (*Armeria*)	10–21 days
Thunbergia (*Thunbergia*)	11–21 days
Thyme (*Thymus*)	15–30 days
Toad lily (*Tricyrtis*)	30–90 days
Torenia (*Torenia*)	7–30 days
Tree mallow (*Lavatera*)	15–20 days
Trillium (*Trillium*)	18 months–3 years
Trout lily (*Erythronium*)	30 days–18 months
Tweedia (*Tweedia*)	10–15 days
Unicorn plant (*Proboscidea*)	20 days
Verbena (*Verbena*)	2–90 days
Veronica (*Veronica*)	15–90 days
Vinca (*Vinca*)	15–20 days
Viola (*Viola*)	10–21 days
Wallflower (*Erysimum*)	5–30 days
Wandflower (*Sparaxis*)	30–90 days
Wild ginger (*Asarum*)	7–18 days
Winter aconite (*Eranthis*)	30–365 days
Wood rose (*Merremia*)	8–35 days
Woodruff (*Asperula*)	21–42 days

Plant	Time to Germination
Yarrow (*Achillea*)	10–100 days
Ylang-ylang (*Cananga odorata*)	10–90 days
Yucca (*Yucca*)	30–365 days
Zahidi date palm (*Phoenix dactylifera*)	30 days
Zinnia (*Zinnia*)	5–24 days

Potting Up Your Seedlings

After your seeds germinate, you need to pot them up—in other words, plant them in small pots. When dealing with small seedlings that are too tiny to handle individually, you can place the entire paper towel full of germinated seeds on top of your seed-starting mixture.

Lightly cover the top of the seedlings on the paper towel with vermiculite to keep them from drying out. Vermiculite is looser than soil and retains moisture better, making it easier for the newly developing roots to spread and grow.

As soon as the roots begin to show, move the germinated seeds from the paper towels into the soil. If it's necessary to accommodate the roots, make a small indentation for them in the soil.

Pick up larger seeds, one by one, with a pair of tweezers, always making sure the tweezers are grasping the seed coat and not the delicate root growth; place one seed per pot. That makes it easier to transplant them or pot them up again later, whenever necessary.

 THE BAD SEED

Never pick up a seedling by its stem or roots. Doing so could cause enough damage to kill the tender plant. Always pick up seedlings by either the seed coat or the plant's leaves.

If you made an indentation in the soil for the roots, gently press the top of the soil over and around them, leaving no space between the root and the soil for air or water; either of these could kill the seedling. Lightly cover the seeds with just enough vermiculite to barely cover the seed coat. You don't want the seed coat visible, nor do you want the seed to be buried too deeply. Too much vermiculite will make it difficult—or impossible—for the plant to emerge.

After the seeds are transplanted, water them from the bottom and keep them moist until the seedlings begin to grow. As the plant's roots begin to show at the bottom (or on the sides if you used peat pellets, peat pots, or another type of biodegradable container), transplant them either one pot size up or into the garden (more on this in Chapter 11).

The Least You Need to Know

- Periodically check the germination rates of the seeds you save.
- Declining germination rates of your saved seeds means it's time to grow them out and save new ones.
- Always give every seed adequate germination time.
- Handle your newly germinated seeds very carefully to avoid damaging the roots and stems.

Scarification and Stratification

In This Chapter

- Encouraging seed germination
- Mastering seed scarification and stratification
- Determining which seeds to stratify or scarify
- Smoking seeds

Seeds are tough. Some of them develop a hard outer coat, known as a seed coat, that even an embryo can't break through without some help. If the embryo can't penetrate the seed coat, it will die trying.

In nature, weather changes, heavy rains, and seed-eating birds or mammals help break down the seed coat. For example, when a bird or mammal eats a seed, the acid in the animal's digestive system breaks down the seed coat. When the bird or mammal eliminates the seed in its scat, the seed is ready to germinate if the right conditions are met. Animals also help break down the seed coat by nicking, scratching, or sanding the outer shell of hard seed coats, which helps weaken them and allows the embryo to push through and begin to grow.

Instead of leaving it up to nature to break down your seeds, you can take matters into your own hands. This chapter shows you how.

Stratification

Seed stratification is a means of using variations in temperature to break down the seed coat so that the embryo can emerge. This could involve giving seeds a prolonged cold treatment, possibly followed by a prolonged warm treatment. To help the seed coat break down, the seeds must be damp during this process. Using temperature to break down a seed's hard coat enables the embryo to emerge and begin to grow. You can stratify seeds in many ways. You can let nature do the work as the seasons change simply using winter sowing techniques (more on this in Chapter 9); this is the easiest way for busy gardeners. Or you can take a more proactive approach.

Temperature Stratification

Refrigerating or freezing damp seeds is one of the most popular ways to stratify them (see Chapter 5 for a list of seeds that can handle freezing).

You can use either of the following freezing techniques:

- Place seeds in an ice cube tray, cover them with water, and then put the trays in the freezer. After two days, remove the trays and allow the ice cubes to melt naturally at room temperature.

- Place seeds on damp paper towels enclosed in a container, and put the container in the freezer. Make sure the container is sturdy enough to keep the seeds from being damaged if something is placed on top of it.

You can use either of the following refrigeration techniques:

- Place seeds on damp paper towels enclosed in a container, and put the container in the refrigerator. Make sure the container is sturdy enough to prevent the seeds from being damaged if something is placed on top of it, and be sure to put a lid on the container.

- Place the seeds in the envelope they came in inside a container and seal it. Make sure the container is sturdy and waterproof. This will stratify the seeds and allow you to plant them whenever you're ready without having to go through this step again.

KNOW THY SEED

Some seeds require several exposures to different temperatures to break down their seed coat. This can be done indoors by moving them from room temperature to either the refrigerator or the freezer, depending on how cold the seeds need to be, and then moving them back to room temperature again.

The following table lists a wide variety of seeds that require temperature stratification to germinate.

Examples of Seeds That Need Temperature Stratification

Plant Type	Recommended Treatment
Arisaema (*Arisaema*)	Refrigerate seeds in moist paper towel for 6 weeks and then store at 55°F–60°F until germination occurs; this may take up to 180 days.
Clematis (*Clematis*)	Place seeds in moist paper towel, put towel in closed container, and freeze for 3 weeks; then keep the seeds warm until germination occurs.
Dogwood (*Cornus*)	Collect ripe seeds. Remove the pulp, clean, and air-dry them, and place the dry seeds in moist paper towel. Refrigerate for 3–4 months.
Flowering onion (*Allium*)	Place seeds in moist paper towel in the refrigerator for 30 days and then move them into 55°F–65°F temperature. The seeds need light and may take up to a year to germinate.
Fragrant snowbell (*Styrax*)	Refrigerate the ripe seeds in damp paper towels for 3 months.
Magnolia (*Magnolia*)	Collect ripe seed. Remove pulp, clean seeds, and place in moist paper towel for 2–4 months.
Masterwort (*Astrantia*)	Place seeds in moist paper towel and refrigerate for 3–5 months.
Trillium (*Trillium*)	Refrigerate in moist paper towel for 3 months. Remove germination container and place seeds in an area with 60°F–70°F for 3 months. Repeat the entire cycle until the seeds sprout.

Whenever freezing or refrigerating any seed, whether on paper towels or not, always keep the seeds in a sealed container. This can be a lidded plastic container or a freezer bag.

Water Stratification

Soaking seeds in water is another way to help break down the seed coat. The best method is to use boiling water the first time you cover the seeds. After that water cools, replace it with hot tap water. Keep the water as warm as possible while the seeds are soaking in it. You can accomplish this by dumping out the water several times a day and pouring fresh hot water over the seeds.

You can also keep the soaking seeds on top of a warm surface, like the top of a refrigerator, or use a heat mat. If you use a heat mat, keep the seeds in a glass container rather than plastic to prevent the container from accidentally melting.

When the seeds begin to swell, stratification has occurred. Most seeds need to be strained and removed at this point, and then planted. A few types of seeds, such as amaryllis, germinate better when left floating on top of the water.

Examples of Water-Germinated Seeds

Plant Type	Recommended Treatment
Amaryllis (*Amaryllis*)	Float seeds on top of water until they germinate.
Antiganon leptopus (*Antiganon leptopus*)	Soak seeds for 24 hours.
Aristolochia (*Aristolochia*)	Soak seeds for 24 hours.
Brunfelsia (*Brunfelsia*)	Soak seeds for 4 days, or until they swell.
Banana (*Musa*)	Soak seeds in hot water for 48 hours; keep moist and warm until germination occurs.
Cassia (*Cassia*)	Soak seeds for 2 days or until swelling occurs
Cestrum (*Castrum*)	Soak seeds for 3 days or until swelling occurs
Clianthus (*Clianthus*)	Soak seeds for 48 hours. May germinate in the water.
Elephant ear tree (*Enterolobium cyclocarpum*)	Soak seeds for 48 hours.
Flowering maple (*Abutilon*)	Soak seeds for 24 hours.

Plant Type	Recommended Treatment
Gum Arabic (*Acacia senegal*)	Soak seeds for 48 hours.
Hedychium (*Hedychium*)	Soak seeds for 72 hours.
Key lime (*Citrus aurantifolia*)	Soak seeds for 72 hours.
Milky Way tree (*Stemmadenia littoralis*)	Soak fresh seeds until they swell.
Oxen red eye (*Mucuna*)	Soak seeds for 48 hours.
Plumeria (*Plumeria*)	Don't soak, but do keep in moist paper towels at room temperature until germination occurs.
Siberian peatree (*Caragana boisii*)	Soak seeds for 24 hours.
Tacca (*Tacca*)	Soak seeds until they swell. May take a week or so.
Ylang ylang (*Cananga odorata*)	Soak seeds for 2 days or until they swell.

Another advantage of using water to stratify seeds is that, within 24 hours, you typically find out which seeds are viable and which are not; the exception is papery seeds, like amaryllis or garlic vine. As the seeds begin to absorb water, the viable seeds sink to the bottom of the container. Seeds that are not viable remain at the top of the jar, floating on the water (again, papery seeds are the exception to the rule). If none of the seeds sink, several possibilities exist:

- The seeds are not viable.

- The seeds are not heavy enough to sink.

- The seeds need more time to absorb more water.

Some seeds can take up to a week to absorb enough water to sink. As a result of having gone into a deep dormancy, older seeds that have been in storage for a long time often take longer to absorb water as well.

A less frequently used method of stratification is running water, which can rid seed coats of chemicals that inhibit germination. If you have access to a natural stream or pond that has constantly moving water, you can simply tie the seeds in a bag, such as one made of cheesecloth, and secure it to the edge of the bank. The water running over the seeds breaks down the inhibitors and washes them away. Or you can place the seeds in cheesecloth or a tea strainer in your sink, turn on the faucet, and allow the water to run over the tops of the seeds; this will run up your water bill, of course, unless you get your water from a well.

One last option is to buy a hydroponics unit used specifically for germinating seeds and rooting cuttings. Worm's Way sells a hydroponics unit called the Rainforest, which is ideal for this. In this unit, the seeds go into a tray at the top of the container, and the unit mists water mixed with nutrients over the top of the seedlings. The germination inhibitors eventually wash off, and the seeds germinate. These units have come down in price in recent years but are still quite expensive. However, if you germinate a lot of seeds or root a lot of cuttings, they are well worth the cost.

Scarification

Hard seed coats, such as flowering sweet peas, need some type of scarification to germinate. Scarification is a process by which you deliberately damage the seed coat through sanding, nicking, or chipping, which enables the embryo to emerge. Nature develops hard seed coats to prevent premature germination. When we remove these seeds from their natural environment, we must somehow let the seed know that it's time to germinate in order for it to break its natural dormancy.

For scarifying your seeds, I highly recommend purchasing a small hand-held rotary tool with a small tip for sanding or grinding. Dremel makes one that works perfectly. They come in corded and cordless varieties and cost less than $20 at discount and craft stores.

Not all seeds need the same treatment. Some prefer to have their seed coat scratched and others need their seed coat to be nicked. For scratching, lightly sand the seed's surface so the embryo can emerge. For seeds that need nicking and chipping, sand the seed's surface slightly deeper until you can see the color change below. When you notice the color of the seed coat changing, you know that you've gone deep enough, and it's time to stop before you damage the embryo.

If you don't have a Dremel tool, you can use sandpaper or soapless scouring pads. A small knife or razor blade also works for nicking the seed coat, but you must be careful not to cut too far into the seed—or cut yourself! If you accidentally cut the embryo, you'll kill the seed.

Examples of Seeds That Need Scarification

Acacia (*Acacia*)

Baobab (*Adansonia digitata*)

Bottle tree (*Callistemon rigidus*)

Caesalpinia (*Caesalpinia*)

Candle bush (*Senna alata*)

Cascalote (*Caesalpinia cacalaco*)

Chinese sweetshrub (*Calycanthus chinensis*)

Goldenrain tree (*Koelreuteria paniculata*)

Illinois bundle flower (*Desmanthus illinoensis*)

Lady's fingers (*Anthyllis vulneraria*)

Lupine (*Lupinus*)

Pelargonium (*Pelargonium*)

Sabal palm (*Sabal palmetto*)

Sweet pea (*Lathyrus*)

Utah loco (*Astragalus*)

GA-3

Seeds that are highly dormant often benefit from being presoaked in a solution of gibberellic acid (GA-3), which is made from naturally occurring growth-stimulating hormones. You can purchase GA-3 from many seed companies and gardening centers.

To scarify seeds in GA-3, you need plastic ice cube trays. If you're treating a lot of seeds, standard trays work fine, but if you're going to treat just a few, use the trays that make smaller cubes.

Before starting, you must prepare the GA-3 by dissolving a 100mg packet of GA-3 powder in 100mL (just less than ½ cup) of clean or distilled water. If you're working with a 1000mg (1 gram) packet of GA-3, add it to 1L of water (about 1 quart plus 1 cup).

Follow these steps:

1. Fold a heavyweight white paper towel in half three times.

2. Moisten it with water, but don't make it wet enough to drip.

3. Cut a piece of plastic, such as that from a grocery bag, into a 3×3-inch square.

4. Open one fold of the paper towel and place the plastic bag square in the center (this provides humidity and keeps the inner pad with the GA-3 from drying out).

5. Cut out a $2\frac{1}{2}×2\frac{1}{2}$-inch square from another paper towel and place this on top of the plastic square.

6. Moisten the small square of paper towel with six drops of water from an eyedropper.

7. Sprinkle 1 mm^3, or the amount of GA-3 that can easily be balanced on the end of a toothpick, on the paper towel square.

8. Place the seeds you want to treat with GA-3 on the paper towel square.

9. To avoid potential problems caused by overexposure to GA-3, remove each seed individually as soon as it begins to sprout.

Example of Seeds That Need GA-3 Treatment

Alpine basil thyme (*Acinos alpinus*)

Azureocereus hertlingianus (*Azureocereus hertlingianus*)

Barrel cactus (*Echinocactus and Ferocactus*)

Belladonna (*Atropa belladonna*)

Bomarea (*Bomarea*)

Butterfly bush (*Buddleia*)

Caper bush (*Capparis spinosa*)

Cardiocrinum cordatum var Glehnii (*Cardiocrinum cordatum* var *Glehnii*)

Common milkweed (*Asclepias*)

Corydalis (*Corydalis*)

Euphorbia inermis (*Euphorbia inermis*)

Euphorbia pentagona (*Euphorbia pentagona*)

Indian tobacco (*Nicotiana*)

Leuchtenbergia principis (*Leuchtenbergia principis*)

Lungwort (*Pulmonaria*)

Meadow rue (*Thalictrum*)

Monkey flower (*Mimulus*)

Opuntia (*Opuntia*)

Orange horned poppy (*Glaucium flavum*)

Penstemon (*Penstemon*)

Poor man's weatherglass (*Anagallis*)

Salvia (*Salvia*)

Stylidium (*Stylidium*)

Tree poppy (*Romneya coulteri*)

Smoking Seeds

A number of seeds are highly dormant and require specific conditions to germinate. In the wild, many of these seeds receive smoke treatment when fires burn off fields. Sometimes this occurs naturally; sometimes the burn is intentional. Either way, the seeds lie dormant until they are smoked.

Smoke seed primer disks are an easy way to smoke seeds. These disks, readily available online from several vendors, dissolve in water. Then you simply soak the seeds in the smoky water for 24 hours. The smoke seed primer disks are made up of an absorbent paper that has been impregnated with fynbos-smoke-saturated water.

Yet another easy (and cheaper) option is to make your own smoky water using natural smoke from the grocery store. In the BBQ or spice section of most grocery stores, you'll find hickory seasoning or liquid smoke. It's a small bottle, but you don't need much. After you mix up the solution, soak the seeds overnight or until they begin to swell; then plant them.

KNOW THY SEED

Here's a formula for making smoky water from liquid smoke: ½ teaspoon liquid smoke plus 4½ teaspoons hot water; if you're making a bigger batch, use nine parts water to one part smoke.

Seeds That Need Smoke Stratification

Kangaroo paw (*Anigozanthos*)

Protea (*Protea*)

Salvia (*Salvia*)

Senna (*Senna*)

Stylidium (*Stylidium*)

Tea tree (*Melaleuca alternifolia*)

Dealing with Double Dormant Seeds

Some seeds require both stratification and scarification to induce germination. Seeds that fall into this category have both an internal and an external dormancy, which is known as a *double dormancy.*

To break double dormancy, you must first scarify the seeds and then stratify them. If you reverse the process and stratify the seed first, the seeds will die.

Examples of Seeds That Have a Double Dormancy

Plant Type	Recommended Treatment
Ajuga pyramidalis (*Ajuga pyramidalis*)	Soak seed in 500ppm of GA-3 and then place on moist paper towels. Put in the refrigerator for 8 weeks.
Beaumontia (*Beaumontia*)	Nick seed coat. Place seed in damp paper towel. Keep moist until germination occurs at room temperature.
Camellia (*Camellia*)	Collect seed before it dries. If the seed is already dry, soak it for 24 hours in warm water. Refrigerate the seed in damp paper towel after soaking until the root (*radicle*) begins to sprout.
Canna (*Canna*)	Chip or nick the seed coat. Soak seed in warm water for 48 hours. Keep seeds moist and in 70°F–75°F temperatures until germination occurs.

Plant Type	Recommended Treatment
Lilies (*Lilium*)	Soak seed in warm water for 24 hours. Place seed in moist paper towel at 70°F for 4 weeks. Move the seeds, whether they are sprouted or not, to the refrigerator for 2–3 months.
Silk tree (*Albizia*)	Nick the seed coat. Soak in warm water overnight.

KNOW THY SEED

You must know which seeds require multiple exposures to different temperatures, or you could end up killing them.

When artificially creating the seasons, be sure you can offer the sprouted seeds a warm place to grow with plenty of light, or they will die off and your work will have been for nothing. An ideal time to work with seeds that require this type of treatment is late fall or early winter so that the seeds can grow during the spring and summer and be ready to go dormant when winter arrives.

Easy Seeds: No Extra Work Required

Not all seeds require stratification or scarification. As soon as conditions are right, some seeds germinate just the way they are. Think about the wide variety of seeds you can direct-sow in the garden without doing anything to encourage them to germinate.

Examples of Seeds That Don't Require Scarification or Stratification

Aster (*Aster*)
Bachelor's buttons (*Centaurea*)
Beans
Broccoli
Calendula (*Calendula*)
Cauliflower
Corn

continues

Examples of Seeds That Don't Require Scarification or Stratification   (continued)

Cosmos (*Cosmos*)

Indian tobacco (*Nicotiana*)

Lettuce

Marigold (*Tagetes*)

Peas

Pumpkin

Radish

Watermelon

Zinnia (*Zinnia*)

The Least You Need to Know

- Seeds removed from their natural environment sometimes need artificial stratification or scarification.
- Understanding how seeds germinate in nature helps you determine the best way to start your seeds at home.
- Water and temperature are reliable stratification methods.
- Chipping and sanding the seed coats of hard seeds are good methods of scarification.

Sowing Seeds Indoors

In This Chapter

- Grasping the fundamentals behind starting plants from seed indoors
- Choosing the best pots for starting your indoor seeds
- Getting the indoor temperature and light right
- Growing healthy, disease-free seedlings

For a gardening geek such as myself, few things in life are as satisfying as growing plants from seed indoors during the off-season. Not only is it fun and economical, but it also gives you the opportunity to grow plants you can't find locally. Starting plants from seeds is one of the most rewarding aspects of gardening. It also allows you to extend the joys of gardening beyond seasonal demands. From saving seeds to germinating, to nurturing seedlings indoors, you can be actively engaged in gardening even when there's three feet of snow on the ground. Some of those indoor seedlings will even begin to flower before you plant them, bringing you more delight.

Of course, there are a lot of fine points of seed starting. You have to use the right seed-sowing medium. You have to decide between plastic pots, peat pots, and peat pellets, making educated decisions about which seed containers are best for your needs. Don't worry, though: I cover all these details and more in this chapter.

Gathering Your Supplies

You need certain basic tools and supplies to start planting your seeds; some are optional, and you probably already have many of them around the house:

- Kelp and/or liquid fertilizer
- Peat moss
- Vermiculite
- Perlite
- Soil (or meat) thermometer
- Compost
- A variety of containers
- Tweezers
- Peat pots and/or peat pellets (optional)
- Heat mat (optional)
- Ceiling hooks (optional)
- Grow lights (optional)
- Light fixture (optional)
- Timer (optional)
- Ladder (optional)
- Fan (optional)

Light, water, soil, nutrients, and temperature all play a critical role in the life of the developing seedling. When a seed first germinates, the *endosperm* contains everything the seed needs to sustain its first few days of growth. This bit of nutrition nourishes the seed until it grows enough to absorb nutrients from the soil through its roots.

DEFINITION

The **endosperm** is the nutrient-packed tissue that surrounds the developing embryo of a seed.

Finding the Right Spot

The ideal spot to start seeds indoors is a low-traffic area that's warm, has plenty of light, and is free of drafts and pests, such as field mice or ants. A spare room is perfect, of course, but if you don't have one, just look around your home to see what space is available to use.

THE BAD SEED

Mice and ants love to eat or carry off seeds, so choose an area they don't frequent. A light dusting of diatomaceous earth (DE) deters ants, but mice are harder to get rid of when they find a source of food.

Walk around your home at different times of the day. Think about the areas that receive large amounts of natural light and how you can set up shelves or tables to hold seed trays full of young seeds or seedlings.

Here are some ideas:

- An empty closet can work well, as long as it's large enough to hold the seedlings, can accommodate grow lights, and gives you the space you need to get into it to tend to the plants.

- The top of a refrigerator, freezer, or water heater can be ideal because these are warm places—as long as you provide adequate light.

- Turn an unused basement into a grow room, as long as the basement is dry and some sort of heat is available.

- Large windows, especially those that face south, are ideal places to start seeds. But because seedlings and plants lean toward the light, you must turn them at least once a day to keep them growing straight, or else they will be crooked. If you can hang grow lights near the window to balance this tendency, you'll be relieved of daily turning tasks.

- Sunrooms or window-lined porches and patios also work well for starting seeds in natural light.

SPROUTING WISDOM

Keep in mind that if you completely fill your planting area with seed trays, you'll run out of room once you start to pot up your seedlings. Picture your storage area after the seedlings have shot up several inches, and design your storage space according to that projection.

Choosing Your Growing Medium

The seed-sowing medium, which is usually a soilless mixture made up of *peat moss*, *vermiculite*, and/or *perlite*, provides a stable growing environment for young plants. However, most seed-sowing media are devoid of nutrients, which means that when the seed sprouts and the roots enter the soil, there's nothing there for the plants to absorb and use for nourishment. To prevent this problem, after the seedlings begin to grow, you need to add nutrients such as *kelp* or a half-strength liquid fertilizer every time you water.

DEFINITION

Peat moss is any of various mosses of the genus *Sphagnum,* which grows naturally in very wet places. Peat moss holds water and any nutrients you add.

Vermiculite is a mineral that expands with the application of heat. Vermiculite creates a sandy, loose soil, making it easier for the plants' roots to develop.

Perlite is an amorphous volcanic glass that has relatively high water content, typically formed by the hydration of obsidian (a naturally occurring volcanic glass). It occurs naturally and has the unusual property of greatly expanding when heated sufficiently. Perlite keeps the soil from compacting, making drainage easier.

Kelp is a rich source of vitamins, minerals, and trace minerals that's made from seaweed. The plants grown in this fertilizer take up the nutrients. When we eat the plants, we get the benefits, too. Plants fertilized with kelp also exhibit more cold-hardiness.

Peruse the shelves of any garden center, and you'll see many varieties of commercial seed-starting mix. Or you can make your own. The key to making your own mix is to make sure the ingredients you use are sterile. You can do this by heating the soil on a grill or in an oven to a temperature of 180°F and maintaining that temperature for 30 minutes. The soil should be laid out no more than an inch thick. The smell of cooking soil is a bit off-putting, so unless you have a very good air vent indoors, it's best to do this outside on a grill or in an outdoor oven.

Here's the list of ingredients for a basic seed-starting mix:

1 cubic foot sterilized peat moss

4 quarts vermiculite

4 quarts perlite

4 cups kelp

While the ingredients are still dry, mix them thoroughly. Then add enough hot water to make the soil mixture slightly soupy. Let the mixture sit overnight; the peat moss will absorb most of the water. If the mixture is too dry the next day, add more hot water.

Feel free to vary this recipe based on your soil conditions, the types of plants you're growing, and the amount of rainfall you get in your area. If you're growing plants, such as cacti, that need superior drainage, add some sand or increase the amount of vermiculite. Feel free to add one part of sterilized compost as well.

You can learn about the needs of various plants from a wide variety of books and online (see Appendix B). Experiment with your homemade seed-starting mix until it works well for the seeds you're planting. Gardening and growing plants from seed is about trial and error.

Housing Your Seeds

You'll find many types and styles of seed-sowing containers on the market: peat pots, peat pellets, plastic pots, flats filled with the latest and greatest seed-starting media, newspaper pots, and even Cow Pots, which are made from—you guessed it—cow manure! With so many products on the market, it can be hard to choose. Some pots work better than others for certain types of seeds, and some pots are recyclable or reusable.

Of course, if you want to get really creative, just look around your house to see what kinds of things you can start your seeds in. Empty eggshells and egg cartons are ideal for starting tiny seeds. The eggshells contain calcium that breaks down in the ground, improves your soil, and helps the plant grow better. Milk cartons, empty toilet paper or paper towel rolls cut down to size, and containers from soft butter, yogurt, and cottage cheese also work well for seed starting. Be sure to punch some holes in the bottom of your containers so excess water can drain off; otherwise, your seeds or young plants could drown.

Plastic Pots

You can reuse plastic pots from year to year, but you must take the time to clean and sterilize them between uses. Plastic pots do a great job of containing the plant's side roots. The roots will eventually find their way to the bottom of the pot, though, and creep out through those holes. When you see the roots down there, it's time to pot the plant into a larger container.

A drawback of plastic pots is that if you don't pay attention, the plant's roots will grow and entangle under the pot, and you'll have to break off some roots when it's time to remove the plant from the pot. This can cause the plant to have a slight delay in growth, but it's unlikely to kill the plant unless it's a plant with a taproot, like a hollyhock. Another problem with plastic pots is that the roots that grow out of the pot are exposed. If you don't keep them dark, cool, and moist, they could dry up—and that could kill the plant.

Peat Pots and Pellets

The greatest benefit of peat pots and peat pellets is that they eliminate *transplant shock* because the entire pot, with the plant intact, goes in the soil.

DEFINITION

Transplant shock is characterized by wilting and a failure of seedlings to thrive after being planted outdoors. It is often caused by root damage when transplanting a seedling or plant.

Peat pots come in a variety of sizes and can be filled with your favorite potting mix.

Peat pellets consist of an oval ball of peat moss inside a netted bag. These are small and expand only when you add water to them. They're easy to use, you don't add any extra soil to them, and they make transplanting into larger pots a breeze.

Both peat pots and peat pellets tend to dry out easily. When planting peat pots or pellets in larger containers, you must make sure they're completely covered with soil, and that the soil around them stays moist. If the tops of the peat pots are left above the soil level, the exposed tops will dry out and wick the water away from the plants roots through the natural process of evaporation, and the organic material in the peat pots will try to keep soaking up moisture to prevent dry-out; this robs the plants' roots of the moisture they need to thrive. Once peat dries out, it's hard to rewet, so even if you catch the problem in time, preventing damage is difficult.

Many plants resist being transplanted. Poppies are notoriously difficult to transplant, for example, as are plants with tap roots, such as hollyhocks; for these types of plants, peat pots are the ideal way to go.

You can start seeds in small peat pots and then put the entire peat pot into a larger one as the plants' roots begin to show. Keep a close eye on the moisture level, especially if you're using them in a greenhouse. In fact, keeping a thin layer of water in the flats they sit in is a good idea. Then you can always rest assured that they'll have enough water to wick up to prevent them from drying out.

Over time, both peat pellets and peat pots will break down. You can speed up the process by tearing away the top edges of the peat pots, or tearing off the bottoms if they're not embedded with plant roots when you plant them in the garden.

Don't throw out what you've torn off and removed! Either bury the peat pot material in a hole in your garden or toss it into the *compost* pile, which you can later use to *mulch* your garden. The earthworms in the soil will incorporate the peat-based matter into your soil, thus improving its natural structure.

DEFINITION

Compost is a mixture of decaying organic matter, anything from leaves to manure to paper products, used to improve soil structure and provide nutrients.

Mulch is a protective covering, usually of organic matter such as leaves, straw, or peat, placed around plants to prevent the evaporation of moisture, the freezing of roots, and the growth of weeds.

Soil Blocks

Soil blocks, made with a soil block maker, are helpful for people who do a lot of seed starting. They're inexpensive to make, but the initial investment in a soil block maker costs somewhere in the neighborhood of $25. (It will more than pay for itself after several seasons, though.) When using soil blocks, you start with a tiny block for your seeds. When you have sprouts, you move them up to a larger block; when they've grown sturdier, you move them up once more before transplanting the entire soil block in the garden. Soil blocks also eliminate transplant shock.

Taking the Soil Temperature

Every type of seed has its preferred germination temperature (this refers to soil temperature, not air temperature). Whether you start seeds indoors or out, you have many ways to adjust the soil's natural temperature to exactly what is needed at the right time. Learning to adjust and maintain soil temperature takes a little practice, but as long as you have a trusty soil thermometer (a meat thermometer works, too), it won't take long for you to master these techniques.

SPROUTING WISDOM

Allow your soil thermometer to remain in the soil for at least 10 minutes to ensure that you get an accurate reading.

Indoor gardeners often use heat mats to keep the soil at a steady temperature. Heat mats are easy to use, easy to clean, and easy to store. Some of the higher-end models have a temperature dial so you can manually adjust the temperature. Less expensive models simply maintain a temperature between 65°F and 75°F. Prices are all over the board, ranging from $17 to $80.

To use a heat mat, place it on a flat, nonflammable surface, plug it in, and set your seed flat on top of it. If you put a clear plastic lid on your seed flat, make sure the lid has a vent; otherwise, too much heat can build up and cook your seeds or young plants.

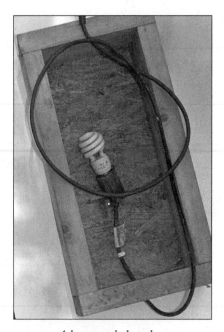

A homemade heat box.

Using Grow Lights

For indoor gardening, adequate light is essential to the health and vigor of seedlings. You can start seedlings in front of a sunny window, but grow lights are the next best thing to natural sunlight. These lights, which are designed to emit all of the various color spectrums that plants need, will keep your plants developing all winter long and even encourage older plants to bloom.

Grow lights are an ideal way to make sure seedlings sown indoors get the light they need to develop into healthy plants. Grow lights are movable—all you need is a horizontal surface from which to hang them. A ceiling or heavy-duty shelf is ideal as long as there's adequate distance between the light and the seedlings. This portability allows you to grow a variety of plants in any room in your home.

SPROUTING WISDOM

Maximize the amount of light the seedlings get by placing a reflective material, such as aluminum foil, under the seed trays. This causes any light that hits the foil to bounce back to the plants. You can also line the back of the seed-starting shelf with foil. If the room is dedicated to seed starting, paint it white, which also reflects more light than darker colors.

A timer is also a good investment if you're planning to use grow lights. When the seeds are germinating and first growing, keep the light on between 14 to 16 hours a day. As the plants begin to mature, cut the light back to 12 hours a day.

Seedlings under grow lights.

For starting seeds that require light to germinate, simply set up the light so that it's 3 inches above the top of the seed-starting container. After the seeds germinate and you move them into pots, keep the lights positioned 3 inches above the top of the foliage. If the foliage begins to look a little brown or dry, move the lights up so that they hang 3 to 6 inches above the tops of the foliage. This keeps the plants growing toward the light but prevents them from getting *leggy*.

DEFINITION

A **leggy** plant has a tall, spindly stem that's too weak to hold itself up, let alone support flowers or fruit.

Grow lights are a good source of additional lighting in greenhouses as well, especially during the winter, when the sun isn't as bright.

You have a number of options when deciding on what kind of bulbs to use, including the following:

- **Fluorescent:** Two-tube 4-foot fluorescent light fixtures are the cheapest option, and they work great. You can buy full-spectrum grow light bulbs for these fixtures, but you can also buy two regular fluorescent bulbs. Use one from the cool end of the spectrum and one from the warm end.

SPROUTING WISDOM

Just like a rainbow, natural light consists of red, orange, yellow, green, blue, indigo, and violet. Plants need this entire range of colors to thrive. Colors in the blue range promote plant growth and photosynthesis. Colors in the red range are responsible for fostering blooming.

- **Metal halide bulbs:** These bulbs emit light from the blue end of the light spectrum and promote strong plant growth. They are ideal for areas that lack any form of natural sunlight, such as a basement without windows. Although they're energy efficient, they cost more initially than fluorescent bulbs and require special fixtures.

- **High-pressure sodium (HPS) lights:** These bulbs produce the full light spectrum, making it easy to fine-tune your lighting system to provide exactly what your plants need in various stages of growth. Additionally, they promote vigorous growth. The drawback is that they require special fixtures.

No matter what kind of bulbs you decide on, make sure they cover both ends of the light spectrum to mimic natural sunlight. The bulb packaging indicates the color spectrum of the bulbs.

SPROUTING WISDOM

When using either metal-halide or high-pressure sodium grow lights in a heated area indoors, use more of the cool spectrum bulbs than the warm spectrum. Areas such as a greenhouse, unheated garage, or basement may benefit more from the use of bulbs in the warm spectrum simply because they produce heat, which can keep young seedlings warm.

Determining Planting Depth

A good rule of thumb is to sow seeds at a depth of two to three times their smallest dimension. Although this is a good general guideline, some seeds, such as celosia or poppy, germinate better on top of the ground and may not germinate at all if they're covered with soil. Seed packets generally recommend the proper sowing depth. If you saved your own seed or were given seed someone else saved, check the seed directories in Chapters 16 through 18 for instructions on planting depth.

KNOW THY SEED

Keep track of any seed packets you sow, especially if you intend to save the seed. They contain essential information about the seeds, including germination time and how deep to sow your seeds. You can tape your empty seed packets into a seed-saver's diary (see Chapter 14) or use them as containers for the seeds you save from year to year.

Planting seeds at the proper depth is important for good growth. Seeds that are planted too deep expend too much energy trying to reach the soil's surface. When they do reach the surface, they're weak and spindly. Seeds that are planted too shallow may begin to root above the soil's surface. Then when the root is exposed to air, it begins to dry up and die.

If you germinate seeds before planting them, add enough additional depth to accommodate the emerging root. Gently pick up the germinated seed with a pair of tweezers, making sure to grab hold of the seed coat, not the roots or stem. Make an indentation in the soil that's large enough to accommodate the root. When the seed is in place, gently push the soil up against the root, but be careful not to break off the root in the process. Loose soil that readily falls against the root is the best type. After you've planted the seed, water it well, even if there's no root to worry about. Watering ensures that the soil and the seed make good contact with one another, which is essential for healthy growth.

Using a tweezers to move seeds that have germinated.

Quenching Your Seedlings' Thirst

Proper watering is just as important to growing healthy plants as the right amount of light, heat, and fertilization. Germinating seeds and the resulting seedlings need moist soil. The ideal moisture level is equal to that of a wrung-out sponge.

Use warm or room-temperature water when watering your seedlings. Cool water chills seeds and seedlings, which delays their growth. While one or two cool waterings might cause a slight delay, continual use of cool water can result in a serious delay. Even after the plants have reached maturity, continue to use room-temperature water. Cold water is not good for a plant.

THE BAD SEED

Peat pots and peat-based seed-starting media don't absorb cool water as quickly as they absorb warm or room-temperature water.

Avoiding Dampening-Off

Overwatering young seedlings or getting water on their foliage can cause them to be attacked by a fungal disease known as *dampening-off*. When this disease strikes, it's too late: the seedlings will die. The good news is that you can avoid this fatal problem in the first place by following these guidelines:

- Always water germinating seeds, young seedlings, and plants from below.

- Avoid splashing water on the stems or leaves of young seedlings.

- When watering seedlings, allow the water to sit in the tray for 15 to 30 minutes; then pour off the excess water. Never allow the seedlings to sit in water for more than 30 minutes. (*Note:* This rule has a few exceptions. Plants that need consistently wet soil, such as aquatic plants, should never have the excess water dumped off.)

DEFINITION

Dampening-off describes a variety of fungal problems that lead to sudden seedling death. The pathogens in the fungi attack the tender stems and roots of the seedlings. Seedlings may look pinched at the base of the stem, flop over, or wither away entirely. When the process is underway, it's hard to save even a few of your plants. Prevention is the best cure.

You can also use a small fan to circulate the air around your plants, to help prevent dampening-off. If moisture forms on the leaves or stems, either from accidental spillage or because of high humidity, the fan will quickly dry it up. In addition to helping prevent dampening-off, fans are useful for hardening off seedlings. When you move them outdoors, they'll already be used to the effects of wind.

Making Your Own Capillary Mat

The best way to water seeds, seedlings, and plants from below is to place a capillary mat in the bottom of a flat. A capillary mat is nothing more than a piece of knit material that absorbs water and then releases it back to the plants placed on top of it as the soil begins to dry out. You can purchase them at most garden supply stores, but why not make your own? Here's how to do it!

1. Cut a piece of knit fabric—old T-shirts are ideal—to fit inside the seed-starting tray. Make sure the fabric is large enough that it can be folded to create a double layer.

2. Drill three ¹⁄₁₆-inch holes in the lid of a jar. Test the lid to see how the water runs out. You want the water to come out fast enough that the material remains moist but not so fast that you can see water beginning to pool in the container. If it runs too fast, start over and drill fewer holes; if it doesn't run fast enough, drill more holes in the lid.

To use the mat, follow these steps:

1. Fill the jar with warm or room-temperature water, put the lid on it, and place it on the fabric with the lid side down.

2. Place the seed or seedling containers on the mat. Keep an eye on them to make sure they're wicking up enough moisture. Feel the soil; it should be moist. If the soil is bone dry or the plants or seedlings are drooping, they are not getting enough water.

When you see algae begin to form on the mat, remove the cloth and replace it with new material.

You can reuse the cloth if you soak it in a 10 percent bleach solution. Be sure to rinse it thoroughly, though: bleach kills plants. When it's dry, it's ready to be used again.

If you don't have a capillary mat, set the containers in a flat or some other shallow dish without holes in the bottom and fill it about half full of water. Set the container with the seeds, seedlings, or plants in the holding pot and allow them to soak up the water for about 15 minutes. Next, remove the containers with the plant material from the holding pots and place them where any excess water can drain out.

The Least You Need to Know

- A sterile seed-starting medium that allows for easy root development is essential to seedling health and vigor.
- Every gardener has a favorite type of seed-starting container. Choose the one that works best for you and your situation.
- Light and temperature play a huge role in seed starting. Understand how to use these factors to your advantage.
- Preventing dampening-off is as simple as providing proper watering and adequate air circulation.

Sowing Seeds Outdoors

In This Chapter

- Winter-sowing your seeds
- Protecting winter-sown seeds and seedlings
- Making mini-greenhouses
- Direct-sowing your seeds
- Choosing the best sowing method by seed type

Winter sowing and direct sowing are two of the easiest methods of germinating seeds. As the seasons change, nature does the hard work of stratification. And you don't have to carry the seedlings in and out of the house to harden them off. Instead, you can plant them in the garden, with or without protection, in the fall, winter, or spring, depending on the type of seed you are working with.

Winter Sowing Success

Winter sowing is nothing more than planting seeds outdoors during winter and letting nature do the work of stratification. This allows the seeds to germinate naturally, just as they would in the wild. Winter-sown seeds do best in mini-greenhouses, which are small protective structures that you can make from recycled materials such as plastic pop or juice bottles (we provide instructions for creating them later in this chapter).

You also need some seed-starting soil. Choose a high-quality, well-draining soil especially recommended for seed starting or make your own (see Chapter 8 for a recipe).

THE BAD SEED

Don't use topsoil for winter sowing. It's too dense, remains too wet, and doesn't allow for good root development of plants, especially seedlings that have delicate roots.

Timing Is Everything

Sowing the seeds at the right time is the biggest key to success. You want to wait until the temperature outside remains cold. Cycles of warm/cold/warm can cause seeds to germinate too early, and your seedlings won't survive. Although you may be eager to get started sowing seeds, be patient and wait until the time is right. Most gardeners consider winter solstice (December 21) to be the first day they can sow their winter seeds, although some seeds can be planted earlier. Winter weather has usually set in by this date, so temperatures are more stable.

Choosing Seeds for Winter Sowing

Quite a few half-hardy annual seeds are ideal for winter sowing. Look around your garden to see what annuals self-sow and add them to the following list. Although it's not necessary to protect these annuals with a mini-greenhouse, since they will come up on their own in your garden, there are advantages to doing so—such as the option to space them better, sell or share some with others, or know that birds, mice, or other critters won't carry away your seeds or eat the young seedlings. By protecting them, you're also helping ensure that severe weather or heavy precipitation won't wash away or kill the seeds.

Winter sowing is also perfect for many perennial seeds because, as mentioned, the weather stratifies them naturally—and this means less work for you. However, perennial seeds that require scarification or have a double dormancy (see Chapter 7) are not ideal for winter sowing. Instead, sow these types of seeds indoors (see Chapter 8).

Half-Hardy Annuals for Winter Sowing

Amaranth (*Amaranthus*)

Baby's breath (*Gypsophila*)

Bells of Ireland (*Moluccella*)

Calendula (*Calendula*)

Candytuft (*Iberis*)

Catchfly (*Lychnis*)

Celosia (*Celosia*)

Chinese foxglove (*Rehmannia*)

Chlorogalum (*Cholorogalum*)

Cleome (*Cleome*)

Coreopsis (*Coreopsis*)

Cosmos (*Cosmos*)

Forget-me-not (*Myosotis*)

Gilia (*Gilia*)

Godeita (*Clarkia*)

Larkspur (*Consolida*)

Love-in-a-mist (*Nigella*)

Mexican sunflower (*Tithonia*)

Mignonette (*Reseda*)

Milkweed (*Asclepias*)

Morning glory (*Ipomoea*)

Nasturtium (*Tropaeolum*)

Nicotiana (*Nicotiana*)

Painted tongue (*Salpiglossis*)

Petunia (*Petunia*)

Phlox (*Phlox*)

Poached-egg plant (*Limnanthes*)

Poppy (*Papaver*)

Rudbeckia (*Rudbeckia*)

Salvia (*Salvia*)

Scabiosa (*Scabiosa*)

Shoo-fly plant (*Nicandra*)

Snapdragon (*Antirrhinum*)

Statice (*Limonium*)

Stock (*Matthiola*)

Strawflower (*Helichrysum*)

Sunflower (*Helianthus*)

Sweet alyssum (*Lobularia*)

Sweet pea (flower) (*Lathyrus*)

Thunbergia (*Thunbergia*)

Torenia (*Torenia*)

Tree mallow (*Lavatera*)

Viola (*Viola*)

Perennials for Winter Sowing

Arisaema (*Arisaema*)

Arum (*Arum*)

Aster (*Aster*)

Balloon flower (*Platycodon*)

Baptisia (*Baptisia*)

Bear's breeches (*Acanthus*)

Bee balm (*Monarda*)

Bellflower (*Campanula*)

Blackberry lily (*Belamcanda*)

Blanket flower (*Gaillardia*)

Blue star (*Amsonia*)

Candylily (*Pardancanda*)

Catchfly (*Lychnis*)

Catmint (*Nepeta*)

Clematis (*Clematis*)

Columbine (*Aquilegia*)

Coneflower (*Echinacea*)

Coral bells (*Heuchera*)

Daisy (*Leucanthemum*)

Daylily (*Hemerocallis*)

Delphinium (*Delphinium*)

Dianthus (*Dianthus*)

Dicentra (*Dicentra*)

Draba (*Draba*)

Edelweiss (*Leontopodium*)

Evening primrose (*Oenothera*)

Evening star (*Mentzelia*)

Foxglove (*Digitalis*)

Gas plant (*Dictamnus*)

Goat's beard (*Aruncus*)

Hellebore (*Helleborus*)

Hollyhock (*Althea*)

Honesty (*Lunaria*)

Hosta (*Hosta*)

Inula (*Inula*)

Iris (*Iris*)

Ladybells (*Adenophora*)

Liatris (*Liatris*)

Lily (*Lilium*)

Lobelia (*Lobelia*)

Lungwort (*Pulmonaria*)

Lupine (*Lupinus*)

Milkweed (*Asclepias*)

Monkey flower (*Mimulus*)

Monkshood (*Aconitum*)

Obedient plant (*Physostegia*)

Penstemon (*Penstemon*)

Peony (*Paeonia*)

Phlox (*Phlox*)

Pocketbook flower (*Calceolaria*)

Poppy (*Papaver*)

Primrose (*Primula*)

Red-hot-poker (*Kniphofia*)

Salvia (*Salvia*)

Sea holly (*Eryngium*)

Sedum (*Sedum*)

Shooting star (*Dodecatheon*)

Solomon's seal (*Polygonatum*)

Spurge (*Eupatorium*)

Valerian (*Centranthus*)

Verbascum (*Verbascum*)

Veronica (*Veronica*)

Viola (*Viola*)

Wallflower (*Erysimum*)

Winter aconite (*Eranthis*)

Wisteria (*Wisteria*)

Yarrow (*Achillea*)

Yucca (*Yucca*)

Protecting Your Seedlings

Seeds and young seedlings greatly benefit from being protected from the elements, pests, and disease. Starting out right with clean seed-sowing containers, sterile soil, and clean seeds goes a long way toward preventing most diseases. With their genetic make-up, seeds collected from diseased plants are more susceptible to developing problems than seeds collected from healthy plants.

Seed-starting soil that you purchase should be sterile, although it is not always weed-free. If you make your own from purchased ingredients, it, too, should already be sterile. However, when you amend the soil with something you've made, like compost, it's best to sterilize it before you add it (see Chapter 8). In fact, compost is best saved for potting up because young seedlings are more susceptible to disease than older plants.

Seeds purchased from a commercial seed source are guaranteed to be clean and free of pests and disease. Seeds that you save yourself or get from another gardener do not carry this guarantee. That's why it's so important to clean and inspect the seeds you save (see Chapter 4).

KNOW THY SEED

When you receive seeds from anyone, inspect them for cleanliness and signs of problems before you store or sow them.

Building Your Mini-Greenhouses

Creating mini-greenhouses out of recycled materials in which to winter-sow seeds saves money, reduces waste, and is an ideal way to protect seeds and the new seedlings they produce. Mini-greenhouses are easy to make out of a variety of materials. Choose clear plastic for plants that thrive in full sun. Use colored plastic only if you're winter-sowing shade-loving plants in an area that receives full sun. In this case, use lightly colored plastic containers to help block some of the sun from these sensitive plants.

Empty 2-liter soda bottles and clear juice containers make excellent mini-greenhouses. The removable cap is ideal for either containing heat or allowing it to escape without having to break the seal on the side of the container that you will create; breaking the seal could overexpose the seedlings to the extreme changes in weather that come so often in late winter and early spring.

You can also use plastic milk jugs, but because they're usually translucent, they don't allow in as much light as 2-liter bottles do. That often makes it hard to see what's happening inside these containers; you might have to remove the cap and peer inside from the top.

THE BAD SEED

Always clean the containers you plan to use in your garden. Dirty containers will attract a variety of pests and possibly promote disease.

To create a mini-greenhouse, grab some empty 2-liter bottles or plastic quart or gallon milk or juice jugs, and follow these steps:

1. Wash the empty containers and caps in warm soapy water.

2. Allow the containers and caps to thoroughly air-dry.

3. With a marking pen, make six evenly spaced dots on the shoulder of the container (the part that begins to widen out, just below the neck) and six dots on the bottom of the container.

Top holes being drilled into a mini-greenhouse.

Bottom holes being drilled into a mini-greenhouse.

4. Use a ⅛-inch drill bit to drill holes where the dots are. This allows for water drainage and air circulation.

5. With the container upright, draw a line with your marker around the center of the container; try to make it as even as possible.

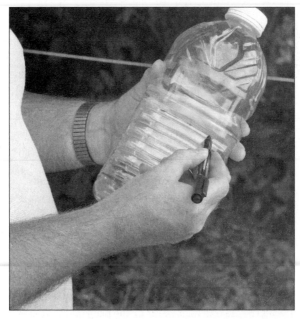

Draw a line before you cut your mini-greenhouse in half.

By leaving a "hinge," you can tip back the top.

6. With a box knife or scissors, cut along the line you just drew, but leave an inch or two uncut on one side. This creates a hinge, allowing you to flip the top back and up again. You now have two connected halves, a top half and a bottom half.

7. Moisten your preferred seed-starting mix and put a couple inches in the bottom half of the container; the soil should come up about halfway to the edge.

8. Sprinkle just enough vermiculite on top of the seed-starting mix to barely cover it. If the seed-starting mix is adequately moist, the vermiculite will absorb some of the water; if it remains dry, gently water it.

9. Plant your seeds according to the package directions. Avoid planting them too close together; they need room to grow and develop. Remember that some seeds need light to germinate, and some need darkness.

10. Place a label inside the container. Use either a botanical pen or a pencil to write. It's a good idea to label the outside of the container as well. Place a piece of clear tape over the label to protect it from fading and water damage.

SPROUTING WISDOM

Cut up old window blinds to make excellent plant markers. Use a pencil or botanical marking pen (permanent marker will fade) to write on your markers. Be sure to include the botanical name of the plant and the date it is sown.

Seeds being sown into a mini-greenhouse.

11. Flip back the top half of your new mini-greenhouse over the bottom half and tape it using clear packing tape. Put the cap back on.

12. Set the container outside in a protected area, such as against the side of your house or a fence. An ideal area will protect the containers from getting too much rain, from too much sun, and from being knocked over.

Monitoring Your Mini-Greenhouses

Check the containers several times a week for the following things:

- Moisture level of soil.

- Heat buildup. If you see too much moisture forming on the side of the bottle, remove the cap.

- Germination. Maturity of the seedling dictates when it's time to be moved.

The following sections discuss these variables in detail.

Adjusting Humidity and Ventilation

The seedlings will burn up if the mini-greenhouse isn't ventilated properly. At first, the air holes you've drilled will suffice, but as the seedlings mature, you need to increase the amount of air they receive. In the beginning, on warm, sunny days, remove the cap of the mini-greenhouse. As the need for ventilation increases, unseal the container and open it a little at a time. You can prop it back on the side of the house or a board.

Remove the tape used to seal the two halves of the mini-greenhouse when the seedlings are big enough.

As you watch the seeds sprout, keep a careful eye on the amount of humidity that builds up inside the mini-greenhouse. Too much humidity could cause disease such as dampening-off. To prevent that from happening, during the day, remove the tape and flip back the top, opening the containers so air can circulate around the young plants; then close up the containers again at night. If it's still too cold outside, remove only the cap during the day, and then replace it at night. If there's still too much humidity inside the containers, as will be evident by signs of heavy water drops building up on the plants and sides of the container, drill additional holes near the top of the container.

Seedlings growing in a mini-greenhouse.

Although you don't want a lot of humidity in the container, you do want some. If in doubt, open the container, place a humidity gauge inside, and see what it says. If the range is in the "normal" section, everything is fine. If not, you need to take steps to get it into the normal range. You can do this by misting or watering the seedlings. If that doesn't do the trick, try taping up some of the holes near the top of the container with clear packing tape.

Watering Winter-Sown Seeds

You should always water seeds and seedlings from the bottom. With winter-sown seeds, set the containers in some type of tray, fill it with water, let the seedlings soak up the water for approximately 15 minutes, and then remove the containers and allow them to drain off the excess water.

It's best to water as early in the morning as possible. This gives you the entire day for the excess water to drain away from the plant's root system. Soil that is too wet will freeze faster, which could damage or kill young plants.

When the seedlings are about a week old, give them a weekly dose of fertilizer. Use *compost tea* or fertilizer. The first week, use only about 10 percent of the recommended dosage. Increase that percentage each week so that by the time the seedlings are 8 weeks old, they are getting a full-strength feeding.

DEFINITION

Compost tea is liquid compost. You can make your own compost tea by filling a pillowcase with a shovel-full of finish compost along with 2 tablespoons molasses, 2 tablespoons fish emulsion, and 2 tablespoons vinegar (white or apple cider). Tie the pillowcase shut and place it in a 5-gallon bucket filed with water. Put an aquarium pump into the bucket and let it oxygenate overnight. The next day you will have compost tea.

Direct Sowing

When you direct-sow seeds you plant the seeds directly into soil—either in the ground or in a pot. It is the easiest method of winter sowing, but remember that good drainage is essential for success. Seeds that are direct-sown into heavy soil that is prone to becoming water logged will rot instead of germinate.

A number of vegetables, flowers, and herbs are perfect for direct sowing.

The first time you direct-sow seeds, it's best to sow just a few, to test the waters.

KNOW THY SEED

Gardeners in extremely cold climates may not be as successful with direct sowing as those in USDA hardiness zone 5 and higher.

Raised beds are ideal for direct sowing. Containers are another option; however, if you use containers, you should wrap them with some type of insulating material to keep the developing plant roots from freezing. Placing a cold frame over the raised beds or containers will help heat the soil faster, resulting in seedlings that germinate and grow faster than direct-sown seedlings that were not protected.

Vegetables

Direct-sowing vegetable seeds in the dead of winter has several advantages over direct sowing in early spring. One of the biggest advantages is that you can work in the garden on warm winter days, getting your crops in the ground and leaving less to plant come spring. It also allows you to avoid the potential of soil that is too wet, which is often a problem at spring planting time.

Vegetable seeds that are direct-sown in winter will germinate and grow when the soil temperature is warm enough for that particular variety. Warm-weather vegetables, such as tomatoes, will generally not emerge until sometime in June. Cool-weather crops will emerge much sooner, sometimes as early as April, even in cold northern climates. These vegetables appear sturdier, produce sooner, and are just as tasty as those sown in spring.

Following is a list of vegetables that are reliable for winter sowing.

Vegetable Sowing Calendar

Vegetable	When to Sow
Arugula	November through February
Beets	November through February
Broccoli raab	November through February
Carrots	November through February
Collards	November through February
Kale	November through February
Lettuce	November through February
Mache	November through February
Mesclun mix	November through February
Orach	November through February
Parsnips	November through February
Peas	November through February
Potatoes	November, December, February
Pumpkins	November through February
Radish	November through February
Rutabaga	November through February
Spinach	November through February
Tomatillo	November through February
Tomato	November through February
Turnips	November through February
Winter squash	November through February

Flowers

Direct-sowing flower seed in winter is a great way to create a lush-looking, colorful garden come spring. While it's tempting to just toss a handful of seeds here and there, remember that if they all germinate, you'll need to thin them out, or else they might choke one another to death (thinning is discussed in detail later in this chapter).

Any flower that self-seeds is ideal for direct sowing, as are a number of perennials. Milkweed, hollyhocks, and other flowering plants with taproots also work well using this method.

KNOW THY SEED

Don't forget to mark the spot where you direct-sow seeds by using plant labels in the ground. As a backup in case your labels break or get moved, make a diagram of your garden to indicate where you've direct-sown seeds.

Flower Sowing Calendar

Flower	When to Sow
Calendula (*Calendula*)	November through February
Celosia (*Celosia*)	November through February
Centaurea (*Centaurea*)	November through February
Cleome (*Cleome*)	November through February
Larkspur (*Consolida*)	November through February
Cosmos (*Cosmos*)	November through February
Sunflower (*Helianthus*)	November through February
Sweet pea (flower) (*Lathyrus*)	November
Sweet alyssum (*Lobularia*)	November through February
Poppy (*Papaver*)	August, November through February
Nasturtium (*Tropaeolum*)	November through February
Viola (*Viola*)	November through February

Herbs

Herbs are also great for direct-sowing in winter. Many will self-sow if allowed to go to seed; however, if your plants did not set seed, you're new to growing herbs, or you simply want to expand your current selection, sow the seeds yourself.

Herb Sowing Calendar

Herb	When To Sow
Dill (*Anethum graveolens*)	November through February
Chamomile (*Anthemis nobilis*)	November through February
Celery (*Apium graveolens*)	November through February
Parsley (*Carum petroselinum*)	August, November through February
Coriander (*Coriandrum sativum*)	November through February
Fennel (*Foeniculum vulgare*)	November through February
Basil (*Ocimum*)	November through February

Thinning Your Young Seedlings

Plants that are transplanted into the garden typically don't need to be thinned. Seeds that were direct-sown, however, often require thinning, unless you spaced them well as you planted. Spacing seeds carefully is time consuming, and if the seeds don't take root, you'll have empty spots in the garden. Most gardeners prefer to sow more seeds than they need and then thin the plants as they begin to grow.

The process of thinning plants requires choosing which ones stay and which ones go. This is an essential step that you should take on with gusto unless you're like me and put one seed per pot or if you use appropriate spacing to start with. The plants often make the selection naturally, as some seedlings thrive and others die off. However, there are advantages to stepping up the action. For instance, young plants grow better if they're given adequate space to develop. The amount of space required depends on the plant (check on the seed packets or look it up online). It's easier for sunlight to reach the leaves of the plants. In fact, the only disadvantage to thinning is the time it takes to do it.

The earlier you begin the thinning process, the better. Don't pull the plants out of the ground; you risk damaging the roots of the plants you want to keep and, worse, you may accidentally pull them up. Instead, use scissors and clip the stems of the seedlings you don't want right at soil level. The plant roots that die underground don't hurt anything and, in fact, add organic matter to the soil.

SPROUTING WISDOM

When you thin young greens such as lettuce, spinach, and kale, don't throw the clipped seedlings in the compost. Instead, use them in a salad. The tender fresh greens are full of flavor and give you your first taste of your garden in the spring.

The Least You Need to Know

- Winter sowing eliminates the need for seed stratification.
- You can save money by making mini-greenhouses out of recycled materials.
- Many seeds can be direct-sown over winter and will germinate the following spring.
- Thin your seedlings to avoid overcrowding, which inhibits plant growth.

When Seeds Become Plants

Learning how to take care of the tiny seedlings that sprout from your saved seeds and nurturing them until they produce vegetables or flowers is one of the most rewarding experiences a gardener can have. Here you'll find all the essentials to help you do it the right way.

You also find out the proper techniques for transplanting, thinning, hardening off, and establishing these tiny seedlings in the garden. You learn how to protect your plants from weather extremes in early spring and fall using cold frames, cloches, and row covers. Finally, you get the scoop on natural ways of dealing with disease, pests, and critters in your garden.

Extending the Growing Season

10

In This Chapter

- Finding Your USDA hardiness zone
- Changing the soil's temperature
- Protecting your plants from the elements with tunnel houses, cloches, and fencing

Winter-sown seedlings (see Chapter 9) are already accustomed to the temperature changes that take place outdoors; however, seedlings sown indoors need to be slowly acclimated to outdoor weather conditions. This is the final stage of raising seedlings, and it's very important.

You have a variety of means at your disposal to protect newly exposed young plants—everything from tunnel houses and cloches to fences and companion planting. This chapter shows you the best ways to ensure the survival of your seedlings.

USDA Hardiness Zones

The U.S. Department of Agricultural issues a map showing hardiness zones across the United States. A hardiness zone designates the various climates in the United States. Each hardiness zone represents a 10°F difference in the average coldest winter temperature.

The map is a good tool for helping you understand what you can grow year-round. Every perennial has a specific hardiness zone rating. For example, purple coneflower (*Echinacea*) grows in USDA hardiness zones 3 through 8. This means it's iffy for gardeners living in USDA hardiness zone 2. They can grow it, but more than likely, the plant will not come back the following year unless it is protected over the winter with a cold frame or is heavily mulched. Most seed and plant labels have a hardiness zone on them. If not, a quick online search, using the botanical name of the plant, will yield results.

Your hardiness zone also lets you know when the first fall frost and the last spring frost will occur. These are important dates for most gardeners, since it is recommended not to plant before the last spring frost and to harvest everything before the first fall frost (unless, of course, you're growing crops that perform better during cooler temperatures or using season extension techniques). Gardeners who use season-extending techniques (discussed later in this chapter) need to be aware of these dates as well so they know when to use cloches, cold frames, greenhouses, row covers, or other devices.

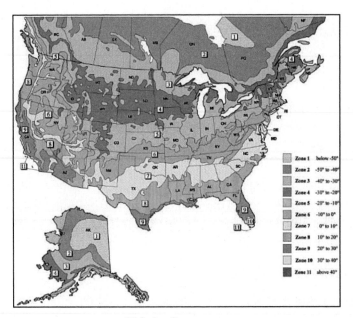

U.S. hardiness zones.

Some Like It Hot, Some Like It Cold

Microbial activity occurs when dead material such as leaves, grass clippings, or old plant roots begin to break down naturally. As these materials break down, nutrients are added to the soil. The closer to the top few inches the nutrients are, the easier it is for young plants to access and benefit from them.

The soil must be at least 40°F for microbial activity to take place. When you add organic matter such as compost to the soil to heat it or cool it, microbes are able to begin to break down the organic matter. This process subsequently causes the soil to heat up again, further encouraging the microbial activity.

DEFINITION

Microbial activity is responsible for the decay of dead material, and it's as vital to the world's ecosystems as it is to your garden. Soil moisture, temperature, and aeration regulate soil microbial activity. It is highest in soils that have a high average annual soil temperature and lowest in soils that have a low average temperature.

Microbial activity is vital because it enables the roots of the plants to get their nutrients. The greater the amount of microbial activity going on underground, the more nutrients are available for the plant. Cooler soil temperatures tend to stabilize microbial activity, while warmer temperatures speed it up. Knowing the preferred temperature range for the plants you're growing gives you the knowledge you need to determine whether to heat or cool the soil. You always want to give plant roots ample opportunity to absorb the maximum amount of nutrients necessary to sustain their growth from seedlings to seed production, and every stage in between.

Different plants prefer different soil temperatures. Some like it hot, some like it cool. Although you can take steps to change the soil temperatures a few degrees, you're always better off planting according to the growing season that best suits the plants. For example, if you're growing crops from late fall through midspring, select plants that prefer cooler soil temperatures. Crops grown from late spring through midfall prefer warmer soil temperatures. The following tables list plants that like cool and warm soil temperatures.

Plants That Like It Cool

Arugula

Beet

Bok choi (pak choi)

Brassica family (cabbage, broccoli, Brussels sprouts, and so on)

Carrot

Chive

Endive

continues

Plants That Like It Cool   (continued)

Garlic

Kale

Leek

Lettuce

Mizuna

Mustard

Onion

Parsley

Potato

Radish

Rutabaga

Sage

Scallion

Snapdragon

Spinach

Stock

Swiss chard

Thymus

Turnip

Viola

Plants That Like It Hot

Basil

Bean

Corn

Cucumber

Eggplant

Marigold

Moonflower

Nasturtium

Pepper

Pumpkin

Sage

Squash
Sunflower
Tomato
Watermelon

Taking the Temperature of Soil

The ideal soil temperature for most plants is 60°F. Plants that prefer cooler tempera-tures don't do well in soil that's more than 5°F warmer than this; in other words, anything over 65°F inhibits healthy growth. Crops that prefer warm soil often toler-ate temperatures of 70°F to 75°F without any problems.

Soil that's too warm promotes rapid plant growth. Although this may not seem like a problem, it can be. Plants that grow too quickly may not develop properly, and when the time comes for them to fruit or flower, they may be incapable of supporting that growth.

> **KNOW THY SEED**
>
> Ideal soil temperatures for cool-loving plants are between 60°F and 65°F.
>
> Ideal soil temperatures for heat-loving plants are between 60°F and 75°F.

To take the soil temperature outside, simply place a soil thermometer in the soil and let it sit for 10 minutes. To get a good idea of the average temperature, take it several times a day over the course of several days. When you know the average temperature range, you can decide whether to plant cool-season or warm-season crops.

If you need to alter the soil temperature for the plants you want to grow, you have several options.

Heating the Soil

A 3-inch layer of compost in early spring helps hold in the soil's heat. Additionally, compost improves your soil structure and suppresses weeds.

You can purchase compost at any garden supply center, but making your own is easy (and less expensive). For more information, see *The Complete Idiot's Guide to Composting* (Alpha Books, 2009).

Black plastic attracts the sun and is a good short-term solution for heating the soil. When the sun beats down on the plastic, it heats the soil and holds that warmth in the soil overnight. The next day, the soil warms some more. The process continues until you remove the plastic.

THE BAD SEED

Never use black plastic as a long-term mulch because it will continue to trap heat and eventually fry your plants' roots—not to mention spoil the soil by killing the good bugs, like earthworms.

Cooling the Soil

During the summer, that same 3-inch layer helps keep the plants' roots cool.

Here are some other ways to help keep the soil cool:

- Install lattice panels.
- Use shade cloth.
- Plant under trees or other structures that create intermittent shade.

Lattice panels, made of crisscrossed wood or plastic slats, filter the amount of sunlight that passes through them, thus creating the perfect environment for plants that prefer to grow in cool soil. Lattice panels look nice and are readily available at most lumberyards. They come in 4×8 sheets, although you may be able to find them in smaller sections; if not, ask if the store will cut them down to the size you need.

Lattice is flimsy, so you must attach it to a sturdy frame made from 2×4s. You can mount the frame upright, creating a trellis or wall, or place it atop some type of structure and use it as a roof.

Shade cloth is a synthetic fabric designed to allow a specific amount of sunlight to penetrate it. Shade cloth is typically used to block the summer sun from entering greenhouses; however, it's ideal for stretching over larger wooden or metal frames. It comes in a variety of sizes and is available in different percentages of shading. The most common percentages are 50 percent, 70 percent, and 80 percent. The right percentage for you will depend on where you live, how hot the area is, and how much shade you actually need for the plants you are growing. For most plants, 50 percent shade cloth will work just fine.

Other options include shade cloth that is part aluminum. This type of shade cloth is better suited to hot climates since the metal reflects some of the sunlight off the shade cloth, making the area underneath considerably cooler. You also need to select either a knitted shade cloth or a woven shade cloth. The advantages of using a knitted shade cloth are you can cut it to size without worrying about it raveling, and it's also lighter and stronger. The downside is that it's usually more expensive.

A third option is to grow your cool-weather crops under the canopy of a large tree. Select an area with intermittent shade whenever possible. This is the type of shade that is created when trees or other large structures block most of the sunlight while still allowing filtered sunlight to hit the ground below. These areas are naturally cooler, but you need to make sure there's enough sunlight to sustain growth. Should the plants become weak or spindly, you know there is too much shade.

Protecting Your Plants from Frost

Floating row covers, tunnel houses, cold frames, and cloches also protect seedlings, young plants, and even mature plants from extreme temperatures, storms, and weeds; they can even prevent soil-borne disease from affecting your plants, as long as proper watering takes place.

The following sections explore these options in detail.

Tunnel Houses

Tunnel houses, also called hoop houses, are similar to greenhouses, except that, unlike the latter, they aren't usually heated. Tunnel houses rely on the sun to provide enough heat to warm up the soil; at night, the soil releases the heat, helping the growth of the plants housed there.

You can buy a kit to make a tunnel house, hire someone to construct one for you, or make your own using materials that are readily available at your local hardware store.

When selecting the location for your tunnel house, choose a spot that receives full sun and, if possible, some protection from high winds. Make sure that the area is accessible, even during winter months, since the plants and seedlings inside the tunnel house require year-round care. During periods of heavy snowfall, you'll need to brush the snow off the top of the roof to prevent collapse. Be sure you have easy access to water, also; in the winter, you may have to carry water to it (even if you plan to leave 55-gallon drums filled with water in the tunnel house, if the outside temperature dips too low, the water will freeze).

The next step is to decide whether you will use raised beds in your tunnel house or work directly in the ground. Both methods have advantages and disadvantages. With raised beds, you don't have to deal with frozen ground, heavy rainfall, or soil that is too heavy to sustain proper plant growth. You can fill the beds with loamy soil that's rich in organic matter, creating a paradise for your plants. Raised beds are easy to work in year-round and don't require rototilling. Simply top the raised beds once or twice a year with freshly finished compost.

On the downside, raised beds dry out quickly because they have such good drainage. If you work directly in the ground, you could have a problem with soil becoming too wet during the rainy season, since soil wicks water. But the biggest advantage of working directly in the ground is that you don't have to build raised beds; that saves you time and money. If you have a very large garden, you won't want to use raised beds.

After you've determined how you will grow your plants, stake off the area where the tunnel house will go and begin preparing the ground. If you're planning to garden in the ground, remove all weeds and turn the soil. If you're using raised beds, position them after building the tunnel house, unless you are using them as the base of the tunnel house (described later in this section). If this is the case, position the raised beds first.

To build an 8' × 6' tunnel house, you need the following materials:

- 15 pieces of 10-foot long metal conduit
- 8 metal conduit connectors
- 2 (12' × 25') rolls of 6 mil. plastic
- 12 (2-inch) carriage bolts and nuts (¼ inch thick)
- Conduit bender

KNOW THY SEED

The type of conduit you select depends on the size of the tunnel house you want to build. For a larger structure, metal conduit (which requires a conduit bender) is better. Plastic conduit (PVC) works well on smaller structures and is easier to work with than metal. The standard length is 8 feet; if you need a longer conduit, you can connect two or more pieces with a special connector.

Here's how to build your tunnel house:

1. Purchase enough conduit to space each rib 2 feet apart for the entire length of the tunnel house. For example, if your tunnel house is 10 feet long, you need at least six pieces of conduit.

2. If you're using metal conduit, figure out the exact angle of the bends you need to make the size and style of tunnel house you prefer.

3. If you're using plastic conduit, stick one end about an inch into the ground and bend it either toward the ground, where you will insert it an inch deep, or toward another length of conduit directly opposite the one you are working with; make sure one of the poles of conduit has a connector attached so you can join the two pieces. Continue placing the conduit into the ground every two feet until it reaches the end of the area designated for your hoop house. Make sure there is a conduit hoop on both ends.

4. When the tunnel house frame is in place, cover it with plastic. Start at one end and gently pull the plastic over the top of the hoops. Be careful and go slowly—plastic tears easily. If it does tear, use clear packing tape to repair it. Be sure to have plenty of extra plastic on either side.

5. Secure the plastic to the ground by placing wood, bricks, sand bags, or another heavy object on the excess plastic along the sides.

   An alternative is to prebuild your raised beds, place the conduit inside them, and secure each end with two-hole strap conduit clips.

KNOW THY SEED

A safe method of securing the plastic to the side of the structure, whether over a raised bed or over a ground-to-ground frame, is to use two 2×4s that run the length of the structure. Place one on each side and roll the plastic around it three or four times, with the crease facing inward.

6. Cover both the front and back. You can do this with plastic. Then use the long peel-and-stick zippers made for tarps to create a door on one end that will open and close (these zippers will last for several years if you're careful when you unzip them). You can also make a door out of wood, securing it with small hook locks.

7. If you're using raised beds, fill them with soil, press the soil down slightly, plant, and water well. If you are using the ground, go ahead and turn the soil, add your amendments, plant, and water well.

That's all there is to it. You can find more detailed instructions online at www. hightunnels.org.

Cold Frames

A cold frame is a small boxlike structure with a clear glass or plastic lid. It's an ideal tool for gardeners who have small spaces or don't plan to grow much at one time.

You can build a bottomless box out of wood or form a structure with bales of straw or any other material you have lying about. In fact, as long as you can place an old window on top or cover it with plastic, almost any sturdy container will work.

Some gardeners who want to grow crops, such as lettuce, during the winter use a cold frame to cover plants growing in the ground. Others place pots, flats, or other containers filled with seeds, seedlings, or more mature plants inside cold frames to protect them from weather extremes or to protect them while they're hardening off.

A disadvantage of cold frames is that they heat up quickly when the sun is out. To avoid burning your plants to a crisp, you have to carefully monitor them and vent whenever they get too warm. Cold frames that you purchase often have preinstalled vents that are easy to open and close. If you make your own cold frame, the easiest way to vent it is to open or slide the top to one side so the hot air can escape. Don't allow too much air in and out, however, especially if it's still chilly outside.

The simplest cold frame to make is created with an old window and four bales of straw. Here's how to do it:

1. Select a spot in full sun.

2. Arrange four bales of straw to make a square slightly smaller than the window you're planning to use.

3. Place the window on top so it lies across the top of the bales of straw.

Cloches

A cloche functions the same way cold frames and tunnel houses do: it traps heat during the day and holds it in at night. Cloches are ideal for protecting plants from slugs, snails, rabbits, and other critters, too.

You can purchase cloches or make them yourself out of plastic milk jugs or 2-liter bottles. Even large drinking glasses work as a cloche.

THE BAD SEED

On a warm day, a cloche can build up too much heat quickly. Cloches need venting, just like cold frames.

To vent a cloche, either remove it completely or put the edges on a brick, 2×4, or other object. Just remember to keep it level so that wind or an animal moving about in your garden won't knock it over and break it.

To make your own cloche out of empty plastic containers, follow these simple instructions:

1. Wash the empty plastic containers (milk jugs, 2-liter bottles, and so on) and caps in warm soapy water.

2. Allow the containers and caps to thoroughly air-dry; then put the caps back on.

3. With the container upright, draw a line with your marker around the lower quarter of the container; try to make it as even as possible.

4. With a box knife or scissors, cut along the line you just drew. You now have two halves, a top half that is about three quarters the height it used to be and a bottom half that is about one quarter the height it once was. Throw away the bottom half or use it for winter sowing.

5. Cover the plants you want to protect with the top half, gently pressing it into the ground.

6. Prevent the cloche from being blown away or knocked over by tying a long string around the neck and securing it to the ground on two sides.

Frost Covers and Row Covers

Frost covers and row covers are similar. The main difference is that row covers primarily serve as an insect guard or barrier, and frost covers protect plants from frost. Both types of covers, which float above the tops of the plants, help hold in heat, keeping the plants and their root systems from freezing even during subzero weather.

Spun-bonded row cover is made of fabric that has been spun into a swirling weblike pattern. It is generally lightweight and see-through; although it may cut down on some of the heat or light that reaches the plants below, it is mainly used to protect plants from insects or to prevent cross-pollination. The heavier the fabric, the more protection (and less light) the plants grown below it receive.

Frost cover is a lightweight, permeable fabric made to protect plants from frost down to 20°F. It is usually a much heavier material than row cover. The temperature under frost cover can be as much as 7°F warmer than the uncovered area.

Either of these two materials must be suspended anywhere from 12 to 36 inches above the ground. The exact height depends on the plants: the cover must sit 4 to 6 inches above the top of the plant. You can use hoops made from plastic conduit (secured the same way as for a tunnel house), tomato cages, or another structure to keep the frost or row cover from touching the plants.

These materials come in different weights, so talk to an experienced nurseryman or extension agent: describe your purpose in using them and ask for advice on the best weight for your particular project.

The Least You Need to Know

- Slowly acclimate seedlings to any new growing conditions.
- Plant cool-weather crops in cool soil; plant warm-weather crops in warm soil.
- You can adjust the soil's temperature by using compost or plastic mulch to heat it up or shade cloth or lattice panels to cool it down.
- Cold frames and tunnel houses are ideal structures for extending the gardening season.

Transplanting
Your Seedlings

In This Chapter

- Proper transplanting methods
- Hardening off seedlings
- Preparing the soil
- Establishing transplants

The health of your plants and the success of your garden depend on using the proper techniques when you move plants outdoors. No matter how nice the young plants look, if you don't take the time to prepare them for their new life outdoors and expose them to the elements, they aren't likely to survive.

Two other essentials for success are properly preparing the soil and planting at the right depth. And even after properly planting your seedlings, you need to give your plants the care they require to become well established during those first vital weeks; this includes making sure they have adequate water and good fertilization.

In this chapter, you find out everything you need to know to move those young plants into the garden and nurture them into full-fledged, healthy plants.

Transplanting

Transplanting does more than just give the plants room to grow. It stimulates the growth of new roots, gives the plants a source of better soil, and gives you the opportunity to weed out seedlings that aren't thriving.

Using the proper transplanting techniques is essential to getting your plants off to a good start. Plants that aren't transplanted correctly often fail to thrive. There's a right way and a wrong way to go about this process, from the handling and planting of seedlings, to smart soil preparation, to the ongoing care required.

Hardening Off

Outdoor conditions such as wind, rain, and fluctuating temperatures are too much for fragile seedlings that have been raised indoors, in a greenhouse, or in a cold frame to handle all at once. Young seedlings need to be *hardened off*, or acclimated to being exposed to the elements.

DEFINITION

Hardening off is the process of adapting a plant that has been sheltered indoors or in a greenhouse to exposure to the elements. Failure to harden off distresses plants, decreasing their ability to survive.

Begin the hardening-off process three weeks before you intend to move the seedlings into the garden. Here's a step-by-step process for proper hardening off:

1. Reduce the frequency of watering and fertilization about a week before you start moving the young plants outdoors. This slows the plants' upward growth, instead causing it to produce more fibrous growth.

2. After a week to 10 days, move the plants outdoors for an hour into a protected area in the shade. A good location might be against the side of your house. Some sunlight is okay, but avoid direct sunlight.

3. Each day for two weeks, gradually increase the amount of outdoors/sunlight time the plants get by an additional hour or so per day (if they are shade plants, slowly expose them to the amount of sunlight they will receive once they are planted in the garden). At the end of the 2-week period, they should be getting 10 hours of sun a day.

4. Observe the young plants closely during this time. Signs of wilting, brown spots on their leaves (caused by too much sun), and other problems are often a sign that you're trying to acclimate them to their new growing environment too quickly. Slow down the process to remedy the situation.

5. At the end of the 2-week period, if the young plants still look healthy, transplant them to their permanent home in the garden.

Prepping the Soil

Before you transplant the young plants into the garden, you should prepare the soil.

Loose, deep soil makes it easier for the roots of young plants to establish. When these tender roots try to establish in soil that is compacted, they must break up the soil as they grow. This takes energy and effort away from the developing plant, which can delay the production of fruits, flowers, or vegetables. It can also hinder the plant's growth.

Double Digging

Double digging, a labor-intensive process using a shovel, is the ideal way to ensure that the soil is loose and ready for young plants. It increases the depth of aerated, loamy soil, which leads to healthier plants. It also improves drainage. Rototillers are unable to turn the soil as deeply as this method.

Here are the steps to follow to double-dig your garden:

1. Mark off the area you will be digging using some sort of visual aid, such as outdoor marking paint, rope, or bamboo stakes.

2. Start at one end of the garden and dig a row all the way across; move the soil into a pile close to the garden. Repeat in rows until you've removed the top layer of soil from the entire garden.

3. Go back to the beginning and dig the garden a second time, moving the second layer of soil into a separate pile.

4. After the entire garden has been dug a second time, incorporate organic matter, such as compost, into both piles, still keeping them separate.

5. Evenly spread the soil from the first pile back into the garden.

6. Evenly spread the soil from the second pile back into the garden.

Avoid walking on the area of the garden you have backfilled as much as possible. You don't want to compact the soil.

THE BAD SEED

Some plants, such as carrots, won't develop properly in soil that's compacted. They may grow, but they often end up smaller than they should be and look deformed. If the soil is too packed, they will not grow at all.

Enriching the Soil

Loamy soil is ideal for growing plants; however, most of us are not blessed with ideal soil, so we must amend it. Compost—otherwise known as black gold—is the best amendment available. Best of all, it's free. Kitchen scraps, leaves, grass clippings, and livestock manure are some of the most common ingredients of compost. If you don't have access to livestock manure, not to worry: most farmers will be delighted to give you as much manure as you can haul away—at no charge. To keep flies away, sprinkle *diatomaceous earth* over the top of the manure before and after you move it onto your compost pile.

DEFINITION

Diatomaceous earth, also known as diatomite or kieselgur, is a naturally occurring substance containing fossilized algae remains; it is easily crumbled into a fine white powder. Diatomaceous earth is used in industry as a filter medium, a mild abrasive, and an insecticide. It is widely available in agricultural feed supply stores.

The proper way to amend soil is to mix in the additive with the soil from your garden. Two to 3 inches of compost mixed into the top layer of soil should suffice. You can blend it into the soil with a shovel or use a rototiller. Gardeners with raised beds or those who choose not to mix their soil annually can top-dress the soil with 3 inches of compost in early spring and let the earthworms incorporate it into the native soil.

Moving Your Plants into the Garden

When your plants are properly hardened off and you've prepared your soil, it's time to move the young plants into the garden.

Extracting the Plants from Their Pots

When removing a plant from its pot, never pick it up by its stem. This could damage or break the stem, which would result in the plant's death. Instead, always hold plants or seedlings by their leaves.

I prefer to place my hand over the top of small pots and turn them upside down. Usually the dirt ball falls forward into my hand. At this point, I remove the pot, still holding on to the soil block, place my other hand on the bottom of the soil block, and using both hands turn the plant right side up. Sometimes it's necessary to remove any roots sticking out of the bottom of the pot before the soil will loosen enough to come out (see the following section).

If the plant will not come out at this point, use a butter knife and gently slide it between the pot and the soil. It is also okay to gently press on the side of the pot to help release the soil block.

Teasing the Roots Free

Young plants grown in pots often end up with a tangled root system. Sometimes the roots begin to wrap around the soil ball, and sometimes they just bunch up in the bottom of the pot. Either way, it's a good idea to tease the plants' roots when you remove them from the pot.

Gently run your fingers back and forth across the bottom of the soil ball, as if you are massaging it. The soil should begin to fall away and the roots fall downward toward the ground. Save whatever soil has fallen away to use in transplant. Continue to massage the roots until they aren't wrapped around the soil ball or one another. Transplant the plant, using the saved soil.

THE BAD SEED

Never pull the roots, because this could damage them. Be patient: roots that are too entangled to easily separate require more time and gentler massaging. If you don't take the time to do this, then instead of growing down into the ground, the roots will continue to wrap around one another, eventually strangling themselves and killing the plant.

Getting the Depth Right

Planting each type of plant at the appropriate depth can make the difference between success and failure. Some plants, such as trees, will not thrive if they are buried too deeply; trees should be buried at the same depth they were in the pot they were seeded in. Other plants, such as tomatoes, thrive best when their stems are buried; in fact, such plants become stronger because their stems send out extra roots. These extra roots help anchor the plant in the ground so strong that winds can't knock it over as easily. The extra roots also take up minerals in the soil, fertilizer, and water.

A young tomato plant being transplanted into a five-gallon bucket,
its permanent home for the rest of the summer.

Vegetables started indoors, in a cold frame, or in a greenhouse, often develop longer stems. When you transplant the vegetables you've grown from seed, you can bury their stems. With the exception of tomatoes, you want the bottom leaves to sit about ⅛ inch above soil level. Tomatoes benefit from having all but the top four leaves removed on the tomato; bury everything below.

The right transplanting depth is a vital means of protecting the plant's roots. Too shallow a depth leaves exposed roots, which can dry out the roots or leave them easily injured by environmental extremes, normal garden chores, or animals. Plants that are planted too deep also experience a wide array of problems: they may not bloom, for example (a common problem with peonies). With some plants, the roots don't develop properly due to a lack of oxygen; these will die.

Transplanting depth is especially important if you're using biodegradable pots. You must completely bury the top of the pot (or remove any exposed areas of it). These types of pots are valued for their ability to wick water from the ground. But if any part of the pot is left exposed to the air, the water continually evaporates until there's no more water for the pots to absorb. At that point, the plant's roots dry out and the plant itself dies.

TLC for New Transplants

The first step to getting your newly transplanted plants off to a good start is to water them well. See if the soil around them has sunk down into the ground. If it has, top-dress the area around the plant with compost and water again.

Regular, deep watering is essential to establishing plants. Most plants prefer an inch of water per week, but this can vary depending on the plant, the amount of precipitation, the air temperature, and other environmental conditions (such as wind, which causes evaporation).

Mulching is a big help because it works to conserve soil moisture and keep the young seedlings' roots cool. Compost, straw, shredded newspapers, (avoid color pages or glossy inserts), grass clippings that have not had chemicals applied to them, and bark chips work well as mulch.

KNOW THY SEED

When laying mulch, be sure to work your way across the garden so that you're laying the mulch in front of you. That way, you walk on the mulch instead of directly on the soil, thus reducing the risk of compacting the soil around the plants' roots.

Some plants, such as corn, are heavy feeders and benefit from a side dressing of a time-release fertilizer in addition to compost. You can side-dress the plants with fertilizer at the time of planting, or wait a week or two to give the plant roots time to establish.

Minimizing Shock

All sorts of commercial preparations promise to help minimize transplant shock. Some work great; others don't seem to help at all. To minimize shock, follow these guidelines:

- Properly harden off the plants.
- Transplant them early in the morning on an overcast day.
- Plant them according to the planting specifications for that particular type of plant, making sure not to damage the roots or stems.
- Water them immediately after you plant them.

Some plants, such as poppies, resent any type of root disturbance. In fact, some will die if they are moved. The best way to deal with these types of plants is to sow their seeds in peat pots, in peat pellets, or directly in the garden. Another option is to make sure the soil around the plant is dry enough that, when you transplant it, none of the soil falls off the roots. If you attempt to move such plants from one area of the garden to another, be certain that you get all the roots, including the smaller feeder roots.

Here's a list of plants that don't transplant well:

Plants That Don't Transplant Well

Balloon flower

Chinese cabbage

Corn

Cucumber

Hollyhock

Melon

Milkweed

Poppy

Pumpkin

Root crops, such as potato and carrot

Squash

Regular Maintenance

As with everything in life, a garden requires regular maintenance, including water, feeding, and weeding.

Mulching

Mulching involves placing a layer of material such as compost, shredded paper, or bark on top of the soil. Mulch helps conserve moisture, enriches the soil, and gives the garden a finished look. You have a plethora of mulch options at your disposal, and many of them are free:

- Compost is the best, since it also encourages microbial activity and provides nutrients for the plants.

- Shredded paper is another option, and one that earthworms love, plus it's a great way to recycle old newspapers. Straw works, too, but it often contains weed seed.

A clean, planted garden bed.

- Some gardeners prefer rocks or small pebbles. Because these don't biodegrade, they can be used again and again; additionally, they don't cause allergy problems.

- Store-bought mulch also works. You can find cedar, eucalyptus, and cacao, which is the ground-up pod of *Theobroma* cacao (chocolate tree).

Watering

Some plants, once established, are drought tolerant, but even they need to be watered during times of extreme drought. Most plants want to be watered at least once a week. A thorough, deep watering that encourages the roots to grow deeper into the ground is best. Plants with shallow roots are not capable of reaching water far below the soil's surface; when drought occurs, these plants are far more likely to die than those with deeper root systems.

Here are some options for keeping your plants properly hydrated:

- **Sprinklers**—Traditional sprinklers are convenient and cheaper than a lot of the other methods, especially if you have a large garden and little time. The downside is that the water goes into the air and much of it evaporates before it reaches the soil. Additionally, sprinklers are not very accurate; they wet the plants' foliage, which can promote disease.

- **Soaker hoses and automatic watering systems**—These basically run themselves if they're set up on a timer. The water is released at soil level so the roots can easily access it. The foliage remains dry. All you have to do is keep an eye on it to make sure everything is working as it should.

- **Watering cans and hoses with sprayers or water wands**—These traditional methods work well for small gardens, greenhouses, tunnel houses, and cold frames. Both methods are time consuming, but you get the opportunity to inspect every plant you're growing as you water.

Weeding

Weeds can choke out young plants. Mature plants are much more tolerant of weeds and often appreciate having them there because they provide shade for their roots. However, you need to remove as many weeds as possible from your garden because you'll have a problem if they go to seed: weed seeds are viable for seven years, sometimes longer, even when they are lying on open ground. When the conditions are right, those weed seeds will germinate, creating a lot of extra work for you.

You can prevent weeds from forming in your garden in many ways, including the following:

- Mulch the soil, thus blocking the sunlight, which often prevents weed seed from germinating.

- Hoe the weeds as soon as they form or pull them out by hand.

 THE BAD SEED

Chemical weed killers, even organic ones, kill not only weeds, but beneficial insects as well. Additionally, spraying them on your vegetables and fruits could make them unsafe to eat.

- Create your own weed cloth by laying several full sheets of newspaper directly on the soil and then laying mulch on top.

- As a last resort, spray weed killer.

Fertilizing

Some plants are heavy feeders and need frequent fertilization, while other plants don't need fertilization at all. Most plants will do just fine if they receive a yearly dressing of compost in early spring. Three inches is all you need. Keep the compost away from the plant stems, since getting it right up against the stem can cause disease to set in.

Pruning

Not all plants need pruning, but those that do must be regularly pruned. Unless you want fruit or seeds to form, the best time to prune is right after the plant flowers.

Flowering shrubs and trees form seeds, then set the next year's flowers, so if you prune too late in the season, you will remove the forming flower buds. For example, lilacs and forsythias require pruning as soon as their flowers fade. If you wait until June, you are going to lose some, if not all, of the following spring's flowers. The plants will produce new foliage, but are unlikely to produce flower buds. Pruning at the right time encourages the plants to bush and produce many more flower buds than if you had not pruned.

SPROUTING WISDOM

The University of Minnesota Extension has a wonderful online resource for pruning trees and shrubs at www.extension.umn.edu/distribution/horticulture/DG0628.html

The Least You Need to Know

- Harden off young plants before transplanting them into the garden.
- Proper transplanting helps get plants off to a good start and minimizes transplant shock.

- Weeds compete for nutrients and water, so remove them as soon as you see them begin to grow.

- Proper watering is essential to the health of your plants, so choose the method that works best for you.

Protecting Your Plants from Diseases, Pests, and Critters

In This Chapter

- Using cages, traps, and fencing
- Using foil, plastic forks, and other prevention methods
- Using companion planting to attract healthy insects
- Using chemicals as a last resort

Disease, insects, and animals can pose a real problem to plants, especially when they're young. Mature plants are far more capable of recovering from damage than young plants. In fact, when immature plants are damaged, they often never fully recover, so even if they manage to survive, they probably won't live up to your expectations.

Prevention is the key to successfully dealing with problems associated with disease, insects, and animals. An excellent way to ensure that plants are more resistant to insects and diseases prevalent in your area is to grow them from seeds you've saved from plants grown in your garden. Nothing you can buy will prove more effective. Of course, proper watering and regular maintenance play a key role in prevention as well.

But there's always an exception to the rule, so it's best to be prepared to deal with disease, insects, and pesky animals in case they become an issue. Fortunately, you have several natural control methods at your disposal that are environmentally friendly; as a last resort, you can always apply chemical substances.

Natural Control

Natural control methods work hand in hand with Mother Nature and are the first choice for organic gardeners. Dealing with disease, pests, and insects as naturally as possible is good for the environment and good for your garden. It usually involves a lot less work, too.

Before selecting the best natural control method, you need to diagnose exactly what ails your garden. The best method in the world is of no avail if you apply it to the wrong problem. If your plants seem to have a disease, identify it; if you're not sure of the disease, bring a leaf to your local nursery for help. If you have an insect infestation or critters are eating your plants, make sure you know which insects or critters you're after. When you know the specifics of the problem, you can wisely apply one of the methods discussed in this chapter.

Dichotomous earth (DE), homemade sprays, hand-picking, cages, and traps are all natural ways to control disease, pests, and critters. The following sections explore each of these methods in detail.

Diatomaceous Earth (DE)

Diatomaceous earth is a natural substance that works wonders in the garden because the tiny grains of powder have sharp edges that slice up soft-bodied insects when they crawl across them. Best of all, it doesn't harm earthworms. Be sure to select food-grade DE if you're using it on edible plants or where animals or children play.

Besides being effective in the garden, it's an ideal material to add to the jars of seeds you've stored (see Chapter 5). DE also works quite well to control fleas and as an internal parasite control for animals, especially livestock. This powder, sprinkled on manure, kills fly larvae, which is why it's a good idea to sprinkle it on any manure that you add to your compost pile. You can purchase DE at most nurseries and feed stores.

THE BAD SEED

Powdered products, including DE, are known to cause irritation to the mouth and nose, so be sure to wear a face mask and gloves when working with them.

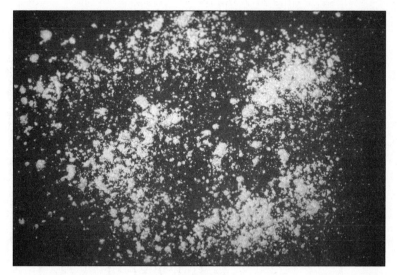

DE is a chalklike, powdery substance made from the fossilized remains of diatoms, a type of hard-shelled algae.

Homemade Sprays

Gardeners have been concocting homemade sprays for centuries. You can find a huge variety of recipes with a simple online search.

One of the simplest homemade sprays to make is an old recipe: put a drop of dish-washing liquid in a spray bottle full of warm water.

Here are some other effective recipes:

Homemade Insecticidal Soap

The vegetable oil clings to both the plant's surface and the insect's body, smothering the insect.

2 TB. liquid dishwashing soap   1 gallon warm water

1 TB. liquid vegetable oil   Dash of Tabasco sauce

1. Fill a clean, empty milk jug with warm water.

2. Add liquid dishwashing soap, liquid vegetable oil, and Tabasco. Put the lid back on the milk jug and shake well.

3. Remove the lid and either put a spray cap on the gallon jug or fill a clean spray bottle with this mixture.

4. Shake well before each use and be sure to coat both the top and bottom of the plants' leaves.

SPROUTING WISDOM

Read the label on your dishwashing liquid to see if it contains anything harmful before you apply it to your garden. Also, test the spray on a single leaf of the plant you intend to spray, to make sure it causes no harm before spraying the entire plant. After half an hour, if the leaf shows signs of damage, such as brown spots that look like sun scald, don't spray the plant with that particular dishwashing liquid; try another.

Repellant for Whiteflies, Aphids, Spider Mites, and Caterpillars

You can make an excellent general insect repellent that's effective on whiteflies, aphids, spider mites, and caterpillars.

1 tsp. hot pepper sauce or Tabasco   Water
4 cloves garlic

1. Add hot pepper sauce and garlic cloves to a blender and blend until smooth.

2. Add enough water to reach the ¼ cup mark on the blender and blend again.

3. Strain mixture to remove any remaining solids.

4. Add ¼ cup of mixture to a gallon of water and spray plants thoroughly.

Traps and Cages

Live traps and cages work well for animals such as raccoons, groundhogs, and rats. A live trap is a cage that catches animals without hurting or killing them. When an animal enters the cage and stands on the cage release, the door snaps shut, containing the animal.

KNOW THY SEED

Before you set up a trap or cage, take the time to find out the local laws pertaining to trapping or caging wild animals, as well as the laws regarding their disposal.

Before you set a live trap for an animal, you should have a plan in place for getting rid of it. Wild animal rescue organizations and businesses in most areas specialize in wild animal removal.

Investigate the best lure for the critter that's munching in your garden. Rats don't eat the same thing as snakes; bats aren't attracted to the same food as squirrels. You can make your own bait, although it can be a messy, smelly business to do so. You can find recipes online for making fish oil (good for raccoons and coyote), rotten eggs (also good for coyote and fox), and various mixtures of oil essences and spices (good for possums and other critters); chocolate and cheese attract mice and other rodents. Check with your fellow gardeners to see what favorite recipes they may have. Of course, you'll also find plenty of commercially made baits and lures at nurseries, at feed stores, and online.

Remember that where there's one animal, there are likely more, so don't remove a cage or trap as soon as you catch the first one; instead, place more bait in it and reset it.

Protecting Young Plants

Creative protection methods for young plants often persuade insects and pesky animals to look elsewhere for an easier meal. Netting, fencing, plastic forks, foil, and paper are just some of the items you can use to protect both young and mature plants from insects and animals.

The first step in combating insect infestation and disease is to make sure you transplant only the most robust plants into the garden, since these problems tend to affect weaker plants first. Healthy plants that have everything they need to thrive are better able to fend off attacks.

Your soil also plays an important role. Good soil is the foundation of your garden. Keep the soil healthy and thriving by top-dressing it with 3 inches of compost every year, working in some organic kelp or other fertilizer, and making sure it has adequate moisture, especially during times of drought.

SPROUTING WISDOM

Kelp contains 70 natural minerals and trace elements, amino acids, vitamins, growth hormones, enzymes, and proteins. These properties increase cold and frost tolerance, make plants better able to resist disease, and accelerate growth. They also increase the number of flowers, fruits, or vegetables each plant produces.

Keep track of what pests and diseases bother your plants on a calendar or in a gardening journal (see Chapter 14). Keep track of dates you apply the various control methods and indicate what worked, what didn't work, and how long it took to work. This is valuable information that will come in handy in years to come. The next time you have a problem, you'll simply have to go back and see what worked and what didn't.

Protected Locations

Planting in protected locations deters a variety of critters and often makes getting rid of insects easier, especially if you remove them by hand. In fact, if the location is really well protected, the insects will have a hard time finding the plants.

Protected locations, such as up against a building or under an established stand of trees, are ideal places for starting seeds, nurturing young plants, or even rooting cuttings.

KNOW THY SEED

Protected areas are often shaded, so there's less chance of the soil drying out.

Barriers from high winds, heavy rains, frost, and other weather extremes are additional benefits of protected locations. Whether you're growing winter-sown seeds, hardening off plants, or trying to grow marginally hardy plants, seek a protected area in your yard for the best outcome.

Netting

Using netting to keep animals from having easy access to your fruits and vegetables is easier than installing a fence. And for those who don't like the thought of traps or cages, netting is a good alternative solution. Fruit tree netting is sort of flimsy compared to regular garden netting, although either one will work for keeping out most animals; critters don't like getting tangled in it.

Secure the ends of the garden netting to conduit hoops with large plastic clamps.

Netting is designed to either lie over plants or attach to something around them. Tomato cages, hoop structures, fence posts, and even a wooden frame are possible choices. When you decide what to attach the netting to, you must figure out how to secure it so animals can't easily crawl beneath it. Anchoring the netting on all four corners with plastic clamps is a good option because it's quick, easy, and secure. Other options include weighting the netting where it touches the ground with bricks, sandbags, or rocks. You want something heavy enough that an animal can't roll it out of the way, but light enough that you can pick it up to access the crops growing underneath.

Fencing

Fencing off your garden is another option for keeping pesky critters out.

A wide variety of fencing material is available. Picket fences add charm but are too short to deter larger animals. Privacy fence can be ideal for gardens in high-traffic areas, but be careful it doesn't block the majority of sunlight from your garden. Chicken wire, farm fence, hardware cloth, and chain-link fence are good options if you want to grow vines on the fence. Another fencing option that's ornamental and keeps out small critters is a brick wall; however, these walls are generally only a few feet tall and don't prevent larger critters from scurrying over the top.

Keep in mind that some animals, such as groundhogs and rabbits, can dig a hole under the fence to access your garden. To prevent them from doing so, dig a channel around your garden deep enough to lay concrete cinder blocks so they're level with the top of the ground, or bury 4 to 6 inches of the fence underground. Keep in mind that deer, cats, and poultry will go over the top of the fence unless it's at least 8 feet high.

> **SPROUTING WISDOM**
>
> Creative gardeners can have growing gourds, squash, or zucchini on their fences. Look for small plastic molds (in garden centers) designed to shape these fruits into faces and other unique objects.

If you don't like looking at fencing, you can camouflage it by planting vines on it. Perennial vines such as clematis, chocolate vine, climbing roses, and passionfruit are ideal for fences that are a permanent part of the garden. Gourds, cardinal climber, morning glories, beans, squash, and zucchini are great annual vines to grow on a fence. Use pantyhose to help support the squash and zucchini. Simply cut off the legs of the pantyhose, lay the wider part of the vegetable in the top half of the pantyhose, gather up the extra material around it, and tie it to the fence.

Plastic Forks

Strange as it may seem, plastic forks prevent cats and other critters that have pads on the bottom of their paws from walking, lying, or digging in the garden. Insert the handle of the fork into the ground. Push it down far enough so no more than an inch of the tines of the fork are above ground. When a padded-paw animal, such as a cat, walks on the tines, it hurts, so they avoid the area.

Make sure the forks are spaced no more than a quarter of an inch apart. If the animal can jump or walk in such a way that they can avoid the forks, they will do so. Keep an eye on the forks and replace any that have broken tines.

Aluminum Foil

When it comes to deterring pests, aluminum foil works wonders in the garden. Aluminum foil is useful in the garden because it is somewhat sturdy, makes noise when it's brushed against, and is reflective.

Consider a couple simple—and inexpensive—uses of this common kitchen item:

- Cut a sheet of aluminum foil into strips approximately $\frac{1}{2}$ inch wide and 4 inches long. Mix these strips into the mulch in your garden. Not only will the strips reflect light back onto the plants, but they will keep some insects and critters at bay because they don't like the reflection or the noise the foil makes when they walk or crawl on it.

- Use aluminum foil to make hanging mirrors that you place throughout the garden. The light these "mirrors" reflect deters insects and critters, especially at night when headlights hit the foil. The critters think there's a predator in the garden and run for cover.

Protecting Your Plants' Stems

Stems do a lot more than just support plants. They carry water and nutrients from the roots up to the leaves, flowers, and fruits. Damaged stems don't always recover, especially on young plants, so protecting them is important.

Small 3×5 index cards work well to protect plant stems and are quite inexpensive compared to other methods. Fold an index card in half lengthwise and then bury about an inch of the card into the soil, keeping it as close to the stem as possible without actually touching it. This dissuades many pests, such as slugs, from chewing plant stems.

You can protect plant stems with aluminum foil, too. Wrap wooden or plastic skewers with aluminum foil and push the skewers into the ground about half an inch away from the plant's stem. Match the size of the skewer to the length and thickness of the stem. The reflective quality of the foil deters pests.

Keeping Pests at Bay

Prevention is the key to keeping pests at bay. Planting healthy plants grown in healthy soil is the best method of prevention, but it is not a cure-all. With urban expansion, critters such as deer are moving into towns at an alarming rate. A neighbor could have an insect infestation in his or her garden, and those insects could easily come into your garden in droves. Knowing what you can do ahead of time if a problem arises is the best way to keep pests at bay. That's why keeping a calendar or journal documenting what you've done in the past is so helpful.

Under most circumstances, just one of the methods mentioned earlier will solve the problem. Sometimes, however, the circumstances are extreme enough that you need to combine methods. If you are dealing with both insects and critters, more than one method of prevention is necessary. If you're still at a loss, you'll need to consider other possibilities.

Electricity

Electric garden fences work well to keep particularly persistent critters out of the garden. They're often sold as moveable chicken fences and come complete with plastic fence posts that are easy to push into the ground. Some of the electric fences run on solar power, and some require electricity. The voltage they require varies depending on the strength of the fence, so if you have only 110 volts available, make sure you don't buy a fence that requires 220 volts. Posting warning signs along the perimeter of the fence is a good idea. After all, you wouldn't want someone to get shocked because they weren't aware the fence had electricity flowing through it.

THE BAD SEED

Electric fences are not an option for everyone. Some cities have ordinances that prohibit their use. Always check with local zoning authorities before you install electric fencing.

Some of these fences are simple strandlike lines that run parallel with the ground from post to post. Others are actual fencing that resemble netting or farm fence. The latter are the best for keeping critters out, since they make it difficult for animals to jump over or crawl under the fence.

Other Measures

Here are some other techniques for deterring pests:

- **Use row covers.**
- **Stake your plants.** Place three or four stakes around the plant, and then wrap yarn, twine, or netting around the outside of the stakes to create a barrier.

- **Plant in protected locations, near your house or outbuildings.** Some animals, such as deer, really dislike humans and won't come close to their living quarters. If you plant your garden near your house or another spot where people are around, you might deter them.

- **Plant early or late in the season.** Bad bugs tend to hang around when a crop is in season. But if there's no food, why would they come? If you plant earlier or later than the norm, you tend to avoid the bugs that prey on certain crops because either the insects haven't yet arrived or they've moved on to greener pastures (more on this later in the chapter).

As a Last Resort: Chemical Defenses

When all else fails, organic or inorganic chemicals are an option. Always read the labels and follow instructions exactly. The law requires it, but mixing or using them incorrectly both is illegal and can harm the environment and possibly the health of the person using them. Wear gloves, long-sleeve clothing, and a face mask when using chemicals, even organic ones. Be sure to spray just the areas that need it. Remember that even organic chemicals will kill the good bugs along with the bad.

THE BAD SEED

Chemicals, organic or not, can kill the good bugs you're trying to encourage to take up residence.

Test an inconspicuous area of the plant you intend to spray before you spray the entire plant. As with homemade chemicals, store-bought chemicals, even those that are premixed, can kill a plant. Whenever possible, begin your line of chemical defense with organic products; use inorganic products only if the organic ones don't solve the problem. Many chemicals remain in the soil for years, and plant roots will absorb those chemicals. When you eat the fruit or vegetables from those plants, you are also eating the chemical residue left behind. That's another reason chemicals should be your last defense.

A Long-Term Solution: Companion Planting

Companion planting is a natural technique in which you plant two or more plants near one another in order to benefit one or both plants. For example, some plants grow better when they are planted together, such as corn, beans, and squash (known as the "three sisters"). Other plants attract or repel insects and, when grown near other crops that those insects love, deter or trap the pests and enable the main crop to thrive.

Companion planting is a simple solution for a lot of pest problems, but it isn't an overnight fix. The full effects often aren't apparent for years, although you will begin noticing a difference within two to three years. During this time, you will need an alternative, nonchemical solution.

Companion planting also increases yield and makes your garden both useful and beautiful. Don't be afraid to intermix herbs, flowers, fruits, and vegetables. This is the best way to increase pollination and get rid of the bad bugs.

Companion Plantings

Plant	With	Known Benefits
Amaranth	Potato Onion Corn	Brings up nutrients from the subsoil
Anise	Coriander	Helps anise seeds germinate better
Basil	Tomato	Prevents insects and disease while improving growth and flavor; also repels flies and mosquitoes
Bean (bush)	Carrot Cauliflower Beet Cucumber Cabbage	Helps beans grow
	Marigold	Repels Mexican bean beetle
	Summer savory	Improves growth and flavor; deters bean beetles
Bee balm	Tomato	Improves growth and flavor
Borage	Tomato	Repels tomato hornworm

continues

Companion Plantings (continued)

Plant	With	Known Benefits
Brassica family (cabbage, kale, cauliflower, kohlrabi, broccoli, collard, Brussels sprout, turnip, rutabaga)	Celery Dill Sage Peppermint Potato Sage	Improves growth
	Chamomile	Improves growth and flavor
	Thyme Wormwood Hyssop Southernwood	Repels white cabbage butterfly
	Onion	Repels rabbits
Calendula		Repels dogs
Carrot	Onion Leek Rosemary Wormwood Sage	Repels carrot fly
Castor bean		Plant around garden perimeter to repel moles and mosquitoes
Chervil	Radish	Improves growth and flavor
Chive	Carrot	Improves growth and flavor
	Apple	Prevents apple scab
Corn	Pea	Restores nitrogen to soil
	Bean	Restores nitrogen to soil; anchors corn to discourage raccoons
	Melon Squash Pumpkin Cucumber	Discourages raccoons
	Odorless marigold	Deters Japanese beetles
	Sunflower	Increases yield

Plant	With	Known Benefits
Cucumber	Radish	Protects from cucumber beetle
Dusty Miller		Repels rabbits
Eggplant	Bean	Prevents Colorado potato beetle
Feverfew		All around insect repellent
Flax	Carrot Potato	Improves growth and flavor; repels the Colorado potato beetle
Foxglove		Repels deer
Fruit trees	Chive Mustard Onion Nasturtium Southernwood Horseradish	Attract pollinators; repels bad bugs
	Garlic	Prevents borers
Garlic	Most anything	Prevents aphids, weevils, and spider mites
	Tomato	Prevents red spiders
	Rose	Increases fragrance; protects against black spot, mildew, and aphids
Horehound	Most anything	Discourages grasshoppers
	Tomato	Improves quality and abundance; promotes longer production
Horseradish	Potato	Prevents disease and blister beetle; improves health
Hyssop	Grape	Increases yield
Lettuce	Radish	Increases succulence
Marigold		Discourages nematodes
	Tomato	Encourages growth and production
	Bean	Protects against Mexican bean beetle
Marjoram		Improves growth and flavor of all plants

continues

Companion Plantings (continued)

Plant	With	Known Benefits
Melon	Corn Sunflower	Improves growth
Mint		Repels ants and aphids
	Tomato	Improves growth and flavor
	Cabbage	Improves growth and flavor; repels white cabbage worm and butterfly
Nasturtium		Repels aphids, whiteflies, and striped pumpkin beetles
	Squash	Repels squash bugs
	Apple	Repels woolly aphids
Oregano	Broccoli	Repels white cabbage butterfly
Parsley	Carrot	Repels carrot flies
	Rose	Repels rose beetles
	Tomato Asparagus	Increases growth
Pennyroyal		Repels ants and mosquitoes
	Broccoli Cabbage Brussels sprout	Protects against cabbage maggot
Sweet pepper	Okra	Pepper plants serve as a windbreak for okra
Potato	Bean Eggplant	Protects against Colorado potato beetles
Radish	Cucumber Squash Melon	Repels striped cucumber beetle
Squash	Icicle radish	Repels insects
	Nasturtium	Repels squash bugs
Tomato	Asparagus	Protects against asparagus beetle
	Gooseberry	Repels insects
	Roses	Prevents black spot

Plant	With	Known Benefits
Yarrow		Attracts beneficial insects; makes plants grown in proximity insect resistant
	Medicinal herbs	Increases essential oils

THE BAD SEED

Any vine will discourage raccoons. The animals get tangled in them. Squash and pumpkin are the best companion plants for corn; interplant them so the vines grow around the corn stalks.

Not all plants make good companions. In fact, some, such as beans and onions, downright hate one another. When two plants are grown together but don't get along, the end result is a decreased harvest and possibly major pest problems. One way to keep these plants apart is to plant a row or two of a neutral plant, such as cosmos, between them.

Avoid Planting These Plants Close Together

Beans and onions

Basil and rue

Beets and mustard

Cabbage and strawberries

Cabbage and tomatoes

Cabbage and pole beans

Carrots and apples

Cauliflower and strawberries

Cauliflower and tomatoes

Cucumbers and potatoes

Cucumbers and aromatic herbs

Fennel and coriander

Peas and onions

Peas and garlic

Potatoes and tomatoes

Tomatoes and corn

The Least You Need to Know

- Start with natural options to control disease, pests, and insect infestations whenever possible.
- Test a single plant leaf before spraying with any product, homemade or not.
- Traps, cages, and fencing are good options for dealing with larger animals.
- Make store-bought organic or inorganic chemical solutions your last option whenever possible.
- Companion planting techniques save time and money by attracting good bugs and eliminating the need for herbicides and pesticides in the long run.

Building Your Seed Future

Part

5

The future of plant diversity and seed saving is in your hands. It's up to all of us to make sure the wide variety of plants our ancestors worked so hard to keep alive remain available for future generations.

This part introduces you to simple cross-breeding techniques to get you started creating your own unique varieties of plants suited to your tastes and growing conditions. You find out how to hand-pollinate your plants to ensure plant purity and take some of the guesswork out of breeding.

A big part of successful seed saving involves keeping good records in a gardening journal. By documenting information about the seeds you save and the plants that sprout from them, you create a historical record of your garden that you can pass down as a family heirloom along with your saved seeds. You can add maps, drawings, photographs, and dried plant material to your journal.

A big part of the joy many people get out of seed saving involves sharing their knowledge—and their seeds—with others. This part gives you pointers on swapping and selling seeds and teaching others, including senior citizens and children, how to save seeds.

Creating New Varieties by Cross Breeding

In This Chapter

- Delving deeper into pollination
- Breeding your own plants
- Avoiding unintentional cross-pollination
- Creating seeds optimized for your garden

Pollination is one of nature's oldest tricks. To survive, plants form seeds so that they can reproduce. As noted in Chapter 2, for plants to produce seed, some form of pollination must take place. This chapter goes into greater detail about pollination and how you can hand-pollinate plants to create brand-new types of plants and then maintain the purity of those plants using a variety of techniques.

It's All in the Breeding

People breed new varieties of edible or ornamental plants for a variety of reasons, including the following:

- To create a vegetable, fruit, or flower of a new color, shape, or size
- To create a plant that has better vigor
- To create a plant that bears more produce
- To create a variety that tastes better

Whatever reason spurs you to experiment with breeding plants, you must take good notes and have a lot of patience. Developing the qualities you want in a new plant can take years. If you haven't fastidiously kept notes, you won't know what worked and what didn't—and you'll have to start your experiment all over again.

Helping Nature Along: Hand-Pollinating and Cross-Pollinating

Someone might want to hand-pollinate a plant for many reasons, but two of the most common reasons are as follows:

- **A lack of necessary pollinators in your area.** Gardeners who grow plants in greenhouses, cold frames, or other protective structures where natural pollinators don't have easy access also use hand pollination. Hand pollination takes the uncertainty out of pollination. If you do it yourself, you can rest assured the plant will produce as expected.

- **A desire to create a hybrid plant.** Gardeners who grow rare or hybrid plants often rely on hand pollination to get their plants to produce seeds. They collect pollen from another plant (or order it from a pollen supplier) and, when the pollen is ripe, use a paintbrush or cotton swab to transfer the pollen from the package to the flower.

Hand pollinating.

KNOW THY SEED

Here's an easy to way distinguish between a male and a female flower: a male flower has a single, pollen-laden stalk inside the center of the flower; this is the stamen. A female flower has several small stalks called pistils that grow from the center of the flower; the pistils have a bulbous base at the bottom, which is the ovary. A plant that has both male and female parts has both the stamen and the pistils on one flower.

You need a few implements for hand pollination: your most important tools are a cotton swab (have plenty on hand) or a fine paintbrush (the type used for watercolors, not house painting) and, of course, a notebook.

The following sections outline two methods you can use to hand-pollinate flowers.

Hand-Pollinating Plants: Method #1

Follow these steps to hand-pollinate your plants:

1. Select two flowers from two different plants of the same species as early in the morning as possible.

2. Locate the male flower part on one plant and the female flower part on the other plant.

3. Use a clean paintbrush or cotton swab to gently remove some of the yellow pollen from the stamen, or male plant part. Cover the brush or swab with pollen.

4. Gently rub the paintbrush or swab across the pistils, or female parts of a flower, that have just opened.

5. Cover the flower you just pollinated with pantyhose, a cloth tea bag, or other material to make sure no additional pollen can reach this plant. If necessary, gently tie a brightly colored ribbon around the plant's stem to help you remember which plants you hand-pollinated.

THE BAD SEED

Don't let any of the pollen get on your hands or clothes. If it does, it could accidentally transfer through wind pollination, or you could accidentally rub against the plant.

If you use cotton swabs to hand-pollinate your plants, use a clean one every time you pollinate. If you use a paintbrush, clean it carefully and thoroughly after each use, to avoid cross-contamination.

Hand-Pollinating Plants: Method #2

Here's a second method for hand-pollinating your plants:

1. Remove the pollen-laden male flower from the plant by cutting it off the stem.

2. Remove all the flower petals on the male plant as well as the male plant part, if there is one.

3. Dab the pollen-laden stamen against the pistils on the female flower.

4. Cover the flower you just pollinated with pantyhose, a cloth tea bag, or other material to make sure no additional pollen can reach this plant. If necessary, gently tie a brightly colored ribbon around the plant's stem to help you remember which plants you hand-pollinated.

Regardless of the method you use, make a tag that includes the name of both parent plants and the date you crossed the plants.

Carefully cut off the pollen-holding stamen.

Cross-Pollinating Plants

The technique for cross-pollinating plants is similar to hand-pollinating, except you're using two different species of plants rather than the same plant. Follow these steps:

1. Select two flowers from two different plants of two different species as early in the morning as possible.

2. Locate the male flower part on one plant and the female flower part on the other plant.

3. Use a clean paintbrush or cotton swab to gently remove some of the yellow pollen from the stamen, or male plant part. Cover the brush or swab with pollen.

4. Gently rub the paintbrush or swab across the pistils, or female parts of a flower, that have just opened.

5. Cover the flower you just pollinated with pantyhose, a cloth tea bag, or other material to make sure no additional pollen can reach this plant. If necessary, gently tie a brightly colored ribbon around the plant's stem to help you remember which plants you cross-pollinated.

Technical Stuff About Plant Chromosomes

Most plants are *diploid*, meaning they have two sets of chromosomes, just like humans. Daylilies, for example, have 11 chromosomes from the male parent and 11 from the female. (Humans, by the way, have 23 pairs.) But some plants are *tetraploid*, meaning that they have four pairs of chromosomes. While you can get some pretty interesting results by crossing a tetraploid with a diploid, the resulting number of seeds produced is few compared with the production resulting from crossing a diploid with a diploid or crossing a tetraploid with a tetraploid. Some plants even have more sets of chromosomes: anything with three or more sets falls under the general category of *polyploids*, a term used to describe cells and organisms containing more than two paired (homologous) sets of chromosomes. Polyploidy is found in some organisms and is especially common in plants.

Because chromosomes are invisible to the eye, you need to do some research to determine whether a plant is a polyploid or a diploid.

Examples of Some Polyploids

Triploid crops (three sets of chromosomes)

Some varieties of apple

Banana

Citrus

Ginger

Watermelon

Tetraploid crops (four sets of chromosomes)

Some varieties of apple

Cabbage

Cotton

Durum or macaroni

Leek

Peanut

Potato

Tobacco

Wheat

Hexaploid crops (six sets of chromosomes)

Bread wheat

Chrysanthemum

Kiwifruit

Oat

Triticale

Octaploid crops (eight sets of chromosomes)

Dahlia

Pansy

Strawberry

Sugar cane

> **DEFINITION**
>
> A **tetraploid** has four times the number of chromosomes in a cell nucleus than normal.
>
> A **diploid** has two separate pairs of chromosomes.
>
> A **chromosome** lives inside the cell's nucleus and is made of different combinations of deoxyribonucleic acid (DNA); chromosomes always exist in pairs.
>
> **Polyploid** is an umbrella term designating any organism with more than two sets of chromosomes.

The other important fact to note is that tetraploids contain lots of genetic material that's quite variable and hard to interpret, even for some genetic research scientists.

Hobby plant breeders are usually a lot less interested in conducting genetic research than trying their hand at creating new varieties. And some of the best hybrids have resulted from their experiments. If creating hybrids inspires you, in just two years' time, you can create a great new edible plant. But don't expect to sell it and get rich; while this isn't impossible, commercial varieties require a level of uniformity that's difficult to achieve as an amateur.

But home gardeners don't do it for the money. It's the thrill of growing something no one else has, something brand-new, something you've created. You can create a variety that is suited to your garden and your climate and your taste. You can create a variety that you can grow organically that's resistant to local pests and disease problems. And you can share the varieties you create with others by trading or selling the seeds on a small scale.

Cross-Breeding Vegetables

Commercial vegetable varieties are bred to have thick skins and hard flesh, enabling harvesting machines to pick them without damaging them. Modern hybrid vegetables have a long shelf life, are uniform in size and shape, and can withstand long shipping distances. Many heirloom vegetables don't have these qualities, which is why they are so hard to find in grocery stores.

Home gardeners don't need such qualities; they can raise vegetables based on visual appeal, smell, and taste. And that's where amateur vegetable breeding comes into play.

Breeding your own vegetables allows you to create plants that are adjusted to the specific growing conditions in your garden. Organic gardeners often find that seed they save from their own garden performs much better than commercial seed because it wasn't bred using chemical fertilizers or pesticides. Plants not grown by relying on chemicals to fend off pests or disease build up resistance on their own, resulting in a healthier plant that produces robust seeds.

Breeding your own vegetables also adds to garden diversity. You can choose the qualities you want your vegetables to have, such as more cold tolerance. Whatever your reason for breeding your own vegetables, there's no better time to start than right now. You never know what fabulous variety you may come up with!

Personalizing Your Produce

If you really like the looks of black tomatoes, but you prefer the taste and size of the yellow pear tomato, you can cross these two varieties by hand-pollinating them and then grow the resulting seeds to see what you get. You might get a tomato with the same size and color of the yellow pear tomato, but the taste of a black tomato—or you might get just what you were hoping for. If you do like the results, allow the plant to self-pollinate to determine whether the cross will remain true. If the cross doesn't set true, or if you're just not happy with it, try crossbreeding again … and again … until you get just the variety of tomato you desire. Don't worry about making mistakes—you can always eat them!

When you get the results you want *and* the plant breeds true, save those seeds so you can sow your new plant again next season. Remember to share your seeds so others can enjoy your new creation.

KNOW THY SEED

You can breed disease and pest resistance into vegetables by crossing them with varieties that have this gene, or, going a step further, breeding them with a wild edible variety, since most wild plants have this quality. Breeding with a wild edible is known as *backcrossing*.

Inbreeding vs. Outbreeding

Before deciding which vegetable varieties to breed, you need to know how each is pollinated. For example, peas, tomatoes, and lettuce are *inbreeders*, meaning that they self-pollinate. Members of the *Allium* family (onion, shallots, and garlic), the *Brassica* family (cabbage, kale, broccoli, cauliflower, Brussels sprouts, and collards), corn, squash, and pumpkin are *outbreeders*, meaning that they cross-pollinate. Outbreeders are easier to hand-pollinate. To cross-pollinate a plant that is an inbreeder you must catch the plant before the pistil fully forms and begins to release pollen. An outbreeder doesn't self-pollinate, so they are easier to cross-pollinate because you do not have to worry about them pollinating themselves.

Vegetables by Pollination Type

Vegetables That Inbreed	Vegetables That Outbreed
Beans	Asparagus
Cowpeas	Beets
Endive	Broccoli
Escarole	Brussels sprouts
Garlic	Cauliflower
Lettuce	Chinese cabbage
Lima beans	Corn
Peas	Cucumber
Peppers	Kale
Soybeans	Kohlrabi
Tomatoes	Melons
	Mustards
	Okra
	Pumpkin
	Rutabaga
	Spinach
	Squash
	Turnips

Cross-Breeding Fruits

Most fruit requires cross-pollination for it to set well, so for open pollination, you generally need to have two plants. This holds true with all varieties of apples, for example, as well as sweet cherries. Bees are the most important pollinators of fruit; unless you're planting a sizeable orchard, wild bees are probably plentiful enough.

If you want to cross-breed, the easiest way to start is to do so with fruits that are related to one another. For example, you might try crossing different varieties of berries to berries, apples to apples, or citrus to citrus. The more initial crosses you make, the greater the chance of getting a successful cross that gives you exactly the plant you were looking for.

SPROUTING WISDOM

Cross-pollinating plants is sort of like having children. One child may be blonde, one may be a redhead, and one may have black hair. Maybe you wanted a child with brown hair, but that gene might not be your genetic make-up, so unless you choose a partner who has that gene you will not get a child with brown hair. And even if you do, it may take several tries to accomplish. Plants are the same way. You don't always get what you want the first time around.

Seed DNA works like human DNA. If you make the same cross, between the same two plants, you will more likely get the exact same variety. If you make several different crosses using different plants, you will more than likely get several different varieties. So if your goal is to create a new plant, make lots of different crosses using a variety of different plants, improving your chances that at least one of the resulting fruits will be what you were hoping for.

After you hand-pollinate, label each cross with a tag, making complete notes either on the tag or in your gardening journal (more on this in Chapter 14). When the fruit starts to develop, don't be in a hurry to pick it. Immature seeds are less likely to sprout, so you want to wait until the fruit is fully ripened on the tree to ensure that the seeds inside the flesh are mature. You can sow the seeds as soon as you harvest them, or you can dry them and sow them later (see Chapter 5). Some seeds, such as citrus, are best sown fresh.

KNOW THY SEED

It is important to know how seeds are produced from the particular type of plant from which you want to save seed. Some plants produce their seeds on the inside of the fruit, and others produce seedpods. Refer to the seed directories in Chapters 17 to 19 for specifics on harvesting seeds from a wide variety of fruits and vegetables.

Don't expect crossed fruit seeds to produce fruits that are the same as the parent plant. Remember, the new plants come from a cross, which opens up the gene pool. Some of the fruit you grow from a crossed seed will be delicious, but some will be undesirable. This is where the selection process begins. To avoid cross-pollination with the fruits you like from the fruits you don't like, simply remove the undesirable plants.

Cross-Breeding Flowers

When a unique flower sprouts in your garden, there's a lot to know about why that particular plant became a *sport*. It could be due to odd cross pollination, it might be a rare mutation, or some environmental factor might be at work. Cold weather, viruses, pesticides, and other environmental factors can change a plant's make-up; such changes aren't passed on from plant to plant, however. Only traits with a genetic basis—those controlled by the plant's genes—can be passed on to future generations.

DEFINITION

A **sport** is a plant that differs in some way from a parent plant. The color of the flower or the foliage may be different, for example, or it may be variegated (or not).

Daylilies (*Hemerocallis*) are one of the easiest groups of flowers for beginning plant breeders to start cross-pollinating because the large floral structures are easy to access. To hand-pollinate a daylily, first determine whether your plants are of the same ploidy. Daylilies are either diploid or tetraploid. As discussed earlier in this chapter, you can cross these two types, but to reap viable seeds, it's better to cross two diploids or two tetraploids. It's possible for the seedpods from two different polyploids to set, but it's unlikely the plant will survive because the seeds inside the pod aren't viable. If you're unsure of the ploidy of your plants and can't find the answer on the Internet or at the library, experiment. Hand-pollinate them and see what happens. If the seedpod dries up and aborts, you know those plants' ploidy are not compatible.

KNOW THY SEED

Daylilies come in a variety of colors, sizes, and flower styles. They are easy to hand-pollinate and are one of the most popular perennial flowering plants in existence.

The American Hemerocallis Society (www.daylilies.org) has an easy-to-use search mechanism that tells you all you need to know about nearly any variety of daylily, including whether it is diploid or tetraploid.

Experiment and see what you get. Try crossing flowers of different petal forms, such as a spider with a double. Cross flowers of contrasting colors. Don't be afraid to try something new. Have fun with it. Think of all the plant diversity we would not have today had gardeners and horticulturists been reticent about trying new ideas. Color combinations that many plant breeders thought were impossible to achieve 20 or 30 years ago are in existence today because someone said, "I've always dreamed of having a candy-cane-striped pansy. Let's see if I can make one."

Variety Is the Spice of Life

Gardeners and natural pollinators have created hundreds of new varieties of fruits, herbs, flowers, and vegetables. Sometimes new varieties are created by accident, such as when natural pollinators spread pollen from one plant to another; other times, the results of a cross is carefully calculated before hand pollination occurs. New varieties of plants create interest in our gardens and give us something new to look forward to each season.

SPROUTING WISDOM

Seed and plant catalogs usually dedicate the first few pages of their publication to the new varieties that are available. This keeps their customers coming back year after year to see what's new and exciting in the gardening world.

The downside of the new varieties is that some of the fine traits of the old plants are lost. Fragrance is often sacrificed for larger flowers, as is an abundance of seeds. The ease of harvesting grains by hand is often traded for crops that are easier to harvest by machine, making home harvesting difficult. Plant breeding is all about making choices. You have to decide which traits you want in a new variety and which traits you are willing to sacrifice to get them.

Commercially, there's more hybridization with edible plants than with ornamentals, leaving that field wide open to hobbyists. There's a broad range of plants to work with and an even broader range of possible results. Lots of gardeners are waiting patiently for the right seedling to grow into a new and exciting plant that they can market. You may not get rich off just one plant introduction, but you will have the thrill of naming that plant—and knowing that you have contributed to plant diversity. This is the joy of creating new plants, whether edible or ornamental—or both.

Maintaining Seed Purity

Maintaining seed purity is essential if you want to keep specific varieties, such as a favorite heirloom plant, from cross-pollinating. Even if you don't grow another variety of that plant, pollen could be brought in on the wind or by pollinating insects. To protect your plant, you should use some type of barrier. Of course, the plant must be pollinated, so if you're really concerned, the best method is to hand-pollinate the entire crop. That's very labor-intensive in large fields, a job few people would choose to do. In a home garden, however, hand pollination of a few plants is very doable.

> **KNOW THY SEED**
>
> If you share seeds with others or with seed banks or seed-saving organizations and you think the seed was contaminated by another crop, let others know so they can either pass the information along or have the seed tested to verify its DNA.

By keeping seed pure, you can count on the continued circulation of crops that have been around for a long time. You also protect them from possible contamination by their GMO counterparts. Every year, hundreds of heirlooms are lost due to accidental cross-pollination. This reduction in our plant diversity could prove to be calamitous. Because of their longevity, many heirloom seeds are resistant to diseases that could wipe out an entire crop of hybrids or GMOs. A time may come when we need to fall back on these heirloom varieties to sustain the human race.

The best way to maintain purity is to grow a single variety of the same crop. If this is the year for beans, grow just one type, unless you can plant another variety far enough away to avoid cross-pollination. The ideal distance is 200 feet, although some say that a mere 50 feet will work.

> **KNOW THY SEED**
>
> When in doubt about the true identity of a seed, you can do a little sleuthing on the Internet. One of the best online identification guides is The Seed Site (http://theseedsite.co.uk).

Even in commercial packaging, contamination can occur if two different types of seed are mixed. If you see any questionable seeds, remove them before they have a chance to grow, cross-pollinate, and contaminate the seed you want to keep pure.

Why Is Seed Purity Important?

Maintaining seed purity is important for preserving plant diversity. By maintaining purity, you're protecting the right of people to choose what they want to grow in their gardens. When seeds lose their purity and cross with another variety, especially a GMO, the entire food chain is affected, including the pollinators. This can lead to serious long-term problems in uncharted territory.

So many serious issues surround seed saving these days. The entire process is in jeopardy as more seeds, including those grown organically, are cross-pollinated with GMO varieties. This limits the consumers' choice to avoid foods that contain GMOs. It limits the farmers' right to save their own seeds. It forces many family farms out of business because, financially, they cannot afford to buy new seed every year (remember, there are legal constraints on propagating GMOs). In addition, the new seed they purchase may not be adapted to their farm, so it may not grow.

> **SPROUTING WISDOM**
>
> Saving seed is essential to saving unique, hard-to-find varieties of plants from extinction. Many varieties have been handed down generation after generation, but eventually no one may be left to keep the tradition alive. These varieties are highly adapted to the specific area where they have been grown for generations; they may be the key to survival of that particular species if modern hybrids are ever wiped out by disease, pests, or other environmental conditions.

Testing for Purity

The only way we can know what we are growing and eating is to maintain the purity of the seed in our gardens. One way to make sure the seed you save is pure is to have the DNA of the seeds you save tested periodically. This can be expensive, although it may be worth it to you to have peace of mind.

A simpler way is to watch the crops you grow. If you see a plant that looks out of place, there's a good chance contamination has taken place. Remove that plant immediately and keep an eye on the remaining plants to see if any other unusual characteristics develop.

Isolating Plants

Isolating plants from one another by distance may seem like the perfect solution to keeping plants pure, but it isn't always effective. Sometimes a neighbor will grow a similar plant, and that pollen can travel into your yard and affect your crop. Wind can move pollen for miles, as can insects. Even if the crops you grow are self-pollinating, as with many tomatoes, accidents still happen. If your strategy to keep seeds pure includes isolation, get to know the crops that grow around you. Talk to the people who are growing similar crops nearby and let them know what you are trying to do. They may be willing to give you pertinent information, such as when they planted their crop or when they intend to do a second or third sowing.

It is possible to plant similar crops at different times so the pollination periods don't overlap. If a plant is already pollinated or not ready to receive pollen, it won't matter whether the pollen from the neighbor's crops—or your own—finds its way into your garden, because nothing will happen.

One surefire way to maintain purity is to grow crops that are less common in your area. For example, most Northern gardeners don't grow cotton or sorghum, so maintaining the purity of these plants would be easier for a Northern gardener than a Southern gardener. Growing crops in tunnel houses (see Chapter 10), out of season, is another isolation technique that works quite well. The only problem might be pollination, but if the crop is small enough, the easy answer is to pollinate by hand.

Caging

For self-pollinating plants, a technique known as caging is an effective barrier from cross-pollination. It is also a useful way to prevent insect-pollinating crops from crossing your plants. Self-pollinating crops can remain under a plastic cover throughout the growing season as long as the plastic is vented (an unvented covering would burn up a crop). If you are using a high tunnel, seal the vents with cloth or window screen, allowing for airflow. The technique varies slightly, depending on whether the crop is self-pollinating or relies on insects for pollination.

KNOW THY SEED

Create your own cages out of plant supports or tomato cages. Simply cover them with row cover (specially designed garden fabrics) or another lightweight, breathable fabric, and secure the entire covered cage about a foot underground by removing some of the soil, placing the plastic in the hole, and covering it with the soil you just removed.

Here's how caging works. Surround a cage, high tunnel, or other frame that fits easily over the plants with plastic, cloth, or window screening. The bottom of the cage should be about a foot below ground to deter ground-dwelling pollinators and determined insects or mammals from getting into them. The best way to secure the material underground is to dig a hole a foot deep around the perimeter of the structure before putting the structure in place. Once the structure is in place, lay the plastic, screening, or other material in the hole. Backfill the hole with the soil you removed. This will secure the material and keep critters out. Self-pollinating plants can be kept caged from the start or right before they begin to flower, which is when you want to prevent them from crossing with any other variety of the same species.

When you have related plants in the same garden, such as kale and cabbage, cucumbers and watermelon, or gourds and pumpkins, use the following alternating caging method: at dusk, cage all the plants. In the morning, remove the covering from, say, the watermelon, thus ensuring that the bees and butterflies that awaken with the sun will be drawn to the flowers on the watermelon plant. That night, cover the watermelon. The next morning, remove the cage from the cucumbers, thus ensuring that the pollinators are drawn to them. Do this as long as new flowers continue to bloom.

If you have a large crop, build separate housing for your different varieties of plants.

One drawback to caging is that you may not get as large a harvest as you would if the plants weren't caged. One way around this problem is to figure out which insects prefer to pollinate the plant in question and put them inside the cage. This method is often used in high tunnels or greenhouses.

Always be sure the cages are properly ventilated so the insects can get plenty of fresh air, or else they will perish.

Bagging

Bagging is a popular method used to maintain the purity of the cross when you use hand pollination. This method also works well for plants that self-pollinate. It's a simple technique that requires covering the female flower with a breathable material of some sort, such as pantyhose, muslin, or other lightweight cloth. Any fabric that allows light and water to penetrate but keeps insects out works well. Gently tie the bottom of the bag to the plant's stem to secure it. A twist-tie works quite well; just be sure to get it snug enough to keep out insects, yet loose enough that you don't damage the stem.

Bagging plants is a great way to stop cross-pollination from occurring and is also a way to deter pests.

Here the pantyhose is halfway over the flower.

Here you see it completely covering the flower, neatly tied at the stem.

This method may not work well for wind-pollinated plants such as corn, chard, beets, or spinach, although it's possible for the grains of pollen to be small enough to find a way inside the bag.

THE BAD SEED

Don't use plastic bags. When the sun hits a plastic bag, an intense heat can build up inside it. This can cause the flower to die before the seeds begin to form.

Bagging also prevents the seeds from scattering once the seedpods begin to split open.

The Least You Need to Know

- You can create your own unique edible and ornamental plants through hand pollination.
- The first cross you make may not give the results you want. Try, try again until you get what you are after.
- Maintaining seed purity is essential to keep some heirloom varieties in existence and avoid GMO contamination.
- A plant's DNA changes while it's growing, which is why the resulting seeds are better suited to your local environment.

Creating a
Gardening Journal

In This Chapter

- Keeping accurate records
- Labeling and mapping your garden
- Choosing between digital documentation and a paper notebook

This chapter shows you how to create your very own gardening journal. A gardening journal is a comprehensive record of every aspect of your garden. In it you list all the plants you're growing in your garden so that, at any given time, you know exactly what's there and what stage it's at. You can add a map showing the exact location of all your plants. And you can include a variety of notes on your plants, including when you crossed plants, when you collected seeds, and much more.

On the Record

Properly recording the data of your seed-saving efforts, including where the original seeds or plants came from, creates a valuable historical record. In addition to recording the basic data, such as crosses, dates the crosses were made, and when the seed was saved, a gardening journal gives you the chance to document the stories that go with the seeds.

Document the following information about each plant or seed:

- Planting date
- Complete botanical name
- Information about the cross, if you've made one

- Germination data for seeds, including number of days to germination

- Planting location

- Other pertinent information, such as performance, fragrance, and taste

Keep a paper trail of each individual plant's performance, especially those from which you intend to save seeds. Label identical plants as a, b, c, and so on so you can tell them apart, and remember to include this data on a paper record as well as on the plant tag.

To have a complete record of your garden, consider including the following information:

- Pest problems or resistance

- Disease problems or resistance

- Growth rate

- Amount of flowers, fruits, or vegetables produced

- Signs of differences between exact varieties

- Anything that you particularly like about the plant

- Length of time from pollination to mature seed

- Length of time for harvest of flowers, fruits, or vegetables

As you gain experience charting your plants' individual performances, you will want to add even more information, such as the way a plant smells or the way the fruits or vegetables look or taste. In hot climates, some full-sun plants actually perform better in partial shade; similarly, you may find that, in cool climates, a shade plant tolerates some sun. These are all important characteristics to make note of.

SPROUTING WISDOM

Document everything you notice about the plant: the seeds, the critters that visit the plant, and even your personal thoughts when you're in the garden. Number each plant in your garden journal, using it as a cross-reference to numbers on your plant tags.

Document as much data as possible on all your seeds, but pay particular attention to those considered to be family heirlooms. Without your notations, no one outside your immediate family will likely know the stories behind the seeds, let alone the names of the seeds or when they were first created. You can note such data in your gardening journal, in your online data, or in a small memo tucked into the seed container.

The Key to Remembering

Labeling and documenting data is the key to knowing what's what. Plants of the same genus look similar enough to one another that you may be able to make a good guess, but seeds vary considerably. Some seeds that are not even remotely connected look alike.

When labeling plant tags, always use a pencil or a botanical pen or marker. Permanent markers tend to fade over time. Check your tags regularly as you walk through your garden. Exposure to weather elements may cause the markers to heave, sink into the ground, or fade with age, even if you've used the proper marking supplies—and critters could carry them off.

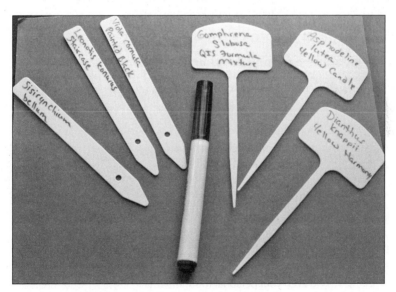

Include the complete botanical name on the plant marker. Use a pencil or
a botanical pen or marker.

Place labels on both the inside and outside of seed-saving containers, flowerpots, and winter-sowing containers. That way, if one tag is lost or damaged, you still have another. And if you have documented the data in a journal, you can cross-reference.

By properly documenting all this information, you will learn from your mistakes and you'll be able to reproduce successful results if unexpected damage occurs to your seed stash.

Create a new record for every new plant or seed that you save.

Organize your records by year and by plant type so that you can more easily find the data you need when you need it.

Plant Pedigrees

Keeping track of the names of the parent plants, including whether they were cross-pollinated, is essential to record keeping. After all, if you don't know who the parents are, you won't know what to expect from the offspring—or even how to label them. This data may not seem important if you're just making crosses for yourself, but if you come up with a really cool plant that you want to reproduce, you need to know its background. Plus, you may want to share or sell seeds someday, and then you'll most decidedly need this data.

When you buy plants or seeds from a commercial company, the data is usually on the plant tag or seed packet. Document this information immediately in your gardening journal. If you're using a paper diary, tape in the tag; you can also create a special binder to hold all your plant tags and seed envelopes.

KNOW THY SEED

Check out the binder section of your local office supply store. You'll find all kinds of notebooks and containers that offer creative ways of keeping your information organized and handy.

Don't forget to document where you're going to plant the parent plants on the map you're creating of your landscape. That will make it even easier to figure out what the parent plants are, in case you forget.

Historical Importance

Every seed and plant has a story. Proper labeling goes a long way toward preserving this story for generations to come. It helps preserve our seed diversity, but most of all, it provides unique genes that can be used to create unique new plants.

KNOW THY SEED

Use a combination of computer records and old-fashioned paper records. Then if something happens to one set of records, you have a backup.

DIY Gardening Journal

Creating a gardening journal is easier than you might think. A gardening journal simply consists of a combination of dates, plant data, photographs, plant tags, and seed envelopes. It can also contain drawings, maps, leaf or flower pressings, or any other pertinent data that you want to document, including personal feelings about your garden.

A leather-bound garden journal makes a beautiful keepsake that will protect your data for years to come. Smartphones are ideal for carrying in the garden to take photos, which enhance the data in your seed saver's diary.

The more data you add to your gardening journal, the more useful it will be in later years. You can create a gardening journal on scraps of paper, in a spiral notebook or three-ring binder, online, on your smartphone, or even in a fancy garden notebook. It doesn't matter how you document the data or how fancy or plain your gardening journal is; what's important is that it's legible and well organized, and includes as much data as possible about every seed you save and every plant you sow.

Parents' Digs

Drawing a map of your garden makes it easier to chart the location of every plant there. Photographs can be a big help, too. A combination of maps and photos is ideal: it's like having a road map and a guidebook. Each serves a different but vital function.

When you have these tools, you don't have to worry when a plant tag gets lost—and they will get lost. During winter, when the ground temperature changes, especially in cold climates, plant tags are often heaved out of the ground. Small animals can scratch about in a garden and dig them up. Sometimes tags just get old and fade or break. Even the expensive metal tags with long stakes or twist ties can get damaged or lost. So although plant tags are great to have, don't rely on them as the sole method of identification for your parent plants.

Dating Mating

Knowing the date cross-pollination took place helps you determine when the seed will be ready to collect, especially when you begin to know how long it takes for the seed of each plant that you grow to mature. Since no hard-and-fast rules apply, when you first begin cross-pollinating, all you can do is to monitor the plant carefully. The seedpod—and often the plant's stem—will begin to turn brown when seed-setting time is near. This is your first indication that it's almost time to collect seeds. Document the dates that you collect seeds.

THE BAD SEED

Don't forget to document data about seeds that abort or fail to germinate. This data is just as important as information about the successful ones.

Keeping track of this information will simplify the seed-collecting process in years to come. You will have a good sense of when the particular cultivar you're working with is going to bloom. You'll know the best time to make a cross, which is especially useful if you're working with a rare plant or one that has a history of seed abortion. You'll know when to cover seed and when to collect the seed, resulting in a higher seed harvest.

Growth Rate

Tracking the growth rates of plants is one of the most important pieces of information you can record. The plants that take off right after the seeds germinate are the most vigorous of the lot; documenting the growth rate helps you make better decisions for seed saving. The faster the plants put out healthy growth, the faster they will mature and begin to produce. In cold climates with short growing seasons, this trait is enormously significant. And in warmer climates with longer growing seasons, such performance could mean a longer harvest period.

Continue to keep track of the growth rate as the plants reach maturity. Some plants will not continue to shoot up in height or put out new side shoots, but will continue to flower and fruit. The ideal plant is stout enough to support the weight of its flowers and fruits without needing staking and is able to produce right up until the first fall frost. You're looking for abundance, especially if you're growing fruits and vegetables.

Be sure to document any and all problems, even if you're able to correct them—and if you did correct the problem, don't forget to document how you did so. Plants prone to disease or pest infestations will pass on this trait through their seeds. You want a healthy plant that can fend off pests and diseases on its own without intervention from you.

Tracking the Harvest

Knowing when to expect the seeds to ripen makes seed harvesting easier. It also gives you the opportunity to prepare. For instance, if you expect heavy storms or rain and your records indicate that the seeds are close to being ready to harvest, you can protect the seeds by covering them.

Another advantage of keeping track of this data is that you know how many seeds to expect. Usually plants set enough seeds for the average home gardener. However, if you're trading or selling, or if you need a specific amount of seed for a certain crop, knowing how many seeds to expect is helpful.

When Seeds Are Sown

Recording the date you sow your seeds helps chart germination times. Every seed has a specific anticipated germination time (see Chapter 6). However, the seeds you grow might germinate faster or slower than the industry standard, especially if you hand-pollinated the parent plants. Such information is essential when it comes to starting seeds in the spring. Seeds started too early are often harder to keep alive indoors and may resent transplanting, especially if they've already begun to flower or fruit. Seeds that take a longer time to germinate need more time to grow before they're ready to transplant into the garden, so they will not flower or fruit as quickly. Knowing all this gives you more control over your garden and its produce.

When you compare the data you've documented from year to year, you will begin to see a pattern of two dates—an early germination date and a late germination date. Combine these two dates to calculate the average time of germination. You can rely on this time for the seeds you save out of your garden.

Your Special Notes

In addition to objective data, recording your personal reasons for choosing certain plants—such as flower colors or fragrance, fruit flavors, and so on—is helpful. Marking down your expectations gives you grounds for comparison when the final results come in. Then you'll know whether you want to plant that seed again or try another.

In years to come, you or someone who reads your gardening journal will find these special notes fascinating. Does a certain plant attract bees? Is it a butterfly magnet, even though you can't find any firm data that proves it should be? Maybe it has an alluring scent after dark. All this data matters. Think of your gardening journal as a book that covers every aspect of your garden!

Drawings

Maps are an ideal way to chart the location of plants in your garden. They are also excellent tools for planning, enabling you to make decisions about companion planting, for example, or size of crop. You can augment your garden map with drawings of the plants, their flowers, or their seedpods.

Drawings add character to the pages of your book. The more detail they show, the better. If you can't draw, don't worry. Maybe you can ask a friend who's a good artist to help, or you can cut out pictures from a seed catalog or simply take photographs of the plants at each stage.

> **THE BAD SEED**
>
> Make copies of your maps and drawings and keep them in a separate and safe file. That way, if you lose your journal or it gets damaged, you'll have a backup copy.

Graph paper is particularly helpful when mapping out your garden. It gives you perspective on size and shape, since you can scale it (for example, one square equals 1 square foot).

If you want your map to be larger than the page in your seed saver's diary, make it a fold-out map.

Hardcopy vs. the Computer

Documenting data on paper is often easier than documenting it on a computer, since you can quickly scribble notes in the sidebars of your gardening journal while you're in the garden. However, there are good reasons for using both hardcopy and a computer to record your data. Using a spreadsheet like Excel, for example, helps you organize and reorganize your data. Database programs like Access work even better.

Advantages of a Paper Notebook

A notebook is usually easier to use in the garden. If you set aside a page per plant, you can quickly flip through and locate just what you want. However, unless you're using a ring binder with loose sheets of paper, you can't easily alphabetize your documentation.

On the downside, working in the garden with any paper product has its risks: you could trip and drop your notebook onto wet earth, or you could be caught in a sudden downpour and your pages could be damaged beyond repair.

Back It Up

Be sure to back up the data you have in your computer: keep a second copy on a thumb drive or disk. If you subscribe to one of the dozens of online backup services available, so much the better. Online records are easy to share, easy to organize, and easy to access from anyplace in the world. Many sites, like Google Docs (www.docs.google.com), will store your data for free, but you must know how large the files are. Other sites may charge a small monthly or yearly fee to store the data.

While this may seem like an unnecessary expense and a lot of extra work, if your paper notebook is damaged or your personal computer crashes, you will be glad you did it.

SPROUTING WISDOM

If you move and have to leave your garden behind, your gardening journal and maps make great gifts for the new homeowners. They can use the journal to find out what the plants on the property are, thus enabling them to continue propagating what you started.

The Least You Need to Know

- Accurate record keeping is the single most important part of a seed saver's diary.
- Document botanical names, which plants were cross-pollinated, and all pertinent dates.
- Use drawings, maps, photos, and seed or plant tags to enhance your seed savers' diary.
- Use a notebook for quick record keeping, but back up your data online.

Sharing Your Knowledge

In This Chapter

- Sharing your seed-saving knowledge
- Getting others involved in seed saving
- Selling and sharing excess seeds

Knowing the proper way to collect, process, dry, and store seeds is only half the battle. The second half is educating others. Think of this scenario: what if something happened to your stash of seeds and all you had to rely on for survival were the other people in your community? How sad would it be if the seeds they saved were not viable because you chose not to share your knowledge? So pass it on—for your sake, for the community's sake, and for the sake of humankind!

Seed saving is more than a hobby or an art: for many, it's a way to survive. It's the best way to keep rare, endangered, and open-pollinated or heirloom seeds in circulation so that future generations can enjoy them. Take advantage of every opportunity you have to share your knowledge by teaching others how to save seed. It's an activity suitable for all ages, male and female; it doesn't matter what color you are, what religion you are, or whether you're differently abled. Gardening and saving seed is for everyone!

Get others involved in the process: teach them to share or even sell their excess seeds and also teach how to create a seed-storage facility. In fact, if you get enough people involved, a community seed-storage facility might not be out of the question at all.

Passing It On

Teaching others how to save seed preserves our garden heritage. It gives folks the opportunity to grow something that they might otherwise not be able to. That's because, if no one saves seeds, some plants could become extinct.

Start simply. You don't want to overwhelm people who are new to seed saving with too much information and too many details. Ask first if they have a favorite plant they would like to grow every year. If so, teach them how to save the seeds from just that one plant. If they ask questions, answer them. When they get the hang of saving seeds, their quest for knowledge will likely continue to grow. This leads to more seeds being saved.

Offering a Class

Teaching seed-saving or seed-starting classes is a great way to interact with others who are interested in learning the art of seed saving or starting. Often people who attend such classes are new gardeners who want to learn as much as they can.

Teaching classes is a good way to earn a little extra income, too. If you prefer not to charge a fee, consider selling some of the seeds you saved from your garden to students.

Local libraries, the YWCA or YMCA, college extension courses, community centers, churches, and other local venues often seek speakers. Usually these places do not have a large budget, so volunteers are always welcome. Keep in mind that attendance can be all over the map: sometimes lots of people will show up, and sometimes no one will attend. To avoid disappointment and keep from wasting your time, ask that people sign up before the event.

SPROUTING WISDOM

The best classes are often hands-on. Consider teaching a class in your own garden.

Classes are a great way to get people involved. Generally, the place you're scheduled to speak will advertise the event, and you'll get to be a local hero by teaching others. You may meet people with similar passions and make new gardening friends. Don't think of offering a class as "teaching": think of it as a great way to share your knowledge and love of gardening with others.

Visual aids enhance any teaching experience, so be sure to take along some seeds you've saved for show and tell. Show off your gardener's journal, too, as well as photographs and whatever you have to illustrate the joys, beauty, and value of gardening and saving seeds.

Involving the Community

Involve the entire community in your seed-saving endeavors by asking for local volunteers to help you collect seed. Set up a booth at local events so you can sell seeds and share your knowledge with others. See if you can organize a communal garden in your neighborhood (what some call a pea patch) so that people who don't have land can grow a garden. The more people you get involved, the more locally grown seeds will be saved. This increases the local seed diversity and takes us back to the days of our forefathers, when almost everyone in a community saved and shared their seeds with one another.

Starting with Kids

A great place to start sharing your knowledge is with children. Whether they're your own children or grandchildren or other kids in your community, youngsters are almost always eager to learn.

Often schools or youth organizations look to members of the community to teach small groups of children about the natural environment. Offer to teach kids how to start seeds.

Sharing seeds with youth groups or even your local elementary school is another great way to get kids involved in gardening. Kids often find the seed-starting process fascinating. Teaching them how to germinate seeds and nurture the resulting plants benefits not only the child, but also the community and the environment.

THE BAD SEED

Working with large groups of young children can be chaotic. Depending on the size of the group, be sure you have at least one other adult to help. Older children are often effective helpers with younger ones.

Sharing Your Knowledge with the Elderly

Seniors are another great population with whom to share your knowledge. Not only can they learn from you, but you might just learn something from them. Your local senior center is an excellent place to offer a program in seed saving. Select seeds that are suitable for container culture, since many elderly people have mobility issues. Some of them may not be aware they can grow a garden in a container on their balcony or deck, or even in window boxes.

Talk to seniors about seed saving. Ask if they had a favorite plant that they used to save seeds from in their younger days. Who knows? Maybe they still grow a garden or have a stash of family heirloom seeds they don't know what to do with. You can give them the opportunity to pass on their precious treasures so they're grown for generations to come.

Dealing with a Surplus of Seeds

Eventually, it's going to happen. You're going to gather more seeds than you could ever use in a lifetime. You need to decide what to do with them. Instead of tossing them, here are some options:

- Share them with others
- Trade them for seeds you want
- Sell them

As long as the seeds are clean, are free of pests or diseases, and are properly labeled, you can even ship them. But before you attempt to do this, check out the laws in both the state you live in and the place they're being sent. You can find the rules in your state by going to the National Plant Board website and downloading the laws for your state at www.nationalplantboard.org/laws/.

When you begin saving seed, especially if you want to sell the seed you save, the benefits of specialization come into play. You may grow 10 different types of vegetables, flowers, or fruits, but do you really know everything there is to know about them? If you specialize in several varieties of a particular *genus*, suddenly you're an expert in the eyes of others.

DEFINITION

A **genus** is a biological classification of a group having common characteristics.

For example, you can choose from many varieties and colors of corn. Instead of growing a single variety, try growing several. Select different-colored corn—black, green, red, white, or yellow—so your customers have a choice. Try your hand at cross-pollinating new varieties as well. For instance, black corn is pretty, but not as sweet as some would like it to be. You could try creating a black-colored sweet corn or a multicolored sweet corn. The opportunities are endless; and once you create a new variety, you get to name it!

Selling Seeds

Selling seeds is a great way to make a little extra money on the side. You're already saving seeds for your own use anyway, and it takes little extra effort to collect, process, dry, store, and label the extra seeds your plants produce.

Put the seeds in small envelopes and include germination time, growing time, spacing, and amount of sun and shade with the seeds. If you've been keeping a gardening journal (see Chapter 14), you can transfer the information from the seed packets to the journal.

To promote ongoing business, be sure to include your contact information on the envelope, too. If you're the creative type, you might want to make your packet attractive using rubber stamps, color printers, or stickers.

Most people will want to know how many seeds they get for the price. Larger seeds, such as sunflowers or pumpkins, are easy to count. Instead of counting small seeds as you place them in the packet, count how many are in a level teaspoon, half-teaspoon, or tablespoon. Then use the measuring spoon to add the seeds to the envelope.

Online

Selling seeds online opens up the whole world to you. Sites such as Local Harvest (www.localharvest.org) that already have a customer base are ideal for starting. You can build your own website as well, but you still need a way to direct traffic to it, and sites like Local Harvest can include a link to your website.

THE BAD SEED

Know the laws on shipping the types of seeds you're selling. You may not be able to sell or ship seeds to certain places. If you don't know this information until after customers buy seeds from you, you're going to have some mighty upset customers on your hands. Seeds, or any produce, that's improperly shipped will be confiscated en route to their destination.

Locally

Selling seeds locally has many advantages. The biggest is that you can advertise that the seeds were locally grown and harvested and so are adapted to the local conditions. This means the plants grown from those seeds are more resistant to pests and diseases in your area, as well as better able to cope with local environmental conditions. These are terrific selling points!

> **KNOW THEY SEED**
>
> Farmers markets and agricultural fairs are good venues for selling local seeds. Check your community's events calendar and book a space well in advance.

Another advantage to selling seeds locally is that you get to know your customers. You can interact with them one on one, be there to answer their questions, and help them learn how to save their own seeds. This may seem like it would hurt your business, but think of it this way: if you run out of seed or decide to take your business global, you'll know where to obtain more seeds.

Sharing Seeds

Gardeners are generous people. They love sharing their favorite plants with their neighbors, friends, and family. Most gardeners share their plants with others by either dividing a plant or sharing seeds.

Local parks, botanical gardens, and other public places are often happy to receive seed donations. In fact, some of these places might even offer you a small garden you can tend. This gives you another opportunity to share your knowledge with others.

Look for local nonprofit groups in your area. Think about correctional facilities, too: gardening is excellent therapeutic work for prisoners. Often such groups grow vegetables and donate them to local soup kitchens. This gives you the opportunity to share your extra vegetable seeds and help others without doing all the work of growing the vegetables yourself.

Swapping Seeds

Seed swaps are a great place to take some of your extra seeds. You can trade them for seeds that other gardeners have saved. Package thoroughly dried seeds and label them. Be sure to include your contact information in case the recipient has questions.

Online opportunities abound. Here are just a few:

- www.seedswaps.com/

- www.garden.org/seedswap/

- www.heirloomseedswap.com/

- www.almanac.com/forums/seed-swap

For exchanges in your community, check your local events calendar or call the agricultural department at your local college.

KNOW THY SEED

When you do a trade, look carefully at the seeds you select to make sure they are, indeed, seeds. Often new gardeners will collect plant material that they think are seeds but are not. Also make sure the seeds you're receiving have been properly dried, clean, and labeled, and aren't moldy.

Becoming Self-Sufficient

Sharing your knowledge about seed saving and starting with others is a great way to teach self-sufficiency. The more you know about the subject, the more capable you'll be of mastering it—and the less you'll have to rely on seeds and plants being shipped in from large nurseries or warehouses thousands of miles away or purchasing them locally for more money than you care to spend.

With prices skyrocketing, jobs becoming scarce, and the local food movement at a peak, there has never been a better time to learn the old ways. Saving seeds and growing your own garden is the best place to start.

The Least You Need to Know

- Share your seed saving and starting knowledge any time you have the opportunity to do so.
- Pass on your surplus seeds by sharing, selling, or donating them.
- Saving and storing seeds is a wonderful way to start down the path toward self-sufficiency.

Seed Directories

The following directories provide information on germinating and sowing a wide variety of flowers, fruits, herbs, and vegetables, as well as the appropriate way to harvest the mature seeds from these plants.

The Herb, Spice, Grain, and Fruit Seed Directory

This directory provides seed-harvesting tips, germination tips, and sowing information for some of the most popular garden produce.

All plants are listed by their botanical names. If you need this same kind of information for a vegetable not listed, first discover its botanical name. For example, if you want to plant oregano, a quick online search will ascertain its botanical name: *Origanum vulgare*. Keep in mind that oregano is sometimes called wild marjoram, which must not be confused with sweet marjoram *(Origanum majorana)*; because you have the botanical name, you can research with assurance that you are getting information on the correct plant.

Herbs and Spices

Herbs and spices are a great way to begin sowing and saving seed. They are practical and easy to grow.

Allium schoenoprasum (Chive)

Seed harvesting Cover seed heads with pantyhose when they are still green, to avoid losing any seeds. Cut off the flower heads as soon as they turn completely brown, hold them over a container, remove the pantyhose, and release the black seeds.

Germinating and sowing Seeds require constant moisture and darkness to germinate, regardless of the sowing method you use. Direct-sow seeds ½-inch deep.

Average germination time 14 to 21 days.

Anethum graveolens (Dill)

Seed harvesting   Allow the seed heads to dry on the plant. Either cover the seed heads with pantyhose before they are fully dry or expect to lose some seeds. When the seed heads are light brown, cut off the seed heads, hold them over a container, remove the pantyhose, and collect the seeds. Remove seeds that remain on the seed head by hand.

Germinating and sowing   As soon as the soil is workable in the spring, direct-sow the seed on the soil surface and press it lightly into the soil. Choose an area where it's okay for the plant to self-seed from year to year as soon as the soil is workable in the spring. Water the seeds well and keep the area moist until the first seedlings begin to appear. Sow a fresh supply of seed every three weeks all summer long to maintain a continuous supply.

Average germination time   21 to 25 days.

Angelica archangelica (Angelica)

Seed harvesting   Seeds typically don't form until either the second or third year. Allow the flower stalk to form, cover the seed head with pantyhose, and allow the seedpods to mature on the plant. As soon as the seeds and about $\frac{1}{8}$ inch of the stem are brown, cut the flower stalk, hold it over a container, remove the pantyhose, and release the seeds into the container.

Germinating and sowing   Seeds require light to germinate, so don't cover them with paper towels, soil, or other seed-sowing medium. Angelica seeds have a very short viability, so it's best to sow the seeds on the soil's surface as soon as you collect them from the plant. If this isn't possible, store the dried seeds in the refrigerator until you're ready to germinate them the following spring.

Average germination time   20 to 60 days.

Anthriscus cerefolium (Chervil)

Seed harvesting   Chervil bolts and produces a seed stalk as soon as the weather begins to warm. Allow the seed heads to form and the seeds to dry on the plant before collecting the seeds.

Germinating and sowing   Chervil seed requires light and constant moisture to germinate. Stored seeds have a reduced germination rate, so direct-sow fresh seed in the fall as soon as it ripens or plant the seeds in peat pots, since chervil doesn't transplant well. To extend the harvest, sow seed every two weeks through mid-July. Begin sowing seed again in mid-August through the end of fall. Some seeds will germinate and produce seeds that you can harvest. Seeds that don't germinate in the fall will overwinter on the ground and grow in spring.

Average germination time   14 days.

Carum carvi (Caraway)

Seed harvesting   As soon as the seed stalks turn brown, cut the stalks, bundle them, and place the seed heads in brown paper bags. Hang the bags in a cool, dark place with good air circulation. When the seeds are fully dry, they will fall into the bottom of the paper bag.

Germinating and sowing   Direct-sow seeds ½ inch deep in spring or fall. Seeds require constant moisture to germinate.

Average germination time   14 days or longer depending on how fresh the seed is.

Coriandrum sativam (Cilantro/Coriander)

Seed harvesting   Harvest the seed heads as soon as they turn brown and before they shatter. Cover the seed heads with pantyhose, to avoid losing any seeds.

Germinating and sowing   Seeds need darkness and temperatures between 55°F and 65°F to germinate. Direct-sow seeds ½ inch deep or start them indoors in peat pots. Cilantro doesn't transplant well, so proper seed spacing is essential.

Average germination time   10 days.

Foeniculum vulgare (Fennel)

Seed harvesting   Cover immature seed heads with pantyhose. When the seed heads turn from a greenish-brown to brown, they are ready to harvest. The seeds have a tendency to fall off as soon as they are ripe.

Germinating and sowing   Seeds require darkness and constant moisture to germinate. Direct-sow seeds ⅛ inch deep in spring or fall; fennel doesn't transplant well.

Average germination time   10 to 14 days.

Levisticum officinale (Lovage)

Seed harvesting Allow the seed heads to mature on the plant. Harvest the seeds as soon as they turn brown.

Germinating and sowing Direct-sow fresh seed ¼ inch deep in late summer or fall where the plant will grow. Fresh seeds germinate best.

Average germination time 10 to 20 days.

Matricaria recutita (Chamomile)

Seed harvesting Remove the dried seed heads from the plants as soon as they turn completely brown.

Germinating and sowing Chamomile requires stratification by either freezing or refrigerating the seeds for four weeks prior to sowing (see Chapter 7). Sow seeds directly on the surface (they require light for germination) in either fall or spring, depending on the variety. *Chamaemelum nobile* (Roman chamomile) performs best when direct-sown in spring. *Matricaria recutita* (German chamomile) performs best when direct-sown in the fall.

Average germination time 7 to 30 days.

Ocimum (Basil)

Seed harvesting Cover the faded flower spikes with pantyhose. The seeds form inside the faded flowers. Collect seed as soon as the seed heads turn brown.

Germinating and sowing Basil seeds need light to germinate, so direct-sow seeds on the soil surface when soil temperature reaches 50°F.

Average germination time 5 to 42 days.

Petroselinum (Parsley)

Seed harvesting Cover seed heads with pantyhose before they mature. When the seeds turn brown, cut the flower stems, place them over a container, remove the pantyhose, and run your hands across the seed heads. The seeds will fall into the container.

Germinating and sowing Seeds require stratification in either a freezer or refrigerator (see Chapter 7) for best results. Seeds require darkness to germinate. Soak older seeds in warm water for 24 hours to encourage germination. Direct-sow fresh seed ¼ inch deep in August where you want the plants to grow the following spring.

Average germination time   21 to 42 days.

Salvia officinalis (Sage)

Seed harvesting   Cover the faded flower heads with pantyhose, since the seeds easily fall out when they are ripe. When the flower spikes dry up, collect the seeds.

Germinating and sowing   Some varieties of Salvia require pre-treatment with GA-3 (see Chapter 6). Seeds need light to germinate, so direct-sow fresh seeds on the surface in the fall where the plants will grow the following spring.

Average germination time   4 to 21 days.

Satureja (Savory)

Seed harvesting   Collect the seeds from the seed heads as soon as they begin to turn brown.

Germinating and sowing   Savory seeds need light to germinate, so direct-sow fresh seeds on the soil surface in the fall. Viability decreases dramatically for seeds more than a year old.

Average germination time   10 to 21 days.

Grains

Grains are more of a specialty crop, although many home gardeners grow them over the winter to enrich their soil. Grains also have ornamental value, and some heirloom varieties are ideal for using in dried flower bouquets.

Amaranthus (Amaranth)

Seed harvesting   Cover the seed heads with pantyhose to prevent loss, since the seed heads don't change color and the seeds fall out when mature.

Germinating and sowing   Plant seeds on the soil surface when the soil temperature is between 65°F and 75°F.

Average germination time   10 to 15 days.

Avena sativa (Oats)

Seed harvesting   Harvest seeds a week after the oat plants have dried by removing the seed heads. Each husk contains one seed. Remove the husk by hand and extract the seed.

Germinating and sowing   Broadcast the oat seeds on top of the soil in early spring or fall, depending on the variety you're growing, and then press them into the soil. Water well.

Average germination time   10 to 90 days.

Triticum aestivum (Wheat)

Seed harvesting   Bend the seed head to one side; if most of the seeds fall out, collect the seeds. Wheat that is allowed to dry in the field will often drop some of its seeds, but not all of them.

Germinating and sowing   Broadcast the wheat seeds on top of the soil. Plant winter wheat 6 to 8 weeks before the soil in your area freezes. Plant spring wheat as soon as the ground can be worked, keeping the seeds moist until they germinate.

Average germination time   2 to 4 days.

Fruits

Although fruits typically don't come true from seed, it's fun to experiment and s ee what you end up with. Sometimes the fruit is really good, and this is how new varieties are developed. If you don't like the fruit, you can simply cull the plant.. To get fruit to grow true, you need to graft it or divide it, topics that are beyond the scope of this book.

Annona muricata (Soursop)

Seed harvesting   Remove seed from the ripe fruit. Wash off all pulp. Dry and plant or store for up to 3 months.

Germinating and sowing   Germinate the seeds in paper towels (see Chapter 6). After the seeds are germinated, carefully remove them from the paper towel, making sure not to break the root. Make a hole in the soil deep enough to accommodate the root, place the seed in the hole, and sprinkle enough vermiculite on top of the seed head to completely cover it.

Average germination time Fresh seeds germinate within 2 to 3 weeks. Older seeds have decreased germination rates.

Citrus (Orange, Lemon, Lime, and so on)

Seed harvesting Remove the seeds from the ripe fruit, wash them under running water, and allow them to dry.

Germinating and sowing Fresh seed germinates best. Use the paper towel germination method (see Chapter 6). After the seed germinates, carefully remove it from the paper towel, making sure not to break the root. Make a hole in the soil deep enough to accommodate the root, place the seed in the hole, and sprinkle enough vermiculite on top of the seed head to completely cover it.

Average germination time 2 weeks to 6 months.

Hylocereus spp. (Dragon Fruit)

Seed harvesting Remove the seeds from the fresh fruit. Rinse them under cold running water, making sure to remove all the flesh. Lay the seeds out to dry.

Germinating and sowing Use the paper towel germination method (see Chapter 6), or plant the seeds on top of the soil and lightly cover them with vermiculite and keep the seeds moist. Seeds that are planted too deep will not germinate.

Average germination time 14 to 28 days.

Malus (Apple)

Seed harvesting Remove the apple seeds from the ripe fruit. Rinse under water and lay out to dry.

Germinating and sowing Seeds require a 3-month stratification period in either the refrigerator or freezer (see Chapter 7). Germinate seeds using the paper towel germination method (see Chapter 6). Once the seed germinates, carefully remove it from the paper towel, making sure not to break the root. Make a hole in the soil deep enough to accommodate the root, place the seed in the hole, and sprinkle enough vermiculite on top of the seed head to completely cover it.

Average germination time 2 weeks.

Musa (Banana)

Seed harvesting   Not all bananas have seeds, but you can save the ones from the bananas that do have seeds. Remove the banana seeds from the fruit, rinse them with water, and lay them out to dry.

Germinating and sowing   Nick and then soak the seeds in hot water until they swell. Use the paper towel germination method (see Chapter 6). Keep banana seeds moist. Once the seed germinates, carefully remove it from the paper towel, making sure not to break the root. Make a hole in the soil deep enough to accommodate the root, place the seed in the hole, and sprinkle enough vermiculite on top of the seed head to completely cover it.

Average germination time   1 to 6 months.

Prunus persica (Peach)

Seed harvesting   The peach seed is inside the pit of the fruit. Wash all the fruit remains off the pit and allow it to dry for several days. Crack open the pit using a nutcracker and remove the seeds. Place the seeds in a sealed container inside the refrigerator.

Germinating and sowing   Seeds require a 3-month stratification period in either the refrigerator or freezer (see Chapter 7). Germinate seeds using the paper towel germination method (see Chapter 6). After the seed germinates, carefully remove it from the paper towel, making sure not to break the root. Make a hole in the soil deep enough to accommodate the root, place the seed in the hole, and sprinkle enough vermiculite on top of the seed head to completely cover it.

Average germination time   2 weeks.

The Vegetable Seed Directory

This directory provides seed-harvesting tips, germination tips, and sowing information for the most popular garden vegetables.

Vegetables are listed by their botanical names. If you need this same kind of information for a vegetable not listed, you first need to find its botanical name. For example, if you want to plant endive, a quick online search will ascertain its botanical name: *Cichorium endivia*. Some people confuse endive with chicory (*Cichorium intybus*), but since you have the botanical name, you can research with assurance that you are getting information on the correct plant.

Allium (Onion)

Seed harvesting   The stalks that bear the flowers are prone to breakage even before the seeds are ready to harvest. When the flower heads show signs of black seeds, place a container under the flower heads to catch any seeds, and cut off the flower heads. Allow the seed balls to dry for 2 weeks, and then rub them until they release the remaining seeds.

Germinating and sowing   Pre-chill the seeds for at least 30 days prior to sowing. Direct-sow seed in the fall ¼ inch deep in heavy soils; sow seeds ½ inch deep in light, sandy soils. Don't cover the seeds until they germinate because they need light to germinate.

Average germination time   14 to 365 days.

Beta vulgaris (Beet)

Seed harvesting   Beets don't set seed until the second season they are grown, so in order to save the seeds, you need to keep the plant alive over the winter. Harvest the beets before the first killing frost in the fall by digging them out of the ground. Cut off the leafy tops, leaving an inch of the stem attached to the root. Store the beets in sand in a root cellar over the winter. Replant them outdoors in the garden the following spring. Remove the seed stalks as soon as the seed at the base of the beet plant is ripe. Winter-sown beet seed often sends up a seed stalk in the spring instead of growing a plant. *Note:* Swiss chard and beets naturally cross-pollinate, so use a caging technique if you are growing both plants and plan to save seeds from both.

Germinating and sowing   Soak seeds for 24 hours before sowing, to hasten germination. Plant seeds ½ inch deep in early spring as soon as the soil can be worked. Tamp the soil down on top of and around the seeds to ensure good contact with the soil.

Average germination time   7 to 14 days.

Beta vulgaris ssp. cicla (Swiss Chard)

Seed harvesting   Swiss chard plants that overwinter in the garden or in a cold frame or tunnel house will set seed the following spring. Mulch around the base of the plants that you want to save seed from in late fall and leave them in the ground. The following spring, new growth will emerge along with a seed stalk. The seed will ripen that summer. Collect the seed after the seed stalk turns brown. *Note:* Swiss chard and beets naturally cross-pollinate, so use a caging technique if you are growing both plants and wish to save seeds from both.

Germinating and sowing   Direct-sow seeds in early spring ½ inch deep.

Average germination time   7 to 14 days.

Brassica oleracea botrytis (Cauliflower)

Seed harvesting   Allow the seedpods that form from yellow flowers to dry on the plant. When they turn brown, remove them. If frost threatens, cut off the pods and take them indoors to finish curing. Never allow cauliflower seed that isn't thoroughly dry to freeze. *Note:* Cauliflower plants that overwinter in the garden, cold frame, or tunnel house will set seed the following spring.

Germinating and sowing   Direct-sow seeds in early spring ½ inch deep.

Average germination time   20 days.

Brassica oleracea capitata (Cabbage)

Seed harvesting   Cabbage sets seed the second year, in the spring. Allow the seed stalks that form to dry on the plant. When they turn brown, remove them. *Note:* Cabbage plants that overwinter in the garden, cold frame, or tunnel house will set seed the following spring.

Germinating and sowing   Direct-sow seeds in early spring ½ inch deep.

Average germination time   5 to 7 days.

> **SPROUTING WISDOM**
>
> Members of the *Brassica* family (kale, cabbage, cauliflower, Brussels sprouts, broccoli, and so on) naturally cross-pollinate, so use a caging technique if you are growing more than one of these plants and want to save seeds from them all.

Brassica oleracea gemmifera (Brussels sprouts)

Seed harvesting   Brussels sprouts plants that overwinter in the garden or in a cold frame or tunnel house will set seed the following spring. Remove the seedpods after they turn light brown; start at the base of the plant and work your way up. Crush the seedpods to release the seeds.

Germinating and sowing   Direct-sow seeds ¼ inch deep.

Average germination time   5 to 10 days.

Brassica oleracea var. acephala (Kale)

Seed harvesting   Allow the plants to overwinter in the garden; the seed stalks will form the following spring. The seeds form inside long seedpods. When these seedpods are dry, harvest the entire pod, open it, and remove the seeds. *Note:* Kale is self-sterile, so to get kale to set seed that is true, you need to grow at least two plants near one another.

Germinating and sowing   Direct-sow seeds in early spring ½ inch deep.

Average germination time   5 to 10 days.

Brassica oleraceae (Broccoli)

Seed harvesting Start plants that you intend to harvest seeds from indoors early in the season. You need at least two plants because broccoli is self-sterile. Instead of picking the broccoli heads, allow them to mature. Yellow flowers will open and seedpods will form. Allow the pods to dry on the plant, and then harvest the entire plant. Hang the plants upside down in a well-ventilated area. Place a paper bag over the seedpods and allow them to dry for 2 weeks, remove the seedpods, open them, and collect the seeds.

Germinating and sowing Direct-sow seeds in the spring ¼ inch deep.

Average germination time 5 to 10 days.

Brassica rapa (Turnip)

Seed harvesting Turnips planted the previous fall or very early in the same season will send up yellow flower stalks. Allow the seedpods to form and dry on the plant. Remove the plant from the ground, stack them in a cool, dark, dry location and allow the seedpods to cure for another week. Cut off the seedpods, open them, and collect the seeds. *Note:* Turnips will cross with mustard, so keep these plants separated or use a caging technique to make sure they don't cross-pollinate.

Germinating and sowing Direct-sow seeds ½ inch deep.

Average germination time 7 to 14 days.

Capsicum annuum (Pepper)

Seed harvesting You can save seeds from dried peppers or fresh peppers. Wait until the peppers turn red; then cut open the pepper and remove the seeds inside. Spread them out on a plate and allow them to dry.

THE BAD SEED

Capsicum oil can burn soft tissue, so wash your hands well after touching peppers. Better yet, wear gloves when handling the seeds and tissue.

Germinating and sowing Direct-sow seeds ¼ inch deep after the last spring frost.

Average germination time 10 to 14 days.

Citrullus vulgaris (Watermelon)

Seed harvesting   Remove the seeds from a ripe watermelon, place them in a mesh strainer, rinse them well under running water, and lay them out on a seed-drying screen to dry.

Germinating and sowing   Direct-sow seeds 1 inch deep after the last spring frost.

Average germination time   7 to 14 days.

Cucumis melo (Melon)

Seed harvesting   Remove the seeds from a ripe melon. Place the seeds in a mesh strainer. Run cold water over the top of the seeds. Make sure you remove all the flesh from these seeds, and then lay them on a seed-drying screen to dry.

Germinating and sowing   Direct-sow seeds 1 inch deep after the last spring frost.

Average germination time   5 to 10 days.

Cucumis sativus (Cucumber)

Seed harvesting   Allow the fruit to mature on the plant. When it turns yellow and fat, remove it from the plant. Cut the cucumber in half and scoop out the seeds. Use the wet processing method before storing (see Chapter 4)

Germinating and sowing   Direct-sow smaller seeds ½ inch deep and larger seeds 1 inch deep after the last spring frost.

Average germination time   7 to 10 days.

Cucurbita pepo (Squash and Zucchini)

Seed harvesting   Collect seeds from the various varieties of winter squash when you are preparing them for a meal. Other types of squash and zucchini should be left on the vine for approximately 8 weeks after they reach the good-eating stage. Cut the vegetables in half, scoop out the seeds, and use the wet processing method. *Note:* Squash, gourds, and zucchini will cross-pollinate, so keep these plants separated or use a caging technique to make sure they don't cross-pollinate.

Germinating and sowing   Direct-sow seeds 1 inch deep after the last spring frost.

Average germination time   7 to 14 days.

Cucurbita spp. (Pumpkin)

Seed harvesting   Select fully ripened pumpkins with a hard outer shell. Cut open the pumpkin, scoop out the seeds, and use the wet processing method. Discard any seeds that look flat instead of slightly round. *Note:* Pumpkins will cross with zucchini, squash, and gourds, so keep them separated or use a caging method to prevent cross-pollination.

Germinating and sowing   Plant seeds 1 inch deep after the last spring frost.

Average germination time   7 to 10 days.

Daucus carota (Carrot)

Seed harvesting   Carrots cross freely with one another and wild Queen Anne's lace, so use the bagging method (see Chapter 13) to prevent this. Either mulch carrots well in the late fall or dig them up, cut the foliage back to 1 inch, and put them in moist sand in a root cellar for the winter. If you dig them up, you will need to replant them the following spring. The carrots will send up a root stalk in late spring or early summer. Allow the first two sets of flowers to mature, and then begin collecting the seeds. Use pantyhose to capture seeds.

Germinating and sowing   Gardeners who have difficulty germinating direct-sown carrot seeds can cut up small sections of paper towel, germinate one seed per section, and then place the paper towel on top of an empty toilet paper roll filled with soil. Lightly cover the germinated seed with vermiculite, and water well from the bottom. The toilet paper roll will absorb water. When the time comes, plant the entire toilet paper roll in the garden. Plant seeds ¼ inch deep as the ground can be worked in early spring.

Average germination time   12 to 15 days.

Lactuca sativa (Lettuce)

Seed harvesting   Allow the plant to bolt (send up a seed stalk). After the yellow flowers turn into a feathery-looking seed head, remove the seed or allow some of it to self-seed in the garden for a continual harvest.

Germinating and sowing   Direct-sow seeds on the soil surface every two weeks year-round for a continual harvest. Plants will need protection in a cold frame during the winter months to survive.

Average germination time   7 to 10 days.

Lycopersicon esculentum (Tomato)

Seed harvesting   Pick tomatoes that are slightly over-ripe. Cut them open and scoop out the seeds. Use the wet processing method before storing (see Chapter 4).

Germinating and sowing   Use the paper towel germination method for best results (see Chapter 6). After the seed germinates, carefully remove it from the paper towel, making sure not to break the root. Make a hole in the soil deep enough to accommodate the root and place the seed in the hole. Sprinkle enough vermiculite on top of the seed to completely cover it. It is best to start tomatoes indoors 6 to 8 weeks before the estimated date of the last spring frost.

Average germination time   3 to 14 days.

Phaseolus vulgaris (Bean)

Seed harvesting   Leave the edible bean pod on the plant for up to 6 weeks after the beans are ready to eat. When the pods turn brown and the leaves fall off the plants, test a pod to see if the seeds are ready to harvest by breaking open a bean pod, removing one seed, and biting into it. If the bean doesn't dent or barely dents, harvest the seeds.

Germinating and sowing   Direct-sow seeds 1 inch deep after the last spring frost.

Average germination time   7 and 10 days.

Pisum sativum (Pea)

Seed harvesting   Allow the peapods to dry on the plants. The plants will die back as well. When the pods are brown and dry, harvest them, remove the seeds from the pods, and use the dry processing method.

Germianting and sowing   Direct-sow seeds 1 to 1½ inches deep as soon as the ground can be worked in early spring. The smaller the seed, the shallower you should plant it.

Average germination time   7 to 14 days.

Raphanus sativus (Radish)

Seed harvesting   Radish that isn't harvested sends up a seed stalk that produces fleshy green, edible pods. When the pods turn brown, harvest them, break them open, and collect the seed inside.

Germinating and sowing   Direct-sow seeds ½ inch deep in early spring as soon as the ground can be worked in early spring.

Average germination time   5 to 7 days.

Solanum melongena (Eggplant)

Seed harvesting   Select past-ripe eggplant that's dull and slightly wrinkled. Cut it open and scrape out the seeds. Use the wet processing method before storing (see Chapter 4).

Germinating and sowing   Use the paper towel germination method for best results (see Chapter 6). After the seed germinates, carefully remove it from the paper towel, making sure not to break the root. Make a hole in the soil deep enough to accommodate the root and place the seed in the hole. Sprinkle enough vermiculite on top of the seed head to completely cover it. It's best to start eggplants indoors 8 weeks before the estimated date of the last spring frost because these plants require a long growing season.

Average germination time   10 to 12 days.

Spinacia oleracea (Spinach)

Seed harvesting   Spinach sends up flower stalks when warm weather arrives. Allow the seed to form, ripen, and dry on the plant. Cut off the seed stalks and harvest the seeds.

Germinating and sowing   Direct-sow seeds ½ inch deep as soon as the ground can be worked in early spring.

Average germination time   7 to 14 days.

Zea mays (Corn)

Seed harvesting   Save seed from open-pollinated varieties only, because most hybrid corn seed is sterile. Select ears that are full and as close to perfect as possible. Allow the corn to ripen on the plant, even if frost threatens (frost doesn't hurt drying corn ears). It takes about a month from the time the corn is ready to eat before it is ready to remove from the plant. To test whether corn is fully dry, remove one kernel and pound it with a hammer. If it turns to powder, it is dry. Corn that is not dry enough will continue to produce heat in storage and possibly ruin your entire harvest.

Germinating and sowing   Direct-sow corn 1 to $1\frac{1}{2}$ inches deep after the last spring frost. Gardeners who watch the soil temperature carefully can plant a month before the last spring frost as long as the ground temperature is 70° F since a light frost will not hurt corn.

Average germination time   7 to 10 days.

The Flower Seed Directory

This directory contains seed-harvesting tips, germination tips, and sowing information for each plant listed. Although it is not comprehensive, it does include some of the most popular flowers.

All flowers are listed by their botanical names. If you need this same kind of information for a flower not listed, the first thing to do is discover its botanical name; then you can research with the assurance that you are getting information on the correct flower.

Abutilon (Flowering Maple)

Seed harvesting   Allow the seedpods to turn brown on the plant, then harvest them and remove the seeds.

Germinating and sowing   Soak seeds in warm water for 24 hours. Sow the seeds in moist paper towels placed inside a plastic container with a lid or a sealed plastic bag.

Average germination time   20 to 90 days.

Achillea (Yarrow)

Seed harvesting   Allow the faded flowers to dry on the plants. When they're dry, place a paper bag over the top of the flower heads. Cut off the stems and, while holding the stems and the paper bag, turn them so the stems are up in the air and the paper bag is right side up. Give the plant material a shake or two, and the seeds will fall to the bottom of the bag.

Germinating and sowing   Seeds require light for germination to occur. Winter-sow or direct-sow outdoors on the soil surface.

Average germination time   10 to 100 days.

Aconitum (Monkshood, Aconite)

Seed harvesting   The seeds form inside the dried flower husks. When the husks are dry, remove and crush the seedpod. The seeds are small and irregularly shaped, and you need to remove the chaff to find the seeds. *Note:* Aconitum is toxic; wear gloves when handling any part of the plant.

Germinating and sowing   Use the paper towel germination method (see Chapter 6), refrigerating for four weeks, or surface-sow the seeds using the winter-sowing technique.

Average germination time   5 to 270 days.

Adenophora (Ladybells)

Seed harvesting   Harvest the dried seedpods. Break them open and blow away the chaff. Use the dry processing method before storing seeds (see Chapter 4).

Germinating and sowing   Direct-sow seeds on the soil surface in fall or early spring. Don't cover the seeds, but do press them into the soil so they make good contact. Plants don't transplant well, so either direct-sow or sow one seed per peat pot.

Average germination time   30 to 90 days.

Agastache (Giant Hyssop, Mexican Hyssop)

Seed harvesting   Cover seed heads with pantyhose to prevent birds from eating them and keep the seeds from falling to the ground. After the flower heads turn brown, cut the stem and shake the seed head so that the seeds fall into the pantyhose.

Germinating and sowing   Direct-sow in the fall, barely covering the seed with soil, or winter-sow. Seeds germinate best when the soil temperature is 55°F.

Average germination time   30 to 90 days

Alcea (Hollyhock)

Seed harvesting   The faded flowers give way to oval, button-shaped seedpods. Allow these pods to mature on the plant. When the seedpods turn completely brown, remove them. Open the seedpods to reveal numerous round, papery seeds.

Germinating and sowing   Seeds require light and prefer soil temperatures between 60°F and 70°F for best germination. Direct-sow seeds on the soil surface in late autumn. *Note:* The long taproot makes transplanting hollyhocks difficult, so either sow the seed in late summer or use peat pots indoors.

Average germination time   10 to 14 days.

Amaryllis (Belladonna Lily, Jersey Lily, Naked Ladies, Christmas Lily)

Seed harvesting   The seedpod turns a light brown or tan and splits open when the thin, papery seeds are mature. To prevent the possible loss of seeds, cover the seedpod with pantyhose while it's still green. Alternatively, cut off the seedpods—stem and all—as soon as they begin to show signs of opening. Place them in a paper bag and hang them in a cool, dark, and dry location. Keep an eye on the seedpods; you should remove the seeds as soon as the seedpods fully open.

Germinating and sowing   Fresh seeds just collected from the plant are the easiest to germinate. Float seeds on top of water until roots emerge, then plant in a seed-starting mix topped with vermiculite. Keep the soil moist by covering the pot with a plastic sandwich bag to hold in humidity. Amaryllis seed germinates best at temperatures that range between 65°F and 75°F. After the seed germinates, carefully remove it from the water using tweezers, making sure not to break the root. Make a hole in the soil deep enough to accommodate the root and place the seed in the hole. Sprinkle enough vermiculite on top of the seed head to completely cover it. These plants can flower and produce seed year-round; plant the seeds as soon as you collect them. *Note:* Plants grown from seed may take 8 years or more to flower.

Average germination time   9 to 120 days.

Amsonia (Blue Star)

Seed harvesting   Cover the long, thin, green seedpods with pantyhose. Harvest the seedpods when they turn brown and remove the seeds.

Germinating and sowing   Direct-sow seeds in the fall or winter-sow, barely covering the seeds with soil.

Average germination time   28 to 42 days.

Anemone (Anemone, Windflower)

Seed harvesting   When faded flowers turn white and fluffy and small brown specks begin to show on top of the white fluff (these are the seeds), remove the entire seed head and pick the seeds off the fluff.

Germinating and sowing   Use the paper towel germination method (see Chapter 6), refrigerating seeds for three weeks. Allow any remaining seeds that didn't germinate in the refrigerator to do so at room temperature. After the seed germinates, carefully remove it from the paper towel using tweezers, making sure not to break the root. Make a hole in the soil deep enough to accommodate the root, and place the seed in the hole. Sprinkle enough vermiculite on top of the seed head to completely cover it. Winter-sow ungerminated seeds. *Note:* Plants grown from seed may take 8 years or more to flower.

Average germination time   15 to 180 days

Antirrhinum (Snapdragon)

Seed harvesting   The faded flower heads give way to round seedpods. Cover the seedpods with pantyhose until they dry. The seedpods are delicate and easily crushed, and they often split open on their own, spilling the tiny black seeds onto the ground or into the pantyhose.

Germinating and sowing   Seeds require light and cool temperatures for germination. Winter-sow seeds on the surface of vermiculite to prevent possible dampening-off. Always water seeds and seedlings from below.

Average germination time   10 and 21 days.

Aquilegia (Columbine, Granny's Bonnet)

Seed harvesting   Allow the seedpods to form on the stems. While still green, cover them with pantyhose. Allow seedpods to turn brown on the plant. When the seeds are mature, the seedpods begin to open at the top; collect the seeds.

Germinating and sowing   Germinate the seeds in paper towels (see Chapter 6), refrigerating seeds for three weeks if you are sowing them indoors; winter-sow ungerminated seeds. An alternative is to direct-sow the seeds on the soil surface using the winter sowing method.

Average germination time   30 to 90 days.

Aristolochia (Dutchman's Pipe)

Seed harvesting   Allow the parachutelike seedpods to develop when the flowers have faded. Be sure to cover those you want to keep with pantyhose. Remove the other developing seeds, since some varieties of this plant are invasive. When the seedpods are dry, remove them from the vine.

Germinating and sowing   Soak the seeds in hot water for 24 hours. Place them in moist paper towels inside a plastic container or bag and keep it in a warm place. Once the seed germinates, carefully remove it from the paper towel using tweezers, making sure not to break the root. Make a hole in the soil it will be planted in that is deep enough to accommodate the root. Sprinkle enough vermiculite on top of the seed head to completely cover it.

Average germination time   4 to 90 days. Patience is required with these seeds, as some varieties take even longer.

Arum (Arum Lily, Lords and Ladies)

Seed harvesting   Cover the berry cluster with pantyhose. Use the wet processing method to remove the flesh from the seeds before drying the seeds (see Chapter 4).

Germinating and sowing   Sow fresh seeds on the soil surface as soon as you harvest them or use the winter sowing method. The seed germinates best when the soil temperature is between 55°F and 65°F.

Average germination time   30 to 180 days.

Asarina (Climbing Snapdragon, Twining Snapdragon)

Seed harvesting   While the seedpods are still green, cover them with pantyhose and allow them to mature on the plant. They are ready to harvest when they are brown and crackle when you squeeze them.

Germinating and sowing   Direct-sow the seeds on the soil surface since they need light to germinate, in late winter or early spring when the average soil temperature range is between 60°F and 75°F.

Average germination time   9 to 21 days.

Asclepias (Butterfly Weed, Milkweed, Silkweed)

Seed harvesting   Cover immature green pods with pantyhose. When the pods are mature, they turn brown and split open. The seeds are at the bottom of the fluffy white fiber. Remove the seeds from the fiber.

Germinating and sowing   Use the paper towel germination method, refrigerating seeds for 10 weeks; some varieties germinate better after being pretreated with GA-3 (see Chapter 7); however, most of the common types do not need this type of treatment. Often seed companies will pre-treat seeds with GA-3. Milkweed resents having its roots disturbed when transplanted, so plant germinated seeds directly in the ground or winter-sow in peat pots.

Average germination time   7 to 90 days

Aster

Seed harvesting   Allow seed heads to dry on the plant; then off cut the dry seed heads and break apart the seed heads to reveal the seeds inside. Use the dry processing method before storing the seeds (see Chapter 4).

Germinating and sowing   Chill the seeds by keeping them stored in the refrigerator. Sow them on damp paper towels. Place the paper towels in a container with a lid or in a sealable plastic bag and place this back in the refrigerator for 2 weeks. After 2 weeks, check for signs of germination and pot up any seeds that are germinated. Wrap up the rest of the seeds in the paper towels, place them back in the container they were in while they were in the refrigerator, and then set this container at room temperature and let them germinate. Seeds germinate best when the room temperature is between 70°F and 75°F.

Average germination time   14 to 36 days.

Beaumontia (Herald's Trumpet, Easter Lily Vine)

Seed harvesting   Allow the fruit to dry on the vine, but keep an eye on it to make sure it doesn't split open naturally; you don't want to lose any seeds. The safest bet is to cover it with pantyhose. When the fruit is dried and brown, cut it open and harvest the seeds inside. The seeds are brown and have a feathery pod on one end that you must remove.

Germinating and sowing   Carefully nick the seed coat using the scarification technique described in Chapter 7). Use the paper towel germination method (see Chapter 6), checking the seeds for germination frequently—at least every couple of days. Once the seed germinates, carefully remove it from the paper towel using tweezers, making sure not to break the root. Make a hole in the soil it will be planted in that is deep enough to accommodate the root. Sprinkle enough vermiculite on top of the seed head to completely cover it.

Average germination time   7 days.

Begonia (Begonia)

Seed harvesting   Allow the papery winglike seedpods to form where the flowers were. Let them dry on the plant, then cut them off and crush the seedpods to release the tiny seeds.

Germinating and sowing   Sow seeds on the soil surface since the seeds require light for germination. Direct-sow outdoors once all danger of frost has passed or sow indoors in January.

Average germination time   15 to 60 days.

Brugmansia and Datura (Angel's Trumpet, Devil's Trumpet, Thorn Apple, Jimson Weed)

Seed harvesting   Use pantyhose to collect the seeds so the pods can split open on the plant. *Note:* The seedpods contain a hallucinogenic substance that readily absorbs into the skin, so use gloves.

Germinating and sowing   Germinate the seeds using the paper towel germination method (see Chapter 6). Brugmansia plants grown from seed take 2 to 5 years to flower. Datura plants grown from seed flower in 14 weeks. Seeds germinate best when the soil temperature is between 68°F and 86°F. Once the seed germinates, carefully remove it from the paper towel using tweezers, making sure not to break the root. Make a hole in the soil it will be planted in that is deep enough to accommodate the root. Sprinkle enough vermiculite on top of the seed head to completely cover it.

Average germination time   21 to 42 days.

Brunfelsia (Yesterday, Today, and Tomorrow; Lady of the Night)

Seed harvesting   Allow the seedpods to dry on the plant, then cut them off and crush them to release the mature seeds.

Germinating and sowing   Soak the seeds in hot water for 4 days, or until the seeds begin to swell. Change the water at least once a day (use a small strainer to catch the seeds when you do so), rinsing the seeds under running water before you put them back into the container. If you notice any type of residue sticking to the seed coat, soak the seeds in hydrogen peroxide for 1 minute, then rinse them again under hot tap water before returning them to the container. Use the paper towel germination method (see Chapter 6). Once the seed germinates, carefully remove it from the paper towel using tweezers, making sure not to break the root. Make a hole in the soil it will be planted in that is deep enough to accommodate the root. Sprinkle enough vermiculite on top of the seed head to completely cover it.

Average germination time   19 days.

Calendula (Pot Marigold, English Marigold)

Seed harvesting   Allow flower heads to dry on the plant, then cut them off and break them apart to reveal the seeds.

Germinating and sowing   Seeds require darkness to germinate. They germinate best once the soil temperature reaches 70°F. Direct-sow seeds ¼ inch deep in autumn or early spring.

Average germination time   6 to 14 days.

Cananga (Ylang-Ylang)

Seed harvesting   Pollinated flowers produce green seedpods that mature to black when ripe. Cut open the seedpod to reveal the brown, flattened seeds inside. Each seedpod contains between 6 and 12 seeds.

Germinating and sowing   Fresh seed germinates easier than older seed. Soak seeds for 48 hours in hot water. Replace the water at least once every 24 hours. If the seeds have not swollen at the end of 48 hours, continue to soak them in hot water until they begin to swell. Remove the swollen seeds, making sure none have germinated, and use the paper towel germination method (see Chapter 6). Once the seed germinates, carefully remove it from the paper towel using tweezers, making sure not to break the root. Make a hole in the soil it will be planted in that is deep enough to accommodate the root. Sprinkle enough vermiculite on top of the seed head to completely cover it.

Average germination time   10 and 90 days.

Canna (Indian Shot)

Seed harvesting   Not all cannas produce viable seeds, so do a germination test before saving or sharing it. The faded flower gives way to a seedpod. Allow the pod to turn brown while still on the plant. When the pod starts to crack open, harvest the black seeds. Some pods produce a single seed; others produce more.

Germinating and sowing   Carefully nick the hard seed coat using the scarification method (see Chapter 7). Place the seeds in a container and fill it with hot tap water. Allow the seeds to soak for 48 hours, making sure to change the water at least once during this time. Canna seed germinates best when the water or soil temperatures range between 70°F and 75°F. If necessary, use a heating pad to keep the seeds and the water warm during the stratification process. Use the paper towel germination method (see Chapter 6). Once the seed germinates, carefully remove it from the paper towel using tweezers, making sure not to break the root. Make a hole in the soil it will be planted in that is deep enough to accommodate the root. Sprinkle enough vermiculite on top of the seed head to completely cover it.

Average germination time   21 to 365 days.

Celosia (Cockscomb)

Seed harvesting   Allow the flowers to dry on the plant. Cover them with pantyhose when the color of the flowers begins to fade. When the flowers are brown, remove the flower head from the plant and shake it from side to side to release the small black seeds into the pantyhose.

Germinating and sowing   Direct-sow seeds on soil surface, pressing the seeds against the soil so they make good contact with it. Keep the seeds moist until germination takes place.

Average germination time   6 and 14 days.

Cestrum (Night Blooming Jasmine)

Seed harvesting   White berries form on the plant. Cut these off when tan spots begin to form, and squish them to release the seeds inside the center of the berry.

Germinating and sowing   Soak the seeds in a container filled with hot tap water for three days or until they begin to swell. At least once a day, change the water and rinse the seeds under hot running water. Use the paper towel germination method (see Chapter 6). Once the seed germinates, carefully remove it from the paper towel using tweezers, making sure not to break the root. Make a hole in the soil it will be planted in that is deep enough to accommodate the root. Sprinkle enough vermiculite on top of the seed head to completely cover it.

Average germination time   5 days.

Clarkia (Godetia, Farewell to Spring, Rocky Mountain Garland)

Seed harvesting   Allow the seedpods to dry on the plant until they turn brown, then remove them and crush them to release the seeds inside.

Germinating and sowing   Direct-sow seeds on top of vermiculite since they need light to germinate, in early spring, making sure the soil temperature is between 55°F and 70°F. The seedlings are highly susceptible to dampening-off, so water them from below only.

Average germination time   5 to 21 days.

Clematis (Leather Flower, Vase Vine, Virgin's Bower, Traveler's Joy, Old Man's Beard)

Seed harvesting   When the fluffy seed heads turn brown, collect the seeds.

Germinating and sowing   Use the paper towel germination method (see Chapter 6), freezing the seeds for 3 weeks. After 3 weeks, remove the container and check to see if germination has occurred. If not, place the container in a warm spot until germination takes place. Once the seed germinates, carefully remove it from the paper towel using tweezers, making sure not to break the root. Make a hole in the soil it will be planted in that is deep enough to accommodate the root. Sprinkle enough vermiculite on top of the seed head to completely cover it. An alternative to germinating seeds indoors is to winter-sow ungerminated seeds in the late fall.

Average germination time   30 to 365 days to germinate.

Cleome (Spider Flower)

Seed harvesting   Long, thin pods form on the flower stalks. Cover these with pantyhose or watch them closely. When mature, they turn brown and begin to split open, releasing the small black seeds.

Germinating and sowing   Use the paper towel germination method (see Chapter 6), refrigerating seeds for two weeks before moving to room temperature. Once the seed germinates, carefully remove it from the paper towel using tweezers, making sure not to break the root. Make a hole in the soil it will be planted in that is deep enough to accommodate the root. Sprinkle enough vermiculite on top of the seed head to completely cover it. An alternative is to direct-sow the seeds on the soil surface after the last spring frost in your area.

Average germination time   10 to 14 days.

Clianthus (Parrot's Beak)

Seed harvesting   A long, beanlike pod forms. Allow it to turn brown on the plant; then split it open to reveal the dark brown seeds.

Germinating and sowing   Soak the seeds in hot water for 48 hours. Replace the water at least once during this time. Place any seeds that didn't germinate in moist paper towels, and put the paper towels inside small plastic containers with lids or sealable plastic bags until they germinate. Once the seed germinates, carefully remove it from the paper towel using tweezers, making sure not to break the root. Make a hole in the soil it will be planted in that is deep enough to accommodate the root. Sprinkle enough vermiculite on top of the seed head to completely cover it.

Average germination time   14 to 30 days

Clivia (Kaffir Lily)

Seed harvesting   After the green berries change to either yellow or orange (berries typically take 9 to 10 months to mature), remove the berries from the plant. The seed is inside the pulp. Wear gloves when separating the seed from the berry.

Germinating and sowing   Always use fresh seeds. The seeds have a "spot" on them. Gently press the seed into the soil, making sure the spot is slightly above the soil surface. Keep the seeds and the surrounding soil moist. A root emerges from the spot on the seed. Sometimes the root grows into the soil on its own, but if it doesn't, tilt the seed sideways so the root touches the soil.

Average germination time   3 days.

Coleus

Seed harvesting   Cover the faded flower stems with pantyhose. Small, papery pods form. Allow these to dry on the plant. When they are dry, cut off the flower stem and shake the dried seed head from side to side inside the pantyhose to release the seeds.

Germinating and sowing   Direct-sow on soil surface since the seeds need light, when the soil temperatures are between 65°F and 75°F.

Average germination time   10 to 20 days.

Consolida (Larkspur)

Seed harvesting   Allow the small, pointy seedpods to form along the flower stems. When they are mature, they turn brown and begin to split open at the top of the pod. Harvest them at this point, crush the pod, and remove the black seeds.

Germinating and sowing   Refrigerate seeds at least 8 weeks prior to Direct-sowing in the spring. To germinate indoors, refrigerate seeds for 8 weeks and then use the paper towel germination method (see Chapter 6), refrigerating seeds for an additional two weeks. After 2 weeks, remove the seeds and plant any seeds that have germinated. Place the remaining seeds in a dark area with temperatures that range between 50°F and 55°F until germination occurs. Direct-sow ungerminated seeds that have been refrigerated for at least 8 weeks on outdoor soil surface immediately. Sow germinated seed in the spring indoors in peat pots.

Average germination time   14 to 21 days.

Dianthus (Pinks, China Pink, Indian Pink, Sweet William)

Seed harvesting   Allow the flower heads to remain on the plant until they are dried and shriveled. Most of the petals likely have fallen off by this time. Cut off the seedpods and turn them upside down inside a baggie to collect the small black seeds.

Germinating and sowing   Winter-sow or start indoors in early spring when the soil temperatures are between 60°F and 70°F; barely cover the seeds with soil.

Average germination time   10 to 21 days.

Dicentra (Bleeding Heart)

Seed harvesting   Tiny, pencil-shaped pods replace the flowers. Cover these pods with pantyhose and allow them to dry on the plant. When they are mature, they turn brown and split open naturally.

Germinating and sowing   Use the paper towel germination method (see Chapter 6), freezing the seeds for 6 weeks. Then remove the container with the seeds in it and place in an area with 55°F to 60°F temperatures until seeds germinate. Once the seed germinates, carefully remove it from the paper towel using tweezers, making sure not to break the root. Make a hole in the soil it will be planted in that is deep enough to accommodate the root. Sprinkle enough vermiculite on top of the seed head to completely cover it. Winter-sow fresh, ungerminated seeds.

Average germination time   30 to 365 days.

Dictamnus (Gas Plant, Dittany, Burning Bush, Fraxinella)

Seed harvesting   Allow the seedpods to dry on the plant, remove them, and crush them to release the small black seeds.

Germinating and sowing   Use the paper towel germination method (see Chapter 6), placing seeds in an area where the temperature range is between 60°F and 65°F. Leave them at this temperature for 2 weeks. At the end of 2 weeks, move them to the refrigerator for 2 weeks. At the end of the 2 weeks, move them back to an area where the temperatures are between 60°F and 65°F for 4 weeks. After 4 weeks, begin the refrigeration process again. Continue alternating temperatures until the seeds germinate. Once the seed germinates, carefully remove it from the paper towel using tweezers, making sure not to break the root. Make a hole in the soil it will be planted in that is deep enough to accommodate the root. Sprinkle enough vermiculite on top of the seed head to completely cover it.

Average germination time   30 to 180 days.

Digitalis (Foxglove)

Seed harvesting   Cover the flower stalks with pantyhose when the small oval green seedpods begin to form. When the seeds are mature, the pods turn brown and begin to split open and release the seeds.

Germinating and sowing   Foxglove seeds require darkness to germinate, so whether you direct-sow them or sow them in flats indoors, cover them with ver-miculite. If sowing in containers, place them in a dark area. Direct-sow the seeds in flats or sow them in moist paper towels. Don't try to separate the young seedlings; let nature take her course. When the seedlings are large enough to pick up easily, separate them

Average germination time   5 to 21 days.

Echinacea (Coneflower)

Seed harvesting   Allow the seed heads to remain on the plant until the stem begins to turn brown, and then cut off the seed heads. Soak the spiny seed heads in hot water for approximately 10 minutes or until the bristles turn limp. Be careful not to leave them in the water too long, or they will not germinate. Pull out the limp bristles to access the seeds below them. Lay the seeds in a warm, breezy area to hasten drying. You can lay them outside on an overcast day or use a fan to help speed up the process.

Germinating and sowing   Winter-sow or direct-sow in either fall or early spring, making sure to plant the seeds ⅛ inch deep since they need darkness to germinate.

Average germination time   10 to 21 days.

Eranthis (Winter Aconite)

Seed harvesting   Allow the seedpods to mature on the plant. Cover them with pantyhose. When the seeds are mature, the seed heads split open to reveal black seeds.

Germinating and sowing   Use the paper towel germination method (see Chapter 6), refrigerating seeds for 3 weeks. Once the seed germinates, carefully remove it from the paper towel using tweezers, making sure not to break the root. Make a hole in the soil it will be planted in that is deep enough to accommodate the root. Sprinkle enough vermiculite on top of the seed head to completely cover it. An alternative is to winter-sow the seeds on the soil surface. Make sure to press them into the top of the soil.

Average germination time   30 days to 1 year.

Eryngium (Sea Holly, Eryngo)

Seed harvesting   Allow the central cone of the flower to mature on the plant. When it turns brown, harvest the seeds. Cut the central cone, hold it over a container, and run your fingers back and forth across it to remove the seeds. Seeds that are difficult to remove are not mature. The seeds look a bit like shuttlecocks or arrowheads.

Germinating and sowing   Use the paper towel germination method (see Chapter 6), refrigerating seeds for 3 weeks. Once the seed germinates, carefully remove it from the paper towel using tweezers, making sure not to break the root. Make a hole in the soil it will be planted in that is deep enough to accommodate the root. Sprinkle enough vermiculite on top of the seed head to completely cover it. Winter-sow or sow germinated seeds in peat pots. Plants have long taproots that make transplanting difficult.

Average germination time   5 to 90 days.

Erysimum (Wallflower)

Seed harvesting   Long, thin seedpods form where the flowers were. Allow them to dry on the plant. When the stems turn brown, cut off the seedpods, stem and all. Remove the seedpods, break them open, and harvest the yellow, disclike seeds.

Germinating and sowing   Direct-sow seeds ¼ inch deep in vermiculite 6 to 8 weeks before the last frost in your area. Seedlings are susceptible to dampening-off, so water from below.

Average germination time   5 to 30 days.

Eupatorium (Joe-Pye Weed, Snakeroot, Hemp Agrimony)

Seed harvesting   Allow the seed heads to mature to the point that they are white and fluffy, sort of like dandelion seed heads. Grab the white fluff and crumble the material in your hands over a container. Allow the fluff to blow away and the tiny brown needlelike seeds to fall into the container.

Germinating and sowing   Seeds require refrigeration for at least 8 weeks before sowing in their dry state. Soak seed in warm water for 2 hours regardless of the germination method used. Plant seeds ¼ inch deep if direct-sown. Winter-sow or sow using the paper towel germination method and refrigerate the seeds in the moist paper towels for an additional 7 days. Once the seed germinates, carefully remove it from the paper towel using tweezers, making sure not to break the root. Make a hole in the soil it will be planted in that is deep enough to accommodate the root. Sprinkle enough vermiculite on top of the seed head to completely cover it.

Average germination time   10 to 28 days

Gaillardia (Blanket Flower)

Seed harvesting   Wear gloves when handling these seed heads, as the small hairs can cause an allergic reaction. Allow the seed heads to turn white and then clip them off. Hold the seed heads over a container and rub them to release the small brown, shuttlecock-shaped seeds.

Germinating and sowing   Direct-sow annual varieties on the soil surface since the seeds need light to germinate, after the last spring frost; direct-sow perennial varieties on the soil surface 6 weeks before the last spring frost.

Average germination time   7 to 20 days.

Gomphrena (Globe Amaranth, Globe Thistle)

Seed harvesting   The color of this plant doesn't change when the seeds are ready to harvest. Instead, watch for the petals to begin blowing off the flowers—this is your cue that the seeds are mature. The seeds are located at the base of the petals. Cut off the flower heads and run your hands along the flowers to release the seeds.

Germinating and sowing   Soak the seeds for 24 hours in warm water before sowing. Sow soaked seeds on soil surface in a container, and place the container in a dark location, making sure the soil temperature remains between 70°F and 75°F until germination occurs.

Average germination time   6 to 15 days.

Gypsophila (Baby's Breath)

Seed harvesting   Place pantyhose over the top of the seed heads and secure the bottom of the pantyhose to the stem of the plant. When the stem is brown, cut it off, remove the pantyhose, and rub your fingers across the seed heads. The fluff comes out with the seeds. You can press the seeds against a strainer to help remove the fluff or pick it off by hand.

Germinating and sowing   The best method of sowing is to direct-sow on soil surface in late spring once the soil temperatures are around 70°F. If you must start them indoors, sow the seeds in peat pots to prevent root disturbance during transplanting. Continue sowing the seeds every 3 weeks through mid-July to ensure continual bloom. A light frost won't harm the seeds or seedlings.

Average germination time   10 to 20 days.

Hedychium (Ginger Lily, White Butterfly Ginger, Butterfly Ginger, Garland Lily)

Seed harvesting   Watch for seedpods to form where the flowers once were. Cover the seedpods with pantyhose and allow them to remain on the plant until they split open. The seeds are bright red.

Germinating and sowing   Soak the seeds for 72 hours; at least once a day, pour off the old water, rinse the seeds under running tap water, and refill the containers with hot tap water. Use the paper towel germination method (see Chapter 6). Once the seed germinates, carefully remove it from the paper towel using tweezers, making sure not to break the root. Make a hole in the soil it will be planted in that is deep enough to accommodate the root. Sprinkle enough vermiculite on top of the seed head to completely cover it.

Average germination time   20 days.

Helianthus (Sunflower)

Seed harvesting   Two different methods of seed harvesting work well for this plant. Choose the one that works best for you:

- Remove the flower heads from the plant once they turn brown. Immerse the dried flower heads in a bucket of water using a rock or brick to keep them submerged for 3 to 4 hours, to loosen the seeds. Remove the seed heads from the water, hold them over a drying screen, and break them up. Dry the seeds by placing them in front of a fan or by placing them outdoors in a shaded area.

- Cover the seed heads with pantyhose and leave them on the plant for at least a month after they are done blooming. By this time, the seed head will be dry enough that you can crush it in your hands to release the seeds.

Germinating and sowing Sow seeds ¼ inch deep in peat pots indoors or direct-sow ¼ deep in the garden.

Average germination time 10 to 14 days.

Helichrysm (Everlasting Flower, Strawflower)

Seed harvesting Allow the flower to completely dry on the plant. When white fluff forms on the seed head, cut off the seed head and remove the fluff. The small black or gray seeds are located underneath the fluff.

Germinating and sowing Direct-sow seeds on the soil surface since they need light to germinate, right after the last frost in your area.

Average germination time 5 to 20 days.

Heliotropium (Heliotrope)

Seed harvesting When the flower head turns completely brown, cut it off, hold it over a container, and roll the dried plant material between your hands to release the small black seeds.

Germinating and sowing Direct-sow, barely covering the seed with soil and keeping the soil evenly moist. Don't let the seedling dry out; if it does, it usually dies.

Average germination time 2 to 42 days.

Helleborus (Hellebore, Christmas Rose, Lenten Rose)

Seed harvesting When center area of the pollinated flower begins to swell, cover the flower with pantyhose. The seedpod releases the seeds when it's mature.

Germinating and sowing Winter sowing is the best method; if you use a mini-greenhouse during the spring, summer, and fall, be sure to vent it. Keeping the soil moist is also essential to success.

Average germination time 30 days to 18 months. Patience is required with hellebore seeds.

Hemerocallis (Daylily)

Seed harvesting   A large green seedpod forms on top of the stalks where the flowers once were. Allow this seedpod to turn brown; then cut it off the plant and open it to reveal the seeds.

Germinating and sowing   Direct-sow seeds ⅛ inch deep in soil or start germinated seeds indoors. You can also winter-sow these seeds. Use the paper towel germination method (see Chapter 6), refrigerating seeds for 6 weeks and then moving them to room temperature until germination occurs. Once the seed germinates, carefully remove it from the paper towel using tweezers, making sure not to break the root. Make a hole in the soil it will be planted in that is deep enough to accommodate the root. Sprinkle enough vermiculite on top of the seed head to completely cover it.

Average germination time   15 to 49 days.

Iberis (Candytuft, Globe Candytuft, Rocket Candytuft, Hyacinth-Flowered Candytuft)

Seed harvesting   Allow the seed heads to dry completely on the plant. Candytuft is a prolific self-seeder, so cover the seed heads with pantyhose to avoid losing seeds. When the seed heads are dry, crush them to remove the seeds.

Germinating and sowing   Direct-sow annual varieties of these seeds ⅛ inch deep; direct-sow perennial varieties ¼ inch deep.

Average germination time   10 to 60 days.

Impatiens (Bizzy Lizzy, Touch-Me-Not)

Seed harvesting   When these seeds are ripe, the pods explode, literally throwing the seeds into the garden; if you want to save the seeds, you must cover them with pantyhose.

Germinating and sowing   Direct-sow on top of vermiculite and water seedlings from below to prevent dampening-off. Seeds require light to germinate, so do not cover the seeds with soil.

Average germination time   7 to 30 days.

Ipomoea (Morning Glory)

Seed harvesting   Collect the small round seedpods as soon as they turn brown (they will self-seed if left on the plant). Crush the seedpod to release the multiple black seeds inside.

Germinating and sowing   Chip the seed coat and soak in warm water for 24 hours. Direct-sow chipped seeds ¼ inch deep.

Average germination time   5 to 21 days.

Lablab (Dolichos Bean, Hyacinth Bean Vine, Lablab Vine)

Seed harvesting   Allow the beanlike pods to completely dry on the plant. When they have turned brown and are crispy, remove them from the vine, split them open, and remove the seeds.

Germinating and sowing   Soak seed in warm water for 24 hours before planting. Sow soaked seeds 1 inch deep.

Average germination time   3 to 30 days.

Lathyrus (Sweet Pea)

Seed harvesting   As soon as the seedpods turn brown, cut them off the vine and remove the seeds. *Warning:* The seedpods resemble edible peas, but don't eat them because all parts of this plant are toxic.

Germinating and sowing   Scarify the seed coat or soak the seeds in hot water overnight. Sow annual seeds ½ inch deep and perennial seeds ¼ inch deep.

Average germination time   10 to 30 days.

Leonotis (Lion's Ear, Lion's Tail)

Seed harvesting   Cover faded flower heads with pantyhose, allowing them to dry on the plant. The seeds often fall out on their own, especially if the flower heads begin to bend toward the ground. To find out if the seed is ready to harvest, simply tilt the flower head to one side. If seed falls out, cut off the seed head and continue to shake the flower head from side to side to release the seeds. The seed head is rather spiny, so use a stick or other object to tap the seed head itself.

Germinating and sowing   Direct-sow the seeds on the soil surface since they need light to germinate.

Average germination time   2 to 21 days.

Leucanthemum (Daisy)

Seed harvesting   Allow the seed heads to dry on the plant until about an inch of the stem is also dry and brown. Cut off the seed heads, crush the head of the dried flower, and press on the center of the flower until the seeds are visible. At this point, run your fingers along the tops and sides of the seeds to release them.

Germinating and sowing   Surface-sow the seeds indoors in peat pots or direct-sow on the soil surface since the seeds need light to germinate.

Average germination time   10 to 14 days.

Liatris (Blazing Star, Gayfeather, Button Snakeroot, Snakeroot)

Seed harvesting   Allow the seed heads to remain on the plant until they are completely brown and the plume is somewhat feathery. Cut off the entire seedpod and run your fingers up and down it to release the seeds.

Germinating and sowing   Winter-sow or direct-sow in late autumn or early spring, barely covering seeds with soil.

Average germination time   20 to 25 days.

Limonium (Statice)

Seed harvesting   Allow the seed heads to dry on the plant, remove them, and then hang them upside down indoors for several more weeks to make sure they are completely dry. Hold the completely dried flowers over a container and roll them between your hands. The seeds, which are slightly curled, are at the base of each flower *floret*.

Germinating and sowing   Direct-sow on the soil surface, barely covering the seeds with vermiculite.

Average germination time   10 to 20 days.

 DEFINITION

A **floret** is a tiny flower. It grows either on a single stem or in clusters to make up one large flower, as with statice and yarrow.

Lunaria (Honesty, Money Plant)

Seed harvesting   Allow the "paper money" to dry on the plant. This round, papery circle contains numerous seeds. When it's dry, you can open the paper circle and remove the seeds.

Germinating and sowing   Direct-sow seeds ⅛ inch deep.

Average germination time   10 to 14 days.

Lupinus (Lupine, Lupin)

Seed harvesting   When the seedpods turn a grayish-black, remove them and lay them out to dry intact. After a week or so, split open the seedpod and remove the seeds.

Germinating and sowing   Scarify the seed coat and soak the seeds for 24 hours (see Chapter 7). Sow scarified and soaked seeds ⅛ inch deep. Sow seeds started indoors in peat pots.

Average germination time   14 to 60 days.

Lychnis (Maltese Cross, Campion, Catchfly)

Seed harvesting   When the tops of the seedpods start to split open, cut them off and turn them upside down to harvest the seeds.

Germinating and sowing   Surface-sow seeds. Winter sow or Direct-sowing in the fall.

Average germination time   21 to 30 days.

Stemmadenia (Milky Way Tree)

Seed harvesting   When the fruits are ripe, harvest them, cut them open, and scrape out the seeds. Put the seeds in a small container, such as a baby food jar, and pour hydrogen peroxide over them; let them sit for 1 minute. Pour the hydrogen peroxide through a strainer so none of the seeds fall down the drain. Repeat this step several times until the seeds are clean, and then give them a final rinse under hot tap water. Either sow the seeds immediately or lay them on a seed-drying rack to dry for 2 weeks.

Germinating and sowing   Put the seeds in a container and cover them with hot tap water. Soak the seeds until they begin to swell. Make sure you change the water at least once a day and replace it with fresh hot tap water. Sow the swollen seeds in a seed-starting mixture inside peat pots. Place the peat pots in a flat with water in the bottom. Use the paper towel germination method (see Chapter 6). Once the seed germinates, carefully remove it from the paper towel using tweezers, making sure not to break the root. Make a hole in the soil it will be planted in that is deep enough to accommodate the root. Sprinkle enough vermiculite on top of the seed head to completely cover it.

Average germination time   2 weeks.

Momordica (Balsam Apple, Balsam Pear)

Seed harvesting   Harvest seeds from the mature fruit and use the wet processing method before storing.

Germinating and sowing   The preferred germination temperature range is between 65°F and 75°F. Germinate the seeds in moist paper towels. Once the seed germinates, carefully remove it from the paper towel using tweezers, making sure not to break the root. Make a hole in the soil it will be planted in that is deep enough to accommodate the root. Sprinkle enough vermiculite on top of the seed head to completely cover it.

Average germination time   14 to 21 days.

Paeonia (Peony, Piney)

Seed harvesting   The seedpods form where the flower was. The pods that contain seeds are plump compared to those that are empty. When the pods turn brown and begin to crack open, harvest the shiny, round, black seeds.

Germinating and sowing   Refrigerate seeds for 10 weeks and use the paper towel germination method (see Chapter 6) making sure not to cover the top of the seeds with paper towel so they can get light), refrigerating seeds for 3 weeks. These seeds can take a long time to sprout and often need a hot/cold/hot/cold period for germination to take place. Sow germinated seeds on top of a seed-starting mix, making sure to just cover the top of the seed head with vermiculite.

Average germination time   30 days to 1 year.

Papaver (Poppy)

Seed harvesting   When the stems and seed heads turn brown, harvest the seed heads, turn them upside down, and shake them gently from side to side to release the seeds.

Germinating and sowing   Direct-sow, barely covering the seeds so they have the darkness they need to germinate. Sow perennial varieties in August and annual varieties in early spring, or sow in peat pots. This plant doesn't transplant well.

Average germination time   10 to 30 days.

Platycodon (Balloon Flower, Chinese Bellflower, Japanese Balloon Flower)

Seed harvesting   Cover the seedpods with pantyhose and allow them to dry on the plant. When the seedpods begin to split open, remove them and harvest the seeds.

Germinating and sowing   Sow seeds on top of vermiculite in peat pots or direct-sow them in the garden on the soil surface in either late fall or early spring. The seeds need light to germinate. The preferred germination temperature of the soil is 70°F.

Average germination time   15 to 30 days.

Tacca (Bat Plant)

Seed harvesting   When the flower fades, a seedpod forms. Cover it with pantyhose and allow the seedpod to completely dry before harvesting the seeds, which often fall out on their own.

Germinating and sowing   Soak fresh seeds in hot water until they begin to swell, which can take several weeks. Change the water at least once a day. When doing so, pour the water through a small strainer to catch the seeds so they don't go down the drain. Rinse the seeds under running water before you put them back into the container. If you notice any type of residue sticking to the seed coat, soak the seeds in hydrogen peroxide for 1 minute and then rinse them again under hot running water. Place the seeds back in the container and refill the container with hot tap water. Germinate the seed using the paper towel method. Once the seed germinates, carefully remove it from the paper towel using tweezers, making sure not to break the root. Make a hole in the soil it will be planted in that is deep enough to accommodate the root. Sprinkle enough vermiculite on top of the seed head to completely cover it.

Average germination time   40 days.

Tagetes (Marigold)

Seed harvesting   When the flowers are completely dry, cut them off, split open the dried flower heads, and remove the seeds from below the flower petals.

Germinating and sowing   Direct-sow, barely covering the seeds with soil. Water from below if planting in pots. These seeds are susceptible to dampening-off.

Average germination time   4 to 14 days.

Verbascum (Mullein)

Seed harvesting   Small, round seedpods form along the flower spike where the flowers once were. When the seedpods are dry, harvest them and crush them to release the tiny round seeds inside.

Germinating and sowing   Seeds germinate best when the soil temperature is between 55°F and 60°F. Direct-sow in early spring, barely covering seeds with soil, or winter-sow.

Average germination time   14 and 30 days.

Verbena (Verbena)

Seed harvesting   The seeds develop where the faded flowers were. When the seeds turn brown, cut off the seed heads and allow them to dry intact for about a week. Crumble the dried seed heads and remove as much chaff as possible.

Germinating and sowing   Seeds require darkness to germinate, so cover the seeds or keep them in a dark place until germination occurs. Use the paper towel germination method, refrigerating seeds for 2 weeks and then moving them into temperatures between 65°F and 75°F. Once the seed germinates, carefully remove it from the paper towel using tweezers, making sure not to break the root. Make a hole in the soil it will be planted in that is deep enough to accommodate the root. Sprinkle enough vermiculite on top of the seed head to completely cover it.

Average germination time   2 to 90 days.

Veronica (Veronica, Speedwell, Birds-Eye)

Seed harvesting   Veronica seeds form where the faded flowers were. They are disk shaped and reddish-brown; however, not all varieties of this plant set seed.

Germinating and sowing   Winter-sow seeds on the soil surface since they require light to germinate. The ideal soil temperature range for germination to occur is between 60°F and 70°F.

Average germination time   15 to 90 days.

Viola (Pansy)

Seed harvesting   Cover the seedpods with pantyhose while they're still green. When the seedpods burst open, cut the pansy stem. Hold the stem over a container, remove the pantyhose, and let the seeds fall into the container.

Germinating and sowing   Viola seeds need soil temperatures between 65°F and 75°F. Winter-sow, planting seeds ¼ inch deep since the seeds need darkness to germinate.

Average germination time   10 to 21 days.

X Pardancanda (Candylily)

Seed harvesting   A large seedpod with numerous seeds forms in place of the faded flowers. When the pod first begins to split open, the seeds are still green. Do not harvest them at this point. Leave them on the plant for approximately one more week until the seeds turn black and the seedpods are completely open.

Germinating and sowing   Use the paper towel germination method, refrigerating seeds for 7 days and then moving them to a location where the soil temperature range is between 70°F and 85°F until they germinate. Once the seed germinates, carefully remove it from the paper towel using tweezers, making sure not to break the root. Make a hole in the soil it will be planted in that is deep enough to accommodate the root. Sprinkle enough vermiculite on top of the seed head to completely cover it.

Average germination time   15 days.

Yucca (Yucca)

Seed harvesting   Large green seedpods form on the tall flower spikes after the flower fades. Allow the seedpods to remain on the plant until they turn brown. When the seedpods begin to split, cut them off, open them up, and harvest the thin black seeds.

Germinating and sowing   Yucca seeds germinate best when temperatures are between 65°F and 75°F. Use the paper towel germination method (see Chapter 6). Once the seed germinates, carefully remove it from the paper towel using tweezers, making sure not to break the root. Make a hole in the soil it will be planted in that is deep enough to accommodate the root. Sprinkle enough vermiculite on top of the seed head to completely cover it. Sow ungerminated yucca seeds in pots, barely covering them with vermiculite. Do not transplant these into the garden until they are 2 to 3 years old.

Average germination time   30 days to a year.

Zephyranthes (Rain Lily, Fairy Lily, Zephyr Lily)

Seed harvesting   The faded flowers form seedpods. When they turn brown, remove them before they start to split open.

Germinating and sowing   The seeds germinate best when soil temperatures are between 60°F and 65°F. Barely cover seeds with vermiculite. Sow seeds in the fall or use the winter sowing method.

Average germination time   120 days, although they can take a lot longer.

Zinnia (Zinnia)

Seed harvesting   Allow the flower heads to remain on the plant until they're completely dry. When the stems turn brown, cut off the brown flower heads, separate the flower petals, and remove the seeds. Use the dry processing method before storing.

Germinating and sowing   Direct-sow seeds ½ inch deep after all danger of frost has passed.

Average germination time   5 to 24 days.

annual   A plant that grows, flowers, sets seed, and dies in one growing season.

biennial   A plant that produces only leaves and roots the first year. The second year it produces flowers, fruits or seeds, and then it dies at the end of the second season.

chaff   Plant debris such as small sections of stems, crushed pieces of the seed pods, bits of leaves, and other natural plant material.

embryo   The living part of the seed that contains the underdeveloped plant. For the embryo to grow into a living plant, it must receive the right combination of moisture, light, and temperature.

endosperm   The nutrient-packed tissue that surrounds the developing embryo of a seed.

fermentation   Naturally occurring process in which mold, fungus, yeast, or other bacteria converts carbohydrates to alcohol or organic acid (carbon dioxide).

genetically modified organism (GMO)   A plant or other living organism that has been genetically altered through DNA transfer. This includes combining genes from plants, animals, or other organisms such as bacteria or chemicals.

genus   A group of closely related plants in the same family. The genus is the first word of the botanical name.

germination   The process that occurs at the exact moment when a seed begins to sprout, or grow, into a plant.

heirloom   A plant or seed from a plant that has been in cultivation for at least 50 years, has been handed down from one generation to another, and is open pollinated.

hybrid   Seeds or plants that have been created by intentionally crossing two similar or different plant species. This usually occurs by humans working in a public breeding program.

nomenclature   The use of Latin names in biology for labeling plants.

open pollination   Open pollination occurs when two plants of the same variety cross naturally without the interference of man. The seeds from open-pollinated plants are not classified as hybrids and often look almost identical to the parent plants.

perennial   A plant that comes back from its own root system year after year.

scarification   The process of nicking or sanding a seed's coat to aid the embryo in the germination process.

seed coat   The protective outer layer of a seed.

seedpod   A protective covering that houses several seeds.

silica gel   A clear, porous, sandlike material capable of absorbing and holding moisture.

sori   Multiple clusters of sorus.

sorus   A cluster of enclosures, called *sporangia*, that protect plant spores while they're developing.

species   A fundamental category of taxonomic classification, ranking below a genus or subgenus and consisting of related organisms capable of crossbreeding.

sporangia   The enclosures that spores grow and develop inside. They are either single celled or multicelled and also are called *spore cases*.

stratification   The process of placing seeds in a moist growing medium in a cool place, such as the freezer or refrigerator, to induce germination.

threshing   The physical process that occurs when a plant's seeds are removed from the seedpods or dried plant material.

vermiculite   A mineral that expands with the application of heat; among its many uses is a planting medium.

viable   The ability of a seed to germinate.

winnowing   The process used to separate the seed from the chaff.

Resources

The books and suppliers listed in this appendix are great resources for additional information as well as seeds, beneficial insects, and gardening supplies.

Books

Coleman, Eliot. *The Winter Harvest Handbook: Year-Round Vegetable Production Using Deep-Organic Techniques and Unheated Greenhouses.* Vermont: Chelsea Green Publishing, 2009.

A guide to extending growing seasons for food plants, from a market-gardener's perspective. Home gardeners should adapt the information to small-scale gardens.

Foster, Catharine Osgood. *Plants-a-Plenty: How to Multiply Outdoor and Indoor Plants Through Cuttings, Crown and Root Divisions, Grafting Layering, and Seeds.* Emmaus, Pennsylvania: Rodale Press, 1977.

A reliable source of information for propagating plants vegetatively.

Franks, Eric, and Jasmine Richardson. *Microgreens: A Guide to Growing Nutrient-Packed Greens.* Utah: Gibbs Smith, 2009.

Market gardeners tell how to grow and use microgreens.

McLaughlin, Chris. *The Complete Idiot's Guide to Heirloom Vegetables.* New York: Alpha, 2010.

This is a wonderful guide to growing heirloom vegetables, with detailed information on many different varieties.

Murphy, Wendy. *Gardening Under Lights.* Virginia, Time-Life Books, 1978.

A timeless guide to growing plants indoors under lights.

Equipment, Supplies, and Tools

Ace, The Helpful Place
www.acehardware.com

A national hardware chain that carries lawn and garden supplies.. Check the website to find the store nearest you.

Charley's Greenhouse and Garden
www.charleysgreenhouse.com

One-stop catalog and online shopping for greenhouse kits, equipment, and gardening supplies, including UV-stabilized bubble-wrap greenhouse insulation, translucent storm tarps, polycarbonate panels, soil thermometers, minimum/maximum thermometers, remote thermometers with low-temperature alarm, rechargeable misters, greenhouse fans, heat mats, rooting hormone, Wall-O-Water, and much more.

Gardener's Supply Company
www.gardeners.com

Earth-friendly gardening supplies, including screen curtain, seed-starting supplies, composters, water barrels, garden fertilizers, amendments, and pest-control products.

Wind and Weather
www.windandweather.com

A catalog and online supplier of electronic weather-watching equipment, like remote sensor thermometers, rain gauges, and garden accessories.

Seed Banks and Organizations

Seed Savers Exchange
www.seedsavers.org

Thomas Jefferson Center for Historic Plants
www.monticello.org

Baker Creek Heirloom Seeds
www.rareseeds.com

Bountiful Gardens
www.bountifulgardens.com

Renee's Garden
www.reneesgarden.com

Seeds of Change
www.seedsofchange.com

J.L. Hudson
www.jlhudsonseeds.net

Sources for Beneficial Insects

Applied Bio-nomics
www.appliedbio-nomics.com

Beneficial Insectary
www.insectary.com

BioBest
www.biobest.be

Biotactics, Inc.
www.benemite.com

The Bug Factory, Ltd.
www.thebugfactory.ca

IPM Laboratories
www.ipmlabs.com

Koppert
www.koppertonline.com

Sterling Insectary
www.sterlingnursery.com

Syngenta Bioline
www.syngentabioline.com

Saving and Starting Spores

C

Some plants, such as orchids, produce spores rather than seeds. This appendix explains how to save spores and propagate them.

Collect spores by placing a sterile plastic bag or pantyhose over the leaves the spores are attached to. When the spores explode, the bag or stocking will capture them.

When cultivating spores, an absolutely sterile growing environment is required for success. Often spores are germinated using tissue-culture methods. But an easier option for home gardeners is to sterilize both the soil and the pots you want to use. (You can buy sterilized soil at nurseries, but this soil is usually filled with weed seed.)

To sterilize pots, wash them with soapy water, thoroughly douse and rinse them with boiling water, and then let them dry.

To sterilize the soil, heat the soil in a single layer—no more than a quarter-inch thick—in a 180°F oven for half an hour. To avoid stinking up your house, you can also heat the soil on an outdoor grill or over a fire pit. Use a soil thermometer to make sure it reaches and maintains 180°. After a half-hour, let the soil cool and put it in one of the sterile pots.

Sprinkle the saved spores on top of the soil and cover the pot with a clear lid or plastic bag so that light can come through. The inside of the lid or bag should always be beaded with humidity; if it isn't, the soil is too dry and the spores will die before they have a chance to germinate and grow. When you water, always do it from the bottom, in the plate or pan holding the pot, and always keep a dab of water in the dish to prevent the soil from drying out completely.

When you see growth, remove the lid. Keep the plants indoors or in a greenhouse until they are several inches tall. Don't expect the tiny seedlings to look anything like the parent plant at this point; only over time do they begin to resemble the parent plant.

THE BAD SEED

Spore cases are similar in appearance to scale, which are oval, hard-shelled insects that feed on plant tissue. These insects range in color from white to brown. Spores, like scale, vary greatly in color, size, and shape, so knowing which plants they grow on and making sure the plants are healthy is the best way to ensure that you are allowing spores to mature and not allowing your plants to be destroyed by scale insects.

Index

C

X-Y-Z

CHECK OUT THESE BEST-SELLERS

More than 450 titles available at booksellers and online retailers everywhere

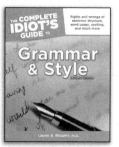

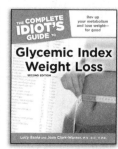
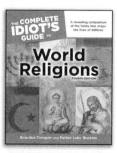

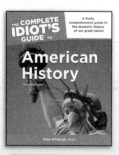

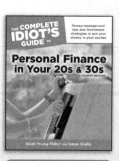

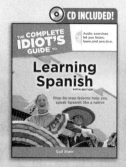
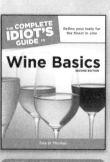

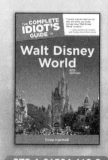

ALPHA

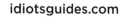 idiotsguides.com